INSPIRE / PLAN / DISCOVER / EXPERIENCE

JERUSALEM
ISRAEL AND THE PALESTINIAN TERRITORIES

DK EYEWITNESS

JERUSALEM

ISRAEL AND THE PALESTINIAN TERRITORIES

CONTENTS

DISCOVER JERUSALEM, ISRAEL AND THE PALESTINIAN TERRITORIES 6

EXPERIENCE JERUSALEM 62

EXPERIENCE ISRAEL AND THE PALESTINIAN TERRITORIES 166

NEED TO KNOW 266

Left: Young Muslim women by the Dome of the Rock
Previous page: Surfers catching waves at sundown, Jaffa, Tel Aviv
Front cover: The Dome of the Rock

DISCOVER

WELCOME TO
JERUSALEM, ISRAEL AND THE PALESTINIAN TERRITORIES

Serene sacred sites and bustling Bauhaus boulevards. Glittering azure seas and dramatic desert outcrops. Magnificent ancient ruins and mouth-watering contemporary cuisine. A meeting place for travellers, traders and worshippers since the dawn of civilization, this land of contrasts is an unforgettable feast for the senses, mind and spirit. Whatever your dream trip to this evocative region entails, this DK Eyewitness Travel Guide is the perfect companion.

1 Floating in the salty waters of the Dead Sea.

2 A pile of freshly baked bagels for sale.

3 The striking façade of the Treasury at Petra.

4 Looking over Jerusalem's historic Old City.

Deeply significant to the Jewish, Christian and Muslim faiths, this ancient land is imbued with a beguiling mix of cultural influences. The fragrant alleyways of Jerusalem's Old City throng with tourists and pilgrims winding their way between holy sites, while the bustling, multicultural modern centre offers an array of eclectic architecture, world-class museums, and hipster bars and cafés. Forward-facing Tel Aviv is Jerusalem's dynamic coastal counterpart, with buzzing beaches and a thriving nightlife.

Traces of civilizations past are evident throughout Israel, but they are at their most picturesque in the north of the country, where balmy Mediterranean waters lap at Roman and Crusader remains, and beautiful churches commemorate Jesus's miracles around the Sea of Galilee. Natural wonders are the draw in the south: snorkel among colourful corals in the Red Sea, roam Negev oases populated by long-horned ibexes or bathe in the salt-rich waters of the Dead Sea. The welcoming cities of the West Bank provide an insight into Palestinian culture, while an excursion to neighbouring Jordan offers the chance to be immersed in an ancient world at the breathtaking ruins of Petra.

From the historic streets of Jerusalem to Bedouin encampments in Wadi Rum, we've broken the region down into easily navigable chapters, with detailed itineraries, expert local knowledge and colourful, comprehensive maps to help you plan the perfect visit. Whether you're staying for a weekend, a week or longer, this DK Eyewitness guide will ensure that you see the very best the region has to offer. Enjoy the book, and enjoy this special part of the world.

REASONS TO LOVE
JERUSALEM, ISRAEL AND THE PALESTINIAN TERRITORIES

Ancient ruins and sacred sites, modern museums and flavoursome food, Mediterranean beaches and desert oases: there are so many reasons to love this evocative region. Here, we pick some of our favourites.

1 **THE VIA DOLOROSA**
There's no better way to feel the passion of Christian pilgrimage to Jerusalem than by joining a procession of the faithful along Jesus's "Way of Sorrow" *(p110)*.

FLOATING IN THE DEAD SEA *2*
Buoy your body and your soul in the salty, soothing waters of the Dead Sea *(p218)*, the lowest point on earth at 431 m (1,414 ft) below sea level.

3 **PETRA**
Truly one of the great ancient wonders of the world, the Nabateans' mysterious rose-red city makes an awe-inspiring short excursion from Israel *(p244)*.

TEL AVIV'S FOOD SCENE 4

Tuck in to Tel Aviv's appetizing array of light, healthy and often vegan fare, comprising an ever-evolving blend of Middle Eastern, Sephardic, Ashkenazi and Mediterranean cooking.

WESTERN WALL 5

Rub shoulders with pilgrims from every corner of the globe at Judaism's holiest place of prayer, surrounded by the sounds of scripture recitals. Here, the faithful slip petitions to the Almighty in between the ancient stones (p88).

DOME OF THE ROCK 6

Topped by a gleaming gold dome, this richly decorated Muslim shrine is the dazzling jewel in the crown of Jerusalem's sacred Temple Mount, or Al-Haram ash-Sharif (p74).

MOUNT OF THE BEATITUDES 7

Enjoy spectacular panoramas of the Sea of Galilee from this serene landscaped hillside – traditionally thought to be the location of Jesus's "Sermon on the Mount" *(p202)*.

ROMAN RUINS 8

Feel the pomp of the Roman Empire come alive as you wander among the ruins of the fascinating ancient cities of Beit She'an *(p204)*, Caesarea *(p190)* and Jerash *(p258)*.

9 MEDITERRANEAN BEACHES

Fine sand and gentle waves make Israel's stunning Mediterranean seashore ideal for swimming, sunbathing and sipping ice-cold lemonade.

10 ISRAEL MUSEUM

Visiting "Israel's Louvre" is like a quick trip to almost any period in Near Eastern and Jewish history you can think of. Make sure not to miss the Dead Sea Scrolls *(p156)*.

SYNAGOGUES OF THE KABBALISTS 11

Envelop yourself in the celestial ambience of Safed's Synagogue Quarter, whose alleyways have been suffused with Kabbalah (Jewish mysticism) since the 16th century *(p206)*.

BAHA'I GARDENS 12

Cascading down the slopes of Mount Carmel, with stunning views of the Mediterranean, the terraces of the Baha'i Gardens are as flowery as they are formal *(p192)*.

EXPLORE
JERUSALEM, ISRAEL AND THE PALESTINIAN TERRITORIES

The region covered in this guide consists of Israel, the Palestinian Territories and western Jordan. We've broken it down into six colour-coded sightseeing areas, as shown on the map below. Find out more about each area on the following pages.

Mediterranean Sea

El-Arish

EUROPE AND THE MEDITERRANEAN REGION

DENMARK

UNITED KINGDOM

NETHER-LANDS

BELGIUM

GERMANY

POLAND

BELARUS

RUSSIA

CZECH REP.

SLOVAKIA

UKRAINE

FRANCE

SWITZ.

AUSTRIA

HUNGARY

CROATIA

ROMANIA

SERBIA

ITALY

BULGARIA

Black Sea

MACEDONIA

GEORGIA

ALBANIA

TURKEY

SPAIN

GREECE

Mediterranean Sea

CYPRUS

SYRIA

IRAQ

MOROCCO

TUNISIA

ISRAEL, THE PALESTINIAN TERRITORIES AND WESTERN JORDAN

SAUDI ARABIA

Nakhl

ALGERIA

LIBYA

EGYPT

Red Sea

Bir Hassana

LEBANON

SYRIA

Tyre

Kiryat
Shmona

Nahariyya

Sasa

Golan
Heights

Akko

Safed

Sheikh Miskin

Karmi'el

Suweida

Haifa

Sea of
Galilee

Ein Gev

MEDITERRANEAN
COAST AND GALILEE
p186

Umm Qais

Zichron Ya'akov

Afula

Irbid

Caesarea

Khadera

Jenin

Beth She'an

El-Mafraq

Netanya

Tul Karem

Jerash

Herzliya

Nablus

El-Hashiniyya

Tel Aviv

WEST BANK
p226

El-Salt

El-Zarqa

TEL AVIV
p168

Ramallah

Amman

JERUSALEM
p62

Jericho

Ashdod

Beit
Shemesh

Jerusalem
Qumran

Madaba

Ashkelon

Bethlehem

Gaza

Qiryat
Gat

Hebron

Dhiban

GAZA

Rahat

Karmel

Dead
Sea

JORDAN

Rafah

ISRAEL

Arad

Tel Be'er Sheva

Kerak

DEAD SEA AND
NEGEV DESERT
p212

Neve Zohar

Nitsana

Yeroham

PETRA AND
WESTERN
JORDAN
p240

Sde Boker

Ovdat

Mitzpe
Ramon

Tsofar

Shobak

Petra

Wadi Musa

EGYPT

Ma'an

Ne'ot Smadar

El-Thamad

0 kilometres   40

N

0 miles   40

Eilat

Aqaba

Rum

GETTING TO KNOW
JERUSALEM, ISRAEL AND THE PALESTINIAN TERRITORIES

The crossroads of three continents, the Holy Land stretches from the Mediterranean in the west to the inland Jordanian deserts, and from Galilee in the north to the balmy Red Sea in the south. At its heart is the ancient city of Jerusalem, just west of the Dead Sea, the lowest point on Earth.

JERUSALEM

PAGE 62

Profoundly sacred to the Abrahamic faiths, Jerusalem's seemingly impossible mix of religions and cultures has been drawing pilgrims and travellers for 3,000 years. In the Old City's quarters, fragrant with spices and incense, a warren of alleys link churches with synagogues, and mosques with markets. Beyond, the neighbourhoods of the New City reflect Jerusalem's motley human tapestry. Ultra-Orthodox Jews lead lives of prayer in Mea She'arim, busy stall-owners sell their wares in the Mahane Yehuda market and Arab East Jerusalem bustles along Salah al-Din Street.

Best for
Encountering history and exploring on foot

Home to
Dome of the Rock, Western Wall, Jerusalem Archaeological Park, Church of the Holy Sepulchre, the Citadel (Tower of David), City of David, Israel Museum

Experience
Splashing through Hezekiah's Tunnel in the City of David

PAGE 168

TEL AVIV

Brash and hedonistic, Tel Aviv is a high-tech powerhouse and proud home of Mediterranean beaches, UNESCO-listed Bauhaus architecture, a Gay Pride Parade, and a world-class restaurant and vegan scene. Creativity abounds, from Old Jaffa's art galleries to the chic boutiques of Neve Tzedek to the Nachalat Binyamin Arts and Crafts Fair. Scoot or cycle between these attractions along the city's shaded boulevards, stopping for freshly squeezed fruit juice, a bowl of Asian noodles or ice cream.

Best for
Sunbathing, dining, LGBT+ life and partying

Home to
Tel Aviv Museum of Art, Rothschild Boulevard

Experience
A sunset walk along the beachfront promenade

PAGE 186

MEDITERRANEAN COAST AND GALILEE

North of Tel Aviv, azure seas lap at Israel's Mediterranean coast, lined with nature reserves, towns and historic sites such as the once-great Roman seaport of Caesarea. Sweeping up the slopes of Mount Carmel, breathtaking Haifa is a religious, cultural and culinary crossroads – and a model of inter-ethnic coexistence. In the Galilee, oak forests, olive groves and vineyards surround Jewish, Arab, Druze and Circassian towns and villages, while the stone alleyways of Safed are suffused with holiness.

Best for
Hiking, dining and shopping for Judaica

Home to
Caesarea, Haifa and Mount Carmel, Akko, Nazareth, the Sea of Galilee, Beit She'an

Experience
Stunning views from Haifa's ornate Baha'i Gardens

→

PAGE 212

DEAD SEA AND NEGEV DESERT

Covering over half of Israel, the rocky, arid expanses of the Negev are home to the soothingly saline waters of the Dead Sea and geographical wonders such as Makhtesh Ramon (a massive crater). Head to the high desert for the well-preserved ruins of Nabatean cities, verdant oases fed by year-round springs, wineries whose grapes flourish thanks to ancient irrigation technology, and the chance to stargaze under some of Israel's darkest skies. In the far south, scuba divers and snorkellers flock to Eilat to explore the spectacular coral reefs and colourful tropical fish of the Red Sea.

Best for
Desert hiking, scuba diving and snorkelling

Home to
Masada, Dead Sea, Eilat

Experience
Floating in the Dead Sea

PAGE 226

WEST BANK

Intended by the international community to be the heartland of a future Palestinian state, the West Bank is a lot more accessible and welcoming to tourists than headlines might suggest. The Old City of Bethlehem still has a small-town vibe and is especially festive around Christmas, while Ramallah, the West Bank's most secular and cosmopolitan city, nurtures the region's liveliest nightlife. In and around quiet Jericho, inhabited for over 10,000 years, cliff-face monasteries evoke the early centuries of Christianity.

Best for
Encountering Palestinian culture

Home to
Bethlehem

Experience
Sipping a local microbrew in a trendy Ramallah pub

PETRA AND WESTERN JORDAN

Hidden away in the rose-red mountains of southern Jordan, Petra keenly conjures the dazzling, lost civilization of the Nabataeans. Monuments carved into solid rock two millennia ago appear around corners without warning, as surprising and improbable today as they were in the time of the Incense Route. Bedouin still live amid the spectacular desert scenery at Wadi Rum and are happy to offer visitors tea – or jeep tours – while at Jerash, the power and pomp of the Roman Empire is recalled by theatres, baths and imposing stone columns. Jordan's urban life is concentrated in the sprawling capital of Amman, where ancient monuments are surrounded by the bustling daily life of a modern Middle Eastern metropolis.

Best for
Nabatean ruins and desert landscapes

Home to
Petra, Wadi Rum, Amman, Jerash, Madaba Mosaics

Experience
Catching your first glimpse of Petra's Treasury as you emerge from the narrow Siq gorge

←

1 Tel Aviv's delightful seafront promenade.

2 ANU - Museum of the Jewish People.

3 Rabin Memorial.

4 A Tel Aviv beach at sunset.

The Holy Land brims with travel possibilities, from short tours around the big cities to odysseys across historic landscapes. These itineraries will help you to chart your own course through this vibrant and varied region.

3 DAYS
in Tel Aviv

Day 1

Morning Stroll down the shaded centre strip of Rothschild Boulevard (p174), stopping at one of the plentiful kiosks for a cool drink or a snack. Call in at Independence Hall, where David Ben-Gurion declared Israel an independent state in 1948, and take time to admire the area's prewar Bauhaus architecture (p175), now some of the city's most coveted real estate.

Afternoon Have lunch at one of the many trendy restaurants on or around Rothschild Boulevard then make your way to Bialik Street (p181) to spend a couple of hours visiting the Rubin Museum and Bialik House. Next, walk along pretty Nachalat Binyamin Street (p183), lined with Eclectic-style buildings (and, on Tuesday and Friday, home to an arts and crafts fair), then head into the produce-filled alleys of Carmel Market (p182).

Evening Amble north along the Tel Aviv beachfront (p178) while enjoying the sunset, then savour a delicious dinner at Kitchen Market (p181), at the Tel Aviv Port.

Day 2

Morning Head to ANU – Museum of the Jewish People (p182) on the campus of Tel Aviv University, to discover the diversity of Jewish diaspora experience. When you're done exploring the exhibitions, have an inexpensive lunch of salad, a schnitzel or a sandwich at a campus cafeteria.

Afternoon Take the bus to Rabin Square (p176), pausing at the Rabin Memorial before hiring a bike or scooter for a leisurely ride along Ben-Gurion Boulevard (p177), which leads directly from the square to the beach. In the late afternoon, when the sun is gentle, take a swim in the Mediterranean.

Evening Watch a play at the Cameri Theater or a performance by the Israeli Opera, both of which reside at the Tel Aviv Performing Arts Center (p177).

Day 3

Morning Peruse the sculptures, paintings and other works by both Israeli and international artists at the Tel Aviv Museum of Art (p172), for a thought-provoking and perhaps provocative start to the day. Round off your visit with an upmarket lunch at Pastel (p181), situated inside the museum's striking Herta and Paul Amir Building.

Afternoon Head to the historic suburb of Neve Tzedek (p180) to visit the Suzanne Dellal Center and the area's creative boutiques. Then walk or take a cab to Old Jaffa (p184) and explore the flea market and art galleries.

Evening Take culinary advantage of the city's seafaring traditions by dining on fish or seafood dinner at the Jaffa port – fishers have been bringing their catch ashore here since at least the time of Jonah.

6 DAYS
in Jerusalem

Day 1

Morning Start at the Western Wall (p88), then make your way up to the Temple Mount, or Al-Haram ash-Sharif (p70), to admire the Dome of the Rock. From there, head to Lion's Gate to embark on a walk along the Via Dolorosa (p110).

Afternoon Stop for lunch in a hummus joint, before continuing along the Via Dolorosa to the Church of the Holy Sepulchre (p106). After visiting the tomb of Christ, head to the Citadel (p112) to enjoy panoramic views from the ramparts.

Evening Walk from Jaffa Gate (p116) to Nachalat Shiv'a, browsing the local galleries before grabbing a simple dinner.

Day 2

Morning Spend the morning delving into the riches of the Israel Museum (p156) – make sure not to miss the Dead Sea Scrolls.

Afternoon Take a taxi to the Old City to explore the Jewish Quarter, including the Four Sephardic Synagogues (p97) and the Cardo (p94). Discover the area's hidden history with a pre-booked tour of the Western Wall Tunnels.

Evening Dine at The Eucalyptus (p145), where the unique menus are inspired by foods mentioned in the Bible.

Day 3

Morning Begin your day perusing the archaeological collection at East Jerusalem's Rockefeller Museum (p149), then visit the attractive grounds of the nearby Garden Tomb (p147) before popping in to Armenian Ceramics (75 Nablus Road) to browse for beautiful souvenirs and gifts. Have an early lunch at the American Colony Hotel (p148).

Afternoon Take a cab to the City of David (p132) and explore the excavations before sloshing through Hezekiah's Tunnel. Then – making sure you have plenty of water – head up the Mount of Olives, with stops at the Church of All Nations (p134), the Garden of Gethsemane (p134) and the Tomb of the Virgin Mary (p136).

Evening Have dinner in West Jerusalem at the First Station (p149), where a dozen restaurants serve a wide array of dishes: everything from hummus to Breton crêpes to Southeast Asian stir-fry.

1 Looking over Temple Mount.

2 The City of David, lit up during the Night Spectacular.

3 The King David Hotel lobby.

4 The interior of the Church of the Nativity, Bethlehem.

5 Entering the Garden Tomb.

Day 4

Morning Visit Yad Vashem (p162), Israel's moving Holocaust memorial and museum, taking in the Valley of the Communities monument and exhibits on European Jewish life before the Holocaust.

Afternoon Take the light rail line to Jaffa Gate and walk along the Old City's ramparts, then head through the bustling souks (markets) of David Street and its nearby alleys to the Muslim Quarter. Visit the beautiful St Anne's Church followed by tea (or something stronger) at the Viennese Café (p80) down the road.

Evening Learn about Jerusalem's history at the Night Spectacular, a lively sound-and-light show at the Citadel (p112).

Day 5

Morning Dedicate today to the modern city centre, starting with a stroll along King David Street to admire the Mandate-era architecture of the King David Hotel (p142) and the YMCA (p142). Continue your walk through the neighbourhood of Yemin Moshe, built – like its distinctive windmill – in the 1890s.

Afternoon Have lunch in one of the trendy restaurants in Mahane Yehuda (p163), then spend a leisurely afternoon exploring the charming alleyways and pretty courtyards of nearby Nakhla'ot.

Evening Take the light rail line down Jaffa Street and have dinner near the Russian Compound (p144).

Day 6

Morning Today brings a change of scene with an excursion to the West Bank. Travel to Bethlehem (p230), passing through Checkpoint 300. Start your tour of the town with its famous Christian sights: the Church of the Nativity, St Catherine's Church and the Milk Grotto Chapel.

Afternoon Have lunch at a local Palestinian restaurant and then soak up the old-world charm of the town centre with a meander through its narrow lanes. Visit the Museum of Palestinian Heritage for a fascinating insight into local culture.

Evening Return to Jerusalem and head to Mahane Yehuda for dinner at a chef-run restaurant, followed by a local beer or wine at one of the area's cutting-edge pubs.

6 DAYS
in the Dead Sea, Negev and Petra

Day 1

Morning Drive from Jerusalem to Qumran National Park *(p218)* to see where the Dead Sea Scrolls were found. Continue to Ein Gedi Nature Reserve *(p219)*, stopping for a short hike through the desert oasis.

Afternoon Head to the hilltop fortress of Masada *(p216)*. Have lunch in the food court and visit the museum before taking the cable car up to the top to explore the ruins and peer down at the remains of the Roman military camps at the base of the mountain.

Evening Take a quick dip in the saline waters of the Dead Sea at Ein Bokek's swish public beach *(p218)*. Enjoy dinner at a nearby restaurant, followed by a post-dinner stroll along the waterfront.

Day 2

Morning Start the day with another swim (or, more accurately, float) in the Dead Sea. Then drive south to the Arava and stop at Kibbutz Lotan *(p224)*, where you can learn about pioneering, low-impact desert technologies on a tour of its Center for Creative Ecology.

Afternoon Continue south to the stunning Timna Park *(p225)*, where the sandy valleys and rocky cliffs come in a magnificent assortment of hues. Admire the scenery on a short desert hike and discover the history of the area at the ancient copper mines.

Evening End the day in Eilat *(p220)*, with dinner on the bustling promenade that runs along North Beach and around the lagoons.

Day 3

Morning Experience the underwater wonders of the Red Sea with a snorkel or dive at the Coral Beach Nature Reserve *(p220)*, teeming with colourful fish and gardens of extraordinary coral.

Afternoon Spend the rest of the day relaxing on Eilat's beaches, indulging yourself with fresh fruit juice to stay hydrated. If you're feeling energetic, have a go at one of the watersports on offer.

Evening Continue the leisurely pace with a stroll in the warm evening air to a café or restaurant in the vicinity of the North Beach Promenade.

1 Floating in the waters of the Dead Sea at Ein Bokek.

2 The museum at Masada.

3 Snorkelling in the Red Sea.

4 Petra's stunning Treasury.

5 Looking out over the Makhtesh Ramon crater.

Day 4

Morning Rise early for a pre-booked tour to Jordan, crossing the border 3 km (2 miles) north of Eilat. Enjoy the scenic drive to Wadi Rum (p252), taking a short hike on arrival to immerse yourself in this desert wilderness.

Afternoon Have lunch with the Bedouin in Rum Village, followed by a jeep tour through the desert to marvel at the changing afternoon colours of the landscape – you can either pre-book or find a driver when you arrive.

Evening Drive to Petra (p244) and dine in one of the many Middle Eastern-style restaurants in Wadi Musa. Grilled meat is the speciality, but fresh mezze salads are also available.

Day 5

Morning Walk from the town of Wadi Musa through the Siq gorge to the ancient ruins of Petra, savouring your first, breathtaking glimpse of the Treasury. Spend the morning visiting the Treasury, the Royal Tombs and the City of Petra.

Afternoon After taking a break with a picnic lunch, make the strenuous but rewarding climb to the Monastery, Petra's most monumental temple.

Evening Drive back to Eilat and have a late dinner in one of the restaurants around North Beach or its lagoons.

Day 6

Morning Drive 150 km (93 miles) north from Eilat to the dramatic Makhtesh Ramon (p224) crater. Take a short walk inside the vast geological marvel for an up-close experience of its unique, otherworldly environment.

Afternoon Have lunch in Mitzpe Ramon's Spice Route Quarter (p223), then visit the ancient Nabatean city of Avdat (p222). Afterwards, drive to Midreshet Sde Boker (p222) to visit the clifftop grave of David Ben-Gurion, Israel's first prime minister, and gaze out across rugged Wadi Tzin. Keep an eye out for ibexes.

Evening Have dinner in one of the small eateries in Midreshet Ben-Gurion's commercial centre, where the options include falafel and pizza.

7 DAYS
in Haifa and Galilee

Day 1

Morning Begin your week in Haifa (p192). Peruse the ancient artifacts at the Hecht Museum), then head to the Baha'i Gardens for a tour of its verdant terraces.

Afternoon Eat lunch in Wadi Nisnas, then visit the Clandestine Immigration and Naval Museum (p194). End the afternoon by taking the cable car to Stella Maris for stunning views of the bay.

Evening Enjoy the Arab fusion food at Shtroudl (p195) followed by a nightcap at the LiBira microbrewery (www.libira.co.il).

Day 2

Morning Take a train or ferry to Akko (p196). Dedicate the rest of the morning to visiting the city's Crusader sites, including the Knights' Halls and the Templars' Tunnel.

Afternoon Have lunch at one of Akko's renowned hummus joints and then explore the rest of the Old City, including the souks, the Mosque of Al-Jazzar and the Citadel (Underground Prisoners Museum).

Evening Dine on seafood at Uri Buri (p197) or Elmārsā (p197) along the waterfront.

Day 3

Morning Head inland to Nazareth (p198) and wander through its historic centre, visiting the Greek Orthodox Church of the Annunciation, the Ancient Bathhouse and the Catholic Basilica of the Annunciation.

Afternoon Have a Nazarene-style Arab lunch at Abu Ashraf (p198), then visit the nearby White Mosque. Explore the lively souk and maze-like alleys of the Old City before checking out the excavations at the Centre International Marie de Nazareth.

Evening Try some of Nazareth's famous Levantine-European fusion cuisine at Tishreen (www.tishreen.rest.co.il), followed by a drink at nearby Avra (www.avra.co.il).

Day 4

Morning Drive east to the pilgrimage site of Mount Tabor (p209), taking time to visit the monastery and church and enjoy the spectacular views of the Jezreel Valley.

Afternoon Head northeast to the holy city of Tiberias (p207) to see the beautiful mosaic in Hamat Tveriya National Park and visit the tombs of Jewish Sages.

1 Haifa's Baha'i Gardens.

2 The elegant Mosque of Al-Jazzar in Akko.

3 Yardenit Baptism Site.

4 Looking over the Jezreel Valley from Mount Tabor.

5 Beit She'an Roman ruins.

Evening Feast on gourmet Galilean-style Arab cuisine at Magdalena (*p207*), under the inspired direction of chef Zuzu Hanna.

Day 5

Morning Drive north from Tiberias along the shore of the Sea of Galilee (*p200*), with stops at Magdala, the Ancient Galilee Boat and Tabgha.

Afternoon After a picnic lunch on the shore, drive up to the Mount of the Beatitudes and enjoy the inspiring views. Continue up the hill to the ruins at Korazim National Park, then loop back to the shore to visit the Roman town of Capernaum.

Evening Dine on St Peter's Fish (tilapia) in Tiberias, at one of the restaurants on the lakefront Yigal Allon Promenade.

Day 6

Morning Drive along the Sea of Galilee's southern shore, stopping at the leafy Kinneret Cemetery, where several notable Israelis are buried. From there continue on to Yardenit Baptism Site (*p203*), where Jesus himself may have been baptized.

Afternoon Lunch at the lovely Beit Gabriel cultural centre (*www.betgabriel. co.il*) at the southern tip of the lake. After soaking up some final sea views, head south towards Beit She'an, calling in at Crusader-era Belvoir Castle (*p208*) for incredible panoramas of the Jordan Valley.

Evening Feast on grilled meat and mezze salads at Shipudei HaKikar (*www.shipudey-hakikar.co.il*) in Beit She'an. Afterwards, take in the She'an Nights sound-and-light show at Beit She'an roman ruins (*p204*).

Day 7

Morning Visit the dazzling ruins of Beit She'an (*p204*), Israel's best-preserved Roman city and explore its almost-intact bathhouses, shops and theatre.

Afternoon Head westward through the farmlands of the Jezreel Valley to see the ancient mosaics at Beit Alpha. Spend the rest of the afternoon exploring the scenic back roads of Mount Gilboa.

Evening Have a quick, cheap dinner in downtown Afula at Falafel Golani (*www. falafel-golani.info*) – said by its many fans to serve some of Israel's best falafel.

◁ Wild Walks

The Hanging Trail at Banias Nature Reserve in the Golan Heights *(p207)* takes you into a veritable tunnel of oaks and fig trees, their branches – like the trail itself – overhanging a gushing, spring-fed stream. In summer, it's all a welcome relief from the heat, sun and parched-brown landscape. Nearby are the remains of an ancient Herodian temple and the thundering Banyas Waterfall, while delicious Druze pitas are often available at both of the reserve's entrances, which also have snack bars.

FAMILY ADVENTURES

The region is a wonderland for children, with beaches on four different seas, child-friendly hikes through spring-fed oases and plenty of museums with creative activities for kids. Whether travelling back in time at ancient sites or exploring the outdoors, a memorable family day out is guaranteed.

▷ Mediterranean Beaches

Israel's Mediterranean coast is lined with fine-sand beaches, from urban lidos in Tel Aviv *(p168)* complete with convenient amenities and people playing *matkot* (Israeli beach tennis) to quiet nature reserves such as Beit Yanai Beach. Even in winter, it's often warm enough to play on the beach, if not to actually swim.

▷ Dead Sea Delights

Floating in the mineral-rich waters of the lowest lake on earth (p218) can be great fun - and because of the elevation, sunburn is much less of a problem than at sea level. On the shoreline, Ein Gedi Nature Reserve (p219) and its spring-fed oasis afford opportunities to spot wild ibexes and scampering dassies, while the ancient fortress of Masada (p216) offers historical drama and a thrilling cable car ride.

◁ Historic Akko

Life in the 13th century is easy to conjure as you uncover the fascinating history of Akko's superbly preserved Crusader sights (p196) - children will delight in imagining knights in clanking armour tramping through the Templars' Tunnel and devouring great banquets in the Knights' Halls. The Ottoman sights of the Old City are equally evocative, while Akko's Baha'i Gardens offer something a little greener and more soothing.

▽ Public Playgrounds

Every city, town and village in Israel has a multitude of playgrounds for children. Some are tiny "pocket parks" hidden away between apartment buildings, others - such as Sarona in Tel Aviv (p176) - have lots of grass and several creative recreational areas. Most shopping malls have air-conditioned areas for the young ones to burn off some energy - a great option for a break on a scorching day.

△ Riveting Ruins

Even children with no declared interest in long-lost civilizations will be captivated by the Roman ruins at Beit She'an (p204), which include a public latrine with marble toilet seats and a vast 7,000-seat theatre.

Picturesque Ruins

As you approach Aqueduct Beach at Caesarea *(p190)*, the azure waters of the Mediterranean are neatly framed by the semicircular stone arches of a Roman aqueduct, built in the 1st century AD to supply fresh water to the new port city. Rarely overcrowded, the captivating site mixes soft, golden sand with a palpable sense of history. Head here in the early evening with your camera for a particularly evocative sunset shot.

→

Caesarea's Aqueduct Beach, with the ancient Roman conduit after which it is named

ON THE COAST

Along the Mediterranean and the Sea of Galilee you can swim, beach-lounge and explore the remains of ancient towns, while the Dead Sea offers bathers the otherworldly experience of being unsinkable. At the Red Sea, it's underwater, among coral reefs, that you'll discover the most dazzling sights.

Relaxing Resorts

Ein Bokek *(p218)* is the best place in Israel for a relaxing dip in the Dead Sea. As you slip into the salty waters, the liquid around your feet is oily and dense, and your body becomes strangely buoyant. Lie back, and enjoy the surreal sensation of floating in this vast natural spa.

→

The salty shoreline of the Dead Sea, with the resort of Ein Bokek in the background

Geological Wonders

Marvel at the power of nature as ultramarine waters crash against chalk-white cliffs at Rosh HaNikra (p211), a promontory that marks the Israel-Lebanon frontier. At the base of the rock face, Mediterranean swells slosh in and out of dramatic, shimmering sea caves, carved into the snowy limestone over the course of thousands of years. Getting to these incredible cave formations is an adventure in itself, involving a thrilling cable car descent from the towering clifftop above.

← The unique rock formations and blue waters of the caves at Rosh HaNikra

TOP 4   MEDITERRANEAN BEACHES

Gordon Beach, Tel Aviv
Lively and packed with amenities, including on-the-sand cafés selling glasses of cool mint-lemonade (p179).

Acadia Beach, Herzliya Pituah
A city beach just north of Tel Aviv, popular with windsurfers and kite surfers.

Beit Yannai Beach
Fringed by sand dunes, this national park between Tel Aviv and Haifa is a short walk from the turtle habitat of Alexander Stream.

Dor HaBonim Beach
An off-the-beaten-track beach south of Haifa, with tidal pools and the ruins of the ancient city of Dor.

Colourful Corals

The Red Sea's reefs are among the richest and most colourful underwater habitats in the world. The water is warm and crystal-clear, so shallow coral communities can easily be explored by both snorkelers and divers. If you've never dived, Eilat's scuba centres offer plenty of chances to learn (p221).

↑ Exploring the spectacular Red Sea coral reefs lying just off the coast of Eilat

Jewish Ritual Objects

For gorgeously creative Judaica – objects used in Jewish religious ceremonies – head to Safed *(p206)*, Nahalat Shiv'a *(p142)* in Jerusalem, and Tel Aviv's Nachalat Binyamin Arts and Crafts Fair *(p183)*. Often beautifully made, the most attractive items include Kiddush (wine) cups, *talits* (prayer shawls), Torah pointers, *shofars* (ram's horns blown for Yom Kippur) and nine-candle *menorahs* and *dreidels* (spinning tops) for Chanukah.

> **HIDDEN GEM**
> **Spice Shop**
>
> In Nazareth, hundreds of pungent, piquant and peppery spices are sold at Elbabour Galilee Mill *(www.elbabour-shop.com)*, family-run for well over a century.

↑ *Kippahs* or *yarmulkes* (brimless caps) for sale at a market in Safed

HANDMADE CRAFTS

Home to bustling souks, modern malls and stylish boutiques, the region is an excellent place for shopping. With a rich heritage of traditional and contemporary crafts, there is a wealth of treasures for souvenir hunters on the lookout for unusual items. Here, we pick some of the best items produced by skilled local artisans.

Jewellery

Modern Israeli jewellery-making began at Jerusalem's Bezalel Academy of Arts and Design; its earliest students included Yemenite silversmiths, famous for their filigree work. Today, you can find items made by Bezalel graduates and others in Jerusalem at Hutzot HaYotzer *(www.artistscolony.co.il)* and in Tel Aviv on Shabazi Street in Neve Tzedek *(p180)*.

←

Baskets of colourful bracelets for sale at a market in Jerusalem

Armenian Ceramics

Decorated with timeless animal and plant motifs, and characterized by the abundant use of blue and yellow, exquisite Armenian ceramics have been produced in Jerusalem for generations. Workshops with the finest-quality products in the city include Balian Ceramics *(www.armenianceramics. com)*, a few hundred metres north of Damascus Gate, just outside the Old City, and Jerusalem Pottery *(www. jerusalempottery.biz)* and Sandrouni Ceramics *(www.sandrouni.com)* in the Christian Quarter.

←

Beautiful plates and dishes, decorated with typical Armenian motifs and colours

→

A woman delicately embroidering fabric with traditional Palestinian geometric designs

JORDANIAN CRAFTS

Jordan is a great place to pick up local, handmade items. In Amman, the Alaydi Jordan Craft Centre *(www.jordancraft center.com)* has an excellent selection of Jordanian, Bedouin and Palestinian crafts, including woven rugs and embroidery, while the not-for-profit Beit al Bawadi *(www.beital bawadi.com)* specializes in ceramics. In Wadi Musa, Made in Jordan sells local products such as soap, embroidery and jewellery. In and around Madaba *(p260)*, craft shops sell locally made mosaics, created using techniques dating to ancient times.

Traditional Palestinian Crafts

Specialty boutiques selling Palestinian items, such as colourful embroidered textiles, can be found in East Jerusalem, Nazareth and Ramallah, as well as in Jordan. Pick up olive-wood and mother-of-pearl ornaments in Bethlehem, beautiful hand-blown glass in Hebron, or soap made with olive oil in Nablus, which has been manufactured here since the 14th century.

The captivating
rust-coloured landscape
of the Wadi Rum desert ↑

THE GREAT OUTDOORS

Walking trails crisscross the region, allowing you to immerse yourself in the sounds, smells and sensations of gushing springs, desert oases and red-rock mountains. The loveliest time to ramble through nature is the early spring, when wildflowers carpet the land.

Canyon Climbing

Israel is a small country but Makhtesh Ramon *(p224)* – an enormous 40-km- (25-mile-) long, 300-m (985-ft) deep crater in the Negev Desert – feels vast and limitless. Sometimes referred to as "Israel's Grand Canyon", this amphitheatre-like valley and its multicoloured sands have ample venues for hiking, mountain biking and abseiling. While exploring, you can overnight in rustic, off-the-grid desert encampments near Mitzpe Ramon *(p223)* and dine in the town's hip restaurants. The stargazing here is some of the best in the region.

→

The view over
Makhtesh Ramon
from the crater rim

Desert Adventures

While ancient Egyptians once went to Timna Park *(p225)* to mine and smelt copper, modern-day travellers flock there to hike, cycle and immerse themselves in the area's pristine desert terrain. In Jordan, meanwhile, dramatic cliffs, blowing sand dunes and weird rock formations make Wadi Rum *(p252)* one of the most enchanting desert landscapes on earth. Explore its vast expanses of rocky reds and sandy tans on a hike or jeep tour with a local Bedouin guide.

← Exploring the dramatic rock formations in Timna Park

BIRDWATCHING

Israel, the Palestinian Territories and Jordan are a birdwatcher's Eden. An amazing 500 million birds – including giant flocks of storks and cranes – migrate through the region twice a year on their way from Eurasia to Africa and back, and there are also many birds of prey that nest here year round. Outstanding spots for birdwatching include the International Birding and Research Center at the salt marshes in Eilat *(p221)* and Hula Nature Reserve *(p208)*, an area of protected wetlands north of the Sea of Galilee.

> 💬 INSIDER TIP
> **Desert Wildlife**
>
> Animals to look out for in the Negev Desert include ibex and hyrax at Ein Gedi *(p219)* and Arabian oryx and African ostrich at Hai Bar Yotvata *(p224)*.

Whitewater rafting through the rapids of the Jordan River ↑

On the River

Two kinds of people are most drawn to the renowned waters of the Jordan River: Christian pilgrims seeking a deeply spiritual experience, and watersports fans in search of an adrenaline rush. Jordan River Rafting *(www.rafting.co.il)* and Kfar Blum Kayaks *(www.kayaks.co.il)* offer rafting and kayak trips down the wild Yarden Harari ("Mountainous Jordan") and the more sedate Hatzbani (Snir) River, a Jordan tributary, further north.

Live Music

Jerusalem is an excellent place to sample Israel's highly creative rock and pop scene, which features an eclectic array of stars ranging from indie guitarists to Ethiopian rappers to 2018 Eurovision winner Netta. Top venues for live music include Yellow Submarine *(www.yellow submarine.org.il)* and Zappa Jerusalem *(www.zappa-club. co.il)*, which also has a sister club in Tel Aviv. Elsewhere in Tel Aviv, the best Israeli talent takes the stage at Barby *(www.barby.co.il)* and Kuli Alma *(www.kulialma.com)*.

←

Crowds enjoying a concert at Barby, a popular music venue in Tel Aviv

AFTER DARK

Buzzing nightlife might not be the first thing that springs to mind when you think of the Holy Land, but Jerusalem and Tel Aviv offer a fabulous smorgasbord of evening entertainment. Chic cafés, hipster pubs and rooftop bars abound, as do nightclubs where talented DJs keep the party going all night long.

INSIDER TIP
West Bank Nightlife

The nightlife scene in the West Bank can be rather limited, but cosmopolitan Ramallah has some lively evening entertainment options. Join the locals quaffing Palestinian and imported beers at an array of pubs, lounges and hipster joints, or attend a concert or film at the A M Qattan Foundation Cultural Centre *(p237)*.

A Nightcap in Tel Aviv

Tel Aviv's nightspots range from sophisticated wine bars to grungy hipster joints to sleek rooftop bars. Shabbat rules don't matter much here so the biggest night out is Friday, with Thursday a close second (the work week begins bright and early on Sunday so Saturday night is relatively quiet). Tel Aviv is open at all hours, so at some bars your last nightcap could begin as late as 5am or 6am.

→

Enjoying a nightcap at one of Tel Aviv's numerous lively bars

Café Culture

Inspired by the historic coffee houses of Central Europe, Tel Aviv's cafés bring together the city's famously gregarious residents. Italian espresso, beer and light meals (including giant salads) can be enjoyed at Paris-style sidewalk cafés and shady Bauhaus gardens, as well as in the lively hipster establishments of south Tel Aviv's edgy Florentin neighbourhood and at centre-strip kiosks on boulevards such as Rothschild *(p174)* and Ben-Gurion *(p177)*.

→

Relaxing with drinks at a pavement café in Tel Aviv's vibrant Florentin neighbourhood

Out on the Town in Jerusalem

Most of Jerusalem's trendiest music pubs, beer bars and tapas spots are in the area around Mahane Yehuda market *(p163)*. The Jerusalem Cinematheque *(www. jer-cin.org.il)* by Mount Zion, meanwhile, is popular with the city's somewhat beleaguered minority of secular lefties.

←

Enjoying an evening out in Mahane Yehuda, a market by day and thriving entertainment spot by night

TEL AVIV PRIDE

Asia's largest gay pride event – a week-long series of festivities and late-night parties – brings a quarter of a million revelers from around the world to the streets of Tel Aviv in a giant celebration of freedom, pluralism and tolerance *(www.tel-aviv.gov.il)*. The city is festooned with rainbow flags, the mayor makes a speech, and carnival-style floats proceed along the beachfront, with live music and flamboyant parties stretching into the early hours of the night. Begun in 1998, the annual event has grown into one of the highlights of the year. It takes place in the second week of June.

IN THE FOOTSTEPS OF JESUS

Many of the locations associated with Jesus's life and ministry have been identified, either by long tradition or by archaeologists (or both), and can easily be visited. Born in Bethlehem *(p230),* he grew up in Nazareth *(p198)* and later preached around the Sea of Galilee *(p200).* He underwent the Transfiguration on Mount Tabor *(p209),* was baptized somewhere along the Jordan River and was crucified in Jerusalem *(p106).*

Jericho's Treasures

Reputedly the world's oldest continuously inhabited city, Jericho *(p234)* has witnessed the entire span of the region's history. Archaeological excavations in and around Jericho have uncovered the world's oldest known stairway, city wall and stone tower, all dated to 8,000 BC, as well as a palace from the time of Cleopatra and Mark Anthony. Don't miss the remains of Hisham's Palace, a richly decorated 8th-century hunting lodge that in its heyday was the "Versailles of the Middle East".

→

The 12th-century Greek Orthodox Monastery of the Temptation at Jericho

UNEARTHING THE PAST

The early humans who lived in the Hula Valley 780,000 years ago left a variety of enigmatic artifacts, as did everyone who followed – including the Israelites, the Romans, the Crusaders and the Ottomans. Few places on earth make so many ancient civilizations feel so proximate and palpable.

Roman Remains

Triumphant and brutal, Roman power – preserved in stone – can be experienced in all its bombast and glory at Beit She'an *(p204),* Caesarea *(p190)* and Jerash *(p258).* The Roman military camps that still surround Masada *(p216)* provide insights into Roman siege tactics and strategy.

→

The elegant Cardo, the main thoroughfare through the Roman city of Jerash

Mysteries of the Israelites

Did King David and his successors rule over a mighty Israelite kingdom or a small, sparsely settled highland territory that benefitted in later centuries from really good PR? Jerusalem's City of David (p132) provides tantalizing clues, as do the excavations at Tel Dan (p209), Megiddo (p206) and Tel Be'er Sheva (p222). The Israel Museum (p156) displays extraordinary archaeological finds dating from the Israelite period.

← Excavations at the ancient fortified city of Megiddo in the the Jezreel Valley

INSIDER TIP
Nabatean Sites

Two millennia ago, Nabatean caravans carried incense across the Negev Desert. Visit the superbly preserved remains of their cities at Avdat (p222), Mamshit and Shivta.

Crusader Monuments

The Crusaders, who ruled parts of the Holy Land from 1099 to 1291, left behind a number of evocative sites. They extensively rebuilt Jerusalem's Church of the Holy Sepulchre (p106), whose desecration helped launch the Crusades; built Belvoir Castle (p208); inspired the Muslims to construct Nimrod Fortress (p207); and ended their days in the Holy Land in Akko (p196), where you can see Israel's most impressive Crusader ruins.

→ The imposing Nimrod Fortress, atop a ridge in the Golan Heights

ISRAELI WINES

Israeli wines have received international acclaim in recent decades, produced by northern wineries on the Dalton Plateau and in the Golan Heights, as well as estates further south in the Jerusalem foothills and the Negev Highlands. In the West Bank, wineries are run by Palestinian Christians near Bethlehem and in Taybeh. A recent trend in the region has been the use of endemic grape varieties such as *marawi (hamdani)* and *jandali*.

FLAVOURFUL FOOD

Contemporary Israeli cuisine melds dishes brought by Jewish immigrants from Europe, North Africa and the Middle East with indigenous Levantine-Arab food and the spices and techniques encountered by Israeli backpackers in South and Southeast Asia. Made with super-fresh local produce, the resulting medley is an irresistible feast for the tastebuds.

Mouthwatering Street Food

Chickpeas take centre stage in two dishes beloved by both Israelis and Palestinians: falafel (deep-fried chickpea balls) and hummus, often served with *fuul* (stewed fava beans). Alternatively, try *Bourekas*, savoury pastries introduced by Sephardic Jews from the Balkans, or *shwarma*, thin slices of grilled meat served in a pita bread.

←

Falafel served in a pita bread with salad, and a drizzle of tahini sauce on top

Levantine and Arab Cuisine

The delicious traditional cuisine of Palestine, Jordan, Lebanon and Syria is available in first-rate Arab restaurants in cities such as Haifa, Akko, Nazareth, Ramallah, Bethlehem and Amman. Mouthwatering dishes include *mansaf* (lamb or chicken cooked with tangy yoghurt and served with rice) – Jordan's national dish – as well as *kibbeh* (ground meat dumplings) and *fattoush* (a vegetable salad made with fried pita chips). For dessert, try deliciously cheesy and gooey *kunafeh* from Nablus.

←

A street stall serving Palestinian food in the Old City of Jerusalem

International Influences

Jewish immigrants and refugees brought with them a wide variety of delectable dishes. Try *tsholnt* (slow-cooked Shabbat stew) from Eastern Europe, flaky *jachnun* pastry from Yemen and spicy dishes served with *injera* (spongy flat bread) from Ethiopia.

←

A traditional Ethiopian dish served with *injera*

Vegetarian Paradise

The region boasts an incredible array of options for vegetarian diners. Most of the street food is vegetarian or vegan, as are the large Israeli salads offered in cafés, and the mezze served in Levantine and Arab restaurants. *Shakshuka*, introduced by North African Jews, is a particular highlight: eggs poached in a tangy sauce of olive oil, chopped tomatoes, onion, sweet peppers and paprika.

→

A tasty family breakfast of *shakshuka*, with bread and hummus on the side

Baha'i Pilgrimages

Followers of the Baha'i faith have been making pilgrimages to the Shrine of the Bab in Haifa's Baha'i Gardens (p192) for over a century. The faithful of all religions or none will find something uplifting and possibly even spiritual among the flowery terraces and fountains cascading down the slopes of Mount Carmel, which afford stunning views of the city and the glittering Mediterranean.

→

The beautifully manicured Baha'i Gardens and the Shrine of the Bab in Haifa

SACRED TRADITIONS

With important sites sacred to five religions – Judaism, Christianity, Islam, and the Druze and Baha'i faiths – the Holy Land offers visitors unsurpassed opportunities to encounter and learn about their own spiritual customs, as well as those of other faiths.

Shabbat in Safed

As sunset nears on Friday, the last shops close and an otherworldly serenity descends on the city of Safed (p206). A siren marks the start of Shabbat, synagogues welcome the Sabbath Queen with mystical liturgy written five centuries ago, and the city takes 25 hours off from the stress of earning a living.

Ultra-Orthodox Jews making their way to prayers in Safed
↓

Iftar Meal

During the Islamic month of Ramadan, observant Muslims fast from sunrise to sundown to cleanse their body, mind and soul (p61). After the sun sets, families joyously break the long hours of abstention from food and water with the Iftar meal. Some Muslim communities in the Palestinian Territories and in towns such as Umm al-Fahm and Jisr az-Zarka in Israel are happy to share an Iftar meal with visitors.

← Muslims breaking their fast near the Dome of the Rock in the Temple Mount compound

→ Christians undergoing baptism in the Jordan River at Yardenit Baptism Site

> **INSIDER TIP**
> ## Shabbat Closures
>
> Shops in almost all Jewish areas are closed during Shabbat (the Jewish Sabbath), which lasts from shortly before sundown on Friday to about an hour after sundown on Saturday. In Orthodox locales all restaurants are closed, so for a meal head to a secular Jewish or Arab area.

KABBALAH

Kabbalah is an ancient, mystical stream of Jewish thought and practice. Safed became the world's premier centre of Kabbalah in the 16th century, following the arrival of Jewish sages expelled from Spain in 1492. Yitzhak Luria (1534–72), also known as the Ari, taught that the world was created through a process known as Tzimtzum, in which the Divinity contracted its infinite light in order to make space for the universe to come into being.

Baptism in the Jordan

Many Christian pilgrims to the Holy Land reaffirm their faith by undergoing baptism in the Jordan River, reenacting Jesus's baptism by John the Baptist in these same waters. In flowing white robes, they immerse themselves at sites including Yardenit (p203), just south of the Sea of Galilee, Qasr al-Yahud on the West Bank and, right across the river, Bethany-Beyond-the-Jordan in Jordan.

Mesmerizing Modern Dance

Israeli choreographers and dancers are a major force on the international modern dance scene. Tel Aviv's Suzanne Dellal Center *(p180)* hosts around 600 performances a year and is home to both the world-renowned Batsheva Dance Company and Israel's first dance company, the Inbal Dance Theater. The leading Kibbutz Contemporary Dance Company *(www.kcdc.co.il)* performs at Kibbutz Ga'aton and around Israel, as well as in Europe and North America.

→

A dance performance in Jerusalem by the innovative Batsheva Dance Company

CAPTIVATING CULTURE

The region has an incredibly rich and varied performing arts scene. Plays – some of them provocative – are widely discussed and debated, while music performances range from Western classical to pop and rap inflected with Hebrew, Arabic, Indian and Ethiopian influences.

Enthralling Theatre

Theatre-going is hugely popular in Israel. In Tel Aviv, the Cameri Theatre *(www. cameri.co.il)* specializes in staging new Israeli plays, while HaBima *(www.habima. co.il)* has been interpreting international classics for over a century; both have performances with English surtitles. Yiddishpiel *(www. yiddishpiel.co.il)* performs musical plays in Yiddish throughout Israel; surtitles are in Hebrew and Russian.

←

The illuminated exterior of the world-class HaBima Theatre in Tel Aviv

The Stirring Sounds of Klezmer

Sometimes referred to as "Jewish soul music", *klezmer* originated in Eastern Europe. Influenced by both Ottoman and Balkan-gypsy music, and starring the clarinet and the violin, it is passionate and soulful and famously able to express both joy and sorrow. Safed hosts a *klezmer* festival (*www.klezmerim.info*) every August, with performances around the city by both Israeli and international artists.

→

Musicians play for the crowds at Safed's *klezmer* festival

East Meets West

The traditional liturgy of the Jews of North Africa, and music from the Magreb, Spain, Egypt, Greece, Turkey and Iraq, is performed with verve by the Jerusalem Orchestra East and West (*www.tjo.co.il*), formerly known as the Orchestre Andalou d'Israël.

←

An outdoor performance by the Jerusalem Orchestra East and West

Western Classical Music

The Tel Aviv-based Israel Philharmonic Orchestra, or IPO (*www.ipo.co.il*), was established in 1936 by German Jews fleeing Nazism. Today, IPO's celebrated concert series includes a performance for children and "IPO in Jeans", intended to appeal to less-formal younger generations.

The Israel Philharmonic Orchestra, conducted by Zubin Mehta ↑

A YEAR IN
JERUSALEM, ISRAEL AND THE PALESTINIAN TERRITORIES

JANUARY

△ **Orthodox Christmas** (*7 Jan*). Orthodox Christians celebrate Jesus's birth with processions in Jerusalem, Bethlehem, Nazareth and Jaffa.

Sea of Galilee Tiberias Marathon (*dates vary*). The lowest marathon in the world.

FEBRUARY

△ **Tu Bishvat** (*dates vary*). The Jewish "new year of the trees" is celebrated by planting trees and hiking.

Tel Aviv Marathon (*dates vary*). Forty thousand runners take to the streets of Tel Aviv.

MAY

Israel Independence Day (*dates vary*). Celebrations usually include an air show by the Israel Air Force.

Lag BaOmer (*dates vary*). Jews celebrate a 2nd-century miracle with bonfires and outings; three-year-old boys are traditionally given their first haircuts.

△ **Eid al-Fitr** (*dates vary*). Muslims celebrate the end of Ramadan with three days of celebrations.

JUNE

Israel Festival (*early Jun*). Israel's largest arts festival brings music, dance and theatre to venues all over Jerusalem.

△ **Tel Aviv Gay Pride** (*second week of Jun*). Around 250,000 revellers flock to the largest LGBTQ+ pride parade in Asia.

SEPTEMBER

△ **Rosh HaShana** (*dates vary*). The Jewish New Year is celebrated with prayers and family outings.

Yom Kippur (*dates vary*). On the solemn Day of Atonement, Jews observe a day-long fast, airports and border crossings close, vehicles stay parked and children ride bicycles on the carless streets.

OCTOBER

Sukkot (*dates vary*). Observant Jews build shelters with branches on top to commemorate the Exodus from Egypt.

△ **International Fringe Theater Festival** (*dates vary*). Akko celebrates the performing arts with street theatre and new plays.

Simchat Torah (*dates vary*). Jews start a new annual cycle of weekly Torah readings.

MARCH

△ **Purim** *(dates vary)*. The deliverance of the Jews of ancient Persia is celebrated with costume parades, especially by children.

French Film Festival *(dates vary)*. Cinematheques all over Israel screen films from France.

APRIL

Passover *(dates vary)*. Celebrations of the Israelites' liberation from slavery in Egypt; as per Jewish law, no bread is sold in Jewish areas.

△ **Good Friday** *(dates vary)*. Processions along the Via Dolorosa in Jerusalem commemorate Jesus's crucifixion.

Easter *(dates vary)*. Jesus's resurrection is marked by parades and church services.

Ramadan *(dates vary)*. A lunar month of dawn-to-dusk fasting by Muslims, with joyous breakfasts held after sundown.

JULY

△ **Jerash Festival** *(late Jul)*. Music, folk dance and theatre performances bring Jordan's finest Roman ruins to life.

Eid al-Adha *(dates vary)*. Muslims honour the willingness of Abraham to sacrifice his son on this holiest of holidays, with celebrations lasting between two and four days.

AUGUST

△ **Safed Klezmer Festival** *(mid-Aug)*. Passionate "Jewish soul music" echoes through the alleys of Safed.

Red Sea Jazz Festival *(late Aug)*. Jazz musicians from around the world jam in Eilat.

NOVEMBER

△ **Yitzhak Rabin Memorial Day** *(dates vary)*. A Tel Aviv rally commemorates Rabin's 1995 assassination by a Jewish opponent of the Oslo peace process.

Open Restaurants Jerusalem *(mid-Nov)*. Top chefs open their restaurant kitchens for workshops and share culinary secrets.

DECEMBER

Chanukah *(dates vary)*. Jews celebrate the victory of the Maccabees over the Seleucid Greeks and the Temple's reconsecration.

Western Christmas *(25 Dec)*. In Bethlehem, Catholic Mass is celebrated at midnight.

△ **Holiday of the Holy Days** *(weekends in Dec)*. Haifa's interfaith celebration of Jewish, Christian and Muslim festivals.

A BRIEF
HISTORY

From the dawn of human history, the land between the Mediterranean and the Jordan River - also known as Canaan, the Land of Israel, Judaea, the Holy Land, Palestine and the State of Israel - has played a major role in human civilization and monotheistic religion.

The Israelites and the First and Second Temples

Between 1200 and 1000 BC, the Hebrew tribes in Canaan merged into a political entity known as Israel and King David established Jerusalem as its capital. After the death of King Solomon, the Israelite kingdom split into Israel in the Galilee and Judaea in Jerusalem and the south. In 586 BC the Babylonians captured Jerusalem and destroyed Solomon's Temple (the First Temple), forcing the Jews of Judaea into exile. After the defeat of the Babylonians by the Persians in 538 BC, the Jews were allowed to return to Israel. They built the Second Temple on the ruins of the First, marking the start of the "Second Temple" period.

1 A historical map of the city of Jerusalem, showing the First Temple.

2 King Solomon, leader of the Israelite Kingdom.

3 A model of the Second Temple in Jerusalem.

4 The siege of Jerusalem during the Great Revolt.

Timeline of events

780,000 BC
Predecessors of *Homo sapiens* live in the Upper Galilee, using sophisticated hand-axes.

10,000 BC
Stone Age hunter-gatherers settle down in Jericho, cultivating crops and domesticating animals.

1500 BC
The Canaanite peoples of the Levant are first mentioned.

1100s BC
The Philistines arrive by sea from the Aegean and settle in and around Gaza.

c 1000 BC
King David makes Jerusalem the Israelite capital; his son Solomon builds the First Temple.

586 BC
The Babylonians destroy the First Temple and exile the Jews in what is known as the "Babylonian Captivity".

2

3

4

The Romans and the Jewish Resistance

Jerusalem was conquered by the legions of Rome in 63 BC.
The Romans' heavy tax burden and insensitive administration
created a volatile social and political climate, into which Jesus
was born, lived and preached as a Jew. In AD 66, a full-scale
Jewish rebellion, known as the Great Revolt (or the First Jewish-
Roman War), broke out, which culminated with the Romans
seizing Jerusalem, destroying the city and demolishing the
Second Temple, leaving only the Western Wall. After crushing a
second Jewish rebellion in the 2nd century BC, Roman Emperor
Hadrian rebuilt Jerusalem as a pagan city that Jews were forbidden
to enter and changed the name of the Roman province of Judaea
(Iudaea) to Syria Palaestina, named after the Jews' great enemies,
the Philistines. During the 2nd and 3rd centuries, there was
virtually no Jewish life in Judaea, but Judaism remained alive in
the Galilee and diaspora communities. In the early 4th century,
Christians were granted freedom of worship by Roman Emperor
Constantine the Great. The doors of the Holy Land were
opened to Christian pilgrims and many Christian churches
were built. Christianity became the official religion of the
Roman Empire in 380, ushering in the Byzantine period.

THE LOST TRIBES

When the Assyrians
conquered the Galilee
around 720 BC, they
exiled the Kingdom of
Israel's ten tribes, who
mysteriously disap-
peared from history.
Groups around the
world, from Ethiopia to
Afghanistan to Nigeria,
claim descent from the
Ten Lost Tribes.

322 BC

Alexander the Great
conquers Judaea, bringing
Hellenistic (Greek) culture.

164 BC

The Maccabees
defeat the
Seleucids,
reestablishing
independence
for Judaea.

63 BC

Roman legions
conquer Jerusalem,
bringing Judaea into
the Roman Empire.

c 4 BC

Jesus is born
in Bethlehem.

AD 66–70

The Great Jewish
Revolt ends with
the destruction of
the Second Temple.

380

Theodosius
proclaims
Christianity
the official
religion of the
Roman Empire.

1

Islam and the Crusades

Following the relative stability and propserity of the Byzantine era, upheaval arrived in 638, when Muslim forces from Arabia conquered Palestine, bringing with them both Islam and Arab culture. Christians and Jews were permitted to live in Jerusalem on payment of an "infidels' tax", and Christian pilgrims from Byzantium and Europe were allowed to visit the Holy Land. Interreligious coexistence ended in 1009, when the sixth Fatimid caliph Al-Hākim destroyed the Church of the Holy Sepulchre. After the Seljuk Turks forbade Christians and Jews from entering Jerusalem in 1071, outraged leaders in Christian Europe launched the first of a series of Crusades to conquer the Holy Land. The First Crusade set off in 1096, capturing the Holy Land in 1099. Crusader control of Jerusalem was ended in 1187 by the Kurdish-Muslim general Saladin (Salah ad-Din), but the Holy Land's Crusader kingdoms survived until 1291. In the wake of the Crusades, Jerusalem slowly declined to the status of a provincial city. The Mamelukes ruled the Holy Land from Egypt, and the Holy City became a place of banishment for officials who fell from court favour in Cairo. However, Christians were once again allowed to visit the Holy Land as pilgrims.

↑ A Byzantine icon of the Madonna and Child, dating to the 6th century

Timeline of events

970

The Fatimids, a Shi'ite dynasty based in Cairo, capture Palestine.

1099

The Crusaders capture Jerusalem and establish a kingdom there.

636

The Battle of the Yarmouk River inaugurates Arab and Muslim rule in the Holy Land.

1187

Saladin defeats the Crusaders and takes Jerusalem.

1260

The Mongols are defeated by the Mamelukes at the Battle of Ein Jalut.

Ottoman Rule and the Birth of Zionism

Four centuries of Ottoman Turkish rule of Palestine began in 1516. Vast architectural projects were carried out in Jerusalem under the sultan Suleyman the Magnificent (1520–66), who built the Old City walls. By the 18th century, however, the Ottoman Empire was seen as weak and vulnerable. With its continuing decline, the European nations, newly empowered by the Industrial Revolution, took a renewed interest in the Holy Land. A British consul arrived in Jerusalem in 1838, followed by diplomats from France and Prussia. Meanwhile, in Western and Central Europe, a movement for Jewish national self-determination, known as Zionism, began growing. Political Zionism, which sought to achieve an independent Jewish state through political and diplomatic initiatives, was founded in 1896 by Theodor Herzl, a Budapest-born Austrian journalist.

Turkish rule of Palestine was ended by the British during World War I. In the Balfour Declaration of 1917, the British government announced its support for "the establishment in Palestine of a national home for the Jewish people", a promise that became part of the British Mandate for Palestine, which was approved by the League of Nations in 1922.

1 An illuminated manuscript showing a battle between Crusaders and Muslims during the Crusades.

2 A portrait of Ottoman sultan Suleyman the Magnificent.

3 Napoleon during his brief conquest of Jaffa in 1799.

4 Jewish immigrant settlers at Rishon Le Zion in the early 20th century.

1291
The last Crusader territories in the Holy Land, including Akko, fall to the Mamelukes.

1516
The Ottomans seize control of Palestine from the Mamelukes.

1799
Napoleon conquers Jaffa, massacring the Ottoman garrison and civilians.

1839
British Jew Sir Moses Montefiore first proposes the idea of a Jewish State.

1882
Following pogroms in Russia, Jews settle in Palestine and establish agricultural villages.

1

Arab-Jewish Conflict

At the outbreak of World War I, some 500,000 Arabs and about 85,000 Jews were living in Palestine. In 1921, the British broke off the eastern section of Palestine to form Jordan. During the 1920s and 1930s, about 250,000 Jews, many of them refugees from Nazi Germany, arrived in Palestine. Each new wave of immigrants increased the tension between the Arab and Jewish communities. The Arab Revolt, launched in 1936, led to violence between Palestinian Arabs and both Palestinian Jews and the British. In 1939, as war neared in Europe, the British government, in an attempt to improve relations with potential Arab and Muslim allies, published a "white paper" drastically limiting Jewish immigration to Palestine – just as the situation of the Jews of Germany was becoming desperate. The immigration ban continued after World War II (including for Holocaust survivors), resulting in a confrontation between the Zionist movement and the British government. The mainstream Jewish community, led by David Ben-Gurion of the socialist Mapai party, largely cooperated with the British, while more radical Zionist groups, such as the right-wing Irgun (Etzel) and the Lehi (Stern Gang), launched

1 Jewish refugees disembarking at Tel Aviv in 1939. ↑

2 A 1947 poster showing Theodor Herzl, founder of Zionism.

3 British troops departing from Palestine in 1948.

4 Ben Gurion officially proclaiming the state of Israel in 1948.

Timeline of events

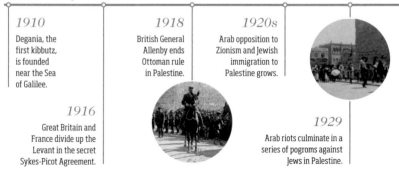

1910
Degania, the first kibbutz, is founded near the Sea of Galilee.

1916
Great Britain and France divide up the Levant in the secret Sykes-Picot Agreement.

1918
British General Allenby ends Ottoman rule in Palestine.

1920s
Arab opposition to Zionism and Jewish immigration to Palestine grows.

1929
Arab riots culminate in a series of pogroms against Jews in Palestine.

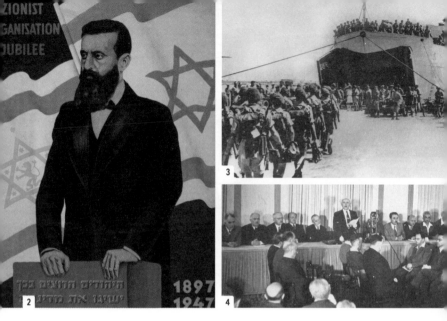

2 1897 1947

3

4

bloody attacks against the British as well as Arabs, including civilians. Unable to control the spiraling situation, the British placed the "Palestine question" before the newly formed United Nations. On 29 November 1947 the UN General Assembly voted for the partition of Palestine into an Arab state and a Jewish state, with Jerusalem under international administration.

The Creation of Israel

Right after the partition vote, the country descended into war. When the British left on 15 May 1948, two things happened immediately: Ben-Gurion declared the establishment of the State of !srael; and the armies of Lebanon, Syria, Iraq, Jordan and Egypt invaded. To the surprise of many, the Israelis held on and even increased the territory under their control. At the end of the 1948 war, Israel controlled 77 per cent of Mandatory Palestine, the West Bank was occupied by Jordan, the Gaza Strip was under Egyptian administration, and Jerusalem was a divided city, with the Old City – including the Western Wall – under Jordanian control. During the fighting some 700,000 Palestinian Arabs fled or were expelled from Israeli territory (about 180,000 remained).

THE GREEN LINE

After the 1948 war, Israeli, Jordanian and Egyptian negotiators used green ink to indicate the armistice lines on maps. The "Green Line" created two new geopolitical entities: the West Bank and the Gaza Strip. Israel has occupied the West Bank since 1967 (it withdrew from Gaza in 2005) but many still see the Green Line as the basis for the borders of a future Palestinian state.

1933
German Jews fleeing the Nazis begin immigrating to Palestine.

1936
The Arab Revolt against the British Mandate and Jewish immigration begins.

1949
Armistice agreements between Israel and its Arab neighbours are signed in Rhodes.

1946
The Irgun (Etzel), a radical Zionist militia, blows up Jerusalem's King David Hotel.

1948
Ben-Gurion declares the establishment of the State of Israel.

1

2

Arab-Israeli Wars after 1948

Upon its establishment, Israel immediately began resettling Jewish refugees from Europe and the Middle East. Over the next two decades, 850,000 Jews fled or were forced to leave the Arab countries, most of them finding refuge in Israel. The state of war between Israel and its Arab neighbours continued. In 1956, the Israeli army swept into Sinai as part of an unsuccessful French and British plan to take back control of the Suez Canal, nationalized by Egypt's President Nasser. In the spring of 1967, Egypt expelled UN peacekeeping forces from Sinai, blockaded the Straits of Tiran to Israeli shipping and sent ground forces into Sinai. In response, Israel launched a pre-emptive attack that destroyed the air forces of Egypt, Syria, Jordan and Iraq on the ground. By the time the Six-Day War ended, Israel had taken control of the Golan Heights from Syria, the Gaza Strip and Sinai from Egypt, and East Jerusalem and the West Bank from Jordan.

The Quest for Peace

The short Yom Kippur War of 1973 between Egypt, Syria and Israel changed little on the ground, but did pave the way for the 1979 Camp David Accords, a peace treaty between Egypt and

Did You Know?

In 1969 Israel's Golda Meir became the world's first female prime minister not from a political dynasty.

Timeline of events

1967
Israel defeats its Arab neighbours in the Six-Day War, tripling the territory under its control.

1977
Israel's right-wing Likud Party comes to power, ending three decades of Labor Party rule.

1993
Israel and the PLO sign the Oslo Accords.

1994
Jordan and Israel sign a peace treaty and open their borders.

1995
Israeli Prime Minister Yitzhak Rabin is assassinated by a right-wing Jewish extremist.

Israel under which Sinai was returned to Egypt. In the late 1980s, the Palestine Liberation Organization (PLO) concluded that their violence against civilians was strengthening Israeli resolve and winning them little international sympathy. Much more effective was the Intifada ("shaking off"), a grass-roots Palestinian revolt against the Israeli occupation in the Gaza Strip and West Bank, which began in late 1987. In the wake of the First Gulf War of 1991, the Europeans secretly brokered a meeting between Israeli and Palestinian delegations that led to the signing of the Oslo Accords in 1993.

Israel and the Palestinian Territories Today

As a result of Israeli anger at Palestinian suicide attacks during the Second Intifada (2000–05), the bitter intra-Palestinian rift between the Fatah-ruled West Bank and Hamas-ruled Gaza, and repeated violent confrontations between Hamas and Israel, the Palestinian-Israeli peace process has broken down. Despite the continued construction of Israeli settlements by Israel's right-wing government – in defiance of the international community – attempts to find a solution that will bring lasting peace to the region persevere.

① Jordanian refugees crossing into occupied Jordan territory during the Six-Day War in 1967. ↑

② Palestinian demonstrations in the Gaza strip in 1988, during the Intifada.

③ The historic handshake between Yitzhak Rabin and Yasser Arafat at the signing of the Oslo Accords in 1993.

④ Present-day residents of Jerusalem shopping at a market in the Old City.

2004
Palestinian President Yasser Arafat dies in a Paris hospital.

2005
Israel unilaterally withdraws from the Gaza Strip.

2006
The Islamist militant group Hamas defeats Fatah in Palestinian Legislative Council elections.

2007
Hamas seizes control of the Gaza Strip from Fatah and the Palestinian Authority.

2020
Israel signs peace agreements with the UAE, Bahrain, Morocco and Sudan.

JUDAISM

Judaism is based on the belief that a single, transcendent God who revealed himself to the prophets of the Hebrew Bible is present in human affairs and maintains a covenantal relationship with the Jewish people. It is the role of the Jews in history to inspire humankind to recognize God's omnipresence and purpose. For traditional Jews, Judaism is an all-encompassing way of life – its legal system, Halacha, guides their conduct, and their identity incorporates a sense of Jewish peoplehood. Whereas Christianity and Islam seek converts, Judaism does not proselytize because, according to the Talmud, "the righteous of all nations have a share in the world to come".

RABBINIC JUDAISM

Jewish worship was originally centered on animal sacrifices offered by priests in the Temple in Jerusalem. After the destruction of the Second Temple in AD 70 *(p48)*, pilgrimages and sacrifices were replaced by prayer and study in local synagogues. The rabbis who led this transformation also wrote down the Oral Law, creating a record of legal deliberations, the Talmud, that is still studied and debated today.

STREAMS IN JUDAISM

Jews have responded to the challenges of modernity in widely divergent ways. Founded in Germany in 1810, the Reform Movement emphasizes Judaism's ethical

↑ Jews praying at the Western Wall in Jerusalem, the most holy site in Judaism

traditions over ritual obligations. The Haredim (ultra-Orthodox) interpret Halacha (Jewish law) very stringently – much more so than the rabbis of centuries past – while Modern Orthodoxy strives to meld adherence to Halacha with life in the modern world. The Conservative Movement believes that for Judaism to remain both authentic and relevant, Halacha is still binding but must evolve.

WOMEN IN JUDAISM

According to traditional Jewish law, Jewish identity is passed down via the mother, but in centuries past women's roles were largely domestic. Today, the Conservative, Reconstructionist, Reform and Jewish Renewal Movements accord full equality to women, and liberal Orthodox streams are searching for ways to be ritually inclusive. The demand that part of the Western Wall in Jerusalem be set aside for gender-egalitarian prayers has been met with strong opposition from ultra-Orthodox political parties (p89).

THE TORAH

The first five books of the Hebrew Bible – Genesis, Exodus, Leviticus, Numbers and Deuteronomy – are known as the Torah (Pentateuch). Judaism's most central and sacred text, it serves as the basis for Judaism's moral code, legal system and theology. The text of the Torah – handwritten on a parchment scroll – is chanted publically in synagogues on Saturday mornings over the course of each year (or, in some communities, three years).

← Women throwing candy during a bar mitzvah by the Western Wall

↑ A group of Orthodox Jews dancing in the plaza in front of the Western Wall

CHRISTIANITY

Initially a sect within Judaism, Christianity grew out of the life and teachings of Jesus of Nazareth, whom Christians believe was anointed by God as the savior of humanity. Christian denominations diverge on significant points of theology, but almost all believe that God, while unitary, exists as God the Father, God the Son (Jesus Christ) and God the Holy Spirit. They also hold that Jesus died a physical death on the Cross to atone for the sins of humanity, was resurrected and ascended into Heaven; and that humanity awaits Christ's Second Coming and the Day of Judgment. Christianity is followed by about 2.4 billion people – one in every three people – among them 1.3 billion Catholics and 920 million Protestants.

JESUS

Jesus of Nazareth was a Jew who lived during the 1st century AD in the Roman province of Judaea (Iudaea). His life and teachings are recounted in the New Testament. Most Christians believe that Jesus was the Incarnation of God and the Messiah (Christ) prophesied in the Hebrew Bible. His birth is celebrated on Christmas, his Crucifixion on Good Friday and his Resurrection on Easter.

↑ The Feast of the Immaculate Conception at St Anne's Church in Jerusalem

THE NEW TESTAMENT

The Christian Bible consists of two parts: the Old Testament (essentially the Hebrew Bible); and the New Testament, whose 27 books include the Gospels ("good news") of Matthew, Mark, Luke and John. Written down in Greek in the late 1st and early 2nd century AD, the New Testament – the

The domes of the ↑
Church of the Holy
Sepulchre in Jerusalem

foundational text of Christian theology – reveals the life and teachings of Jesus and his apostles.

CHRISTIANS IN THE HOLY LAND

About 160,000 Christians, 80 per cent of them Arabic-speaking, live in Israel. Constituting 2 per cent of the population, 60 per cent are Melkite (Greek) Catholics and 30 per cent are Greek Orthodox. Of the West Bank's 50,000 Christians – 1.7 per cent of the population – about half are Greek Orthodox and a third are Catholics, mostly Eastern but also Roman (Latin). Other Christian denominations in the Holy Land include Anglicans, Armenians, Copts, Ethiopians, Lutherans, Maronite Catholics, Russian Orthodox and Syriacs.

THE EUCHARIST

Also known as Holy Communion, the Eucharist is a Christian ritual in which bread (or a wafer) and wine (or grape juice) are consumed as a memorial for Jesus's sacrifice on the Cross. It commemorates Jesus's Last Supper, at which he identified bread with his body and wine with his blood. Most denominations believe that Jesus is present, either literally or symbolically, at the Eucharist.

ICONS

A central feature of Eastern and Oriental Orthodox church decoration, icons are visual representations of Jesus, Mary, the saints and the angels that worshippers venerate in order to help them feel the presence of God's holiness. In Orthodox churches, an icon-adorned wall called an iconostasis (icon screen) – inspired by the architecture of the Temple in Jerusalem *(p48)* – stands between the nave, where lay worshipers pray, and the sanctuary, where the priest conducts part of the service.

The cross is used to symbolize the Crucifixion of Christ.

Domes have been a feature of Christian church architecture since the Byzantine era.

↑ Praying with a cross while undertaking a pilgrimage along the Via Dolorosa

ISLAM

Islam is an Abrahamic religion whose core belief is the absolute oneness and uniqueness of God (Allah), who is both all-powerful and merciful. The Arabic word *islam* means "submission to the will of God", revealed in the Qu'ran (Koran) through the Prophet Muhammad – the last in a series of prophets that began with Adam and includes Noah, Abraham, Moses, Solomon and Jesus. The Islamic legal code, Shari'a, governs every aspect of traditional Muslims' day-to-day life. According to Islamic theology, on the Day of Resurrection the righteous will be rewarded and sinners punished. About one in four people – some 1.8 billion people – follow Islam worldwide.

THE PROPHET MUHAMMAD

Believed by Muslims to be God's final prophet, Muhammad (c 570–632) began receiving revelations at the age of 40. In 622 he was forced to flee to Medina because of opposition by pagans, an event known as the Hijra (Hegira). Muhammad conquered Mecca in 630, and by the end of his life Islam ruled much of Arabia. Sayings and traditions associated with Muhammad, known as Hadith, serve as an authoritative source of moral guidance and law second only to the Qu'ran.

THE QU'RAN

The Qu'ran, the holy book of Islam, is regarded as the final revealed word of God, transmitted verbally to the Prophet Muhammad by the Archangel Jibril (Gabriel). It is divided into 114 *suras* (chapters) that are arranged roughly from longest to shortest. Many figures from the Hebrew Bible and the New Testament appear in the Qu'ran in narrative passages that differ in various details from their Jewish and Christian counterparts.

↑ The beautiful interior of the Mosque of Al-Jazzar in Akko

THE MOSQUE

The interior of a mosque (*masjid* in Arabic) usually includes a *mihrab*, a niche that indicates the direction of Mecca (the holiest city of Islam), and a *minbar*, a raised pulpit from which the imam delivers his Friday sermon. Many mosques also have a minaret, a spire from which the call to prayer is issued five times a day.

The King Abdullah ↑ Mosque in Amman, with its decorative blue dome

THE FIVE PILLARS OF ISLAM

Shahadah - The Muslim declaration of faith: "There is no god but God (Allah) and Muhammad is the messenger of God."

Salah - Set daily prayers, performed in the direction of the Kaaba, a shrine near the centre of the Great Mosque in Mecca (Saudi Arabia), five times a day.

Zakat - The giving of a set proportion of one's wealth to charity.

Sawm - Fasting during daylight hours for the entire holy month of Ramadan, the ninth month of the Islamic calendar.

Hajj - The pilgrimage to the holy city of Mecca, which all Muslims, if they are able, are enjoined to undertake at least once in their lives.

1 *Zakat* donations are collected.

2 Worshippers pray at Jerusalem's Al-Aqsa Mosque while observing the *sawm* during the holy month of Ramadan.

3 Thousands of Muslim pilgrims circle the Kaaba in the Great Mosque in Mecca, Saudi Arabia, while undertaking the *hajj*.

Did You Know?

Mosques are decorated with patterns and calligraphy because Islamic law forbids images of sentient beings.

EXPERIENCE
JERUSALEM

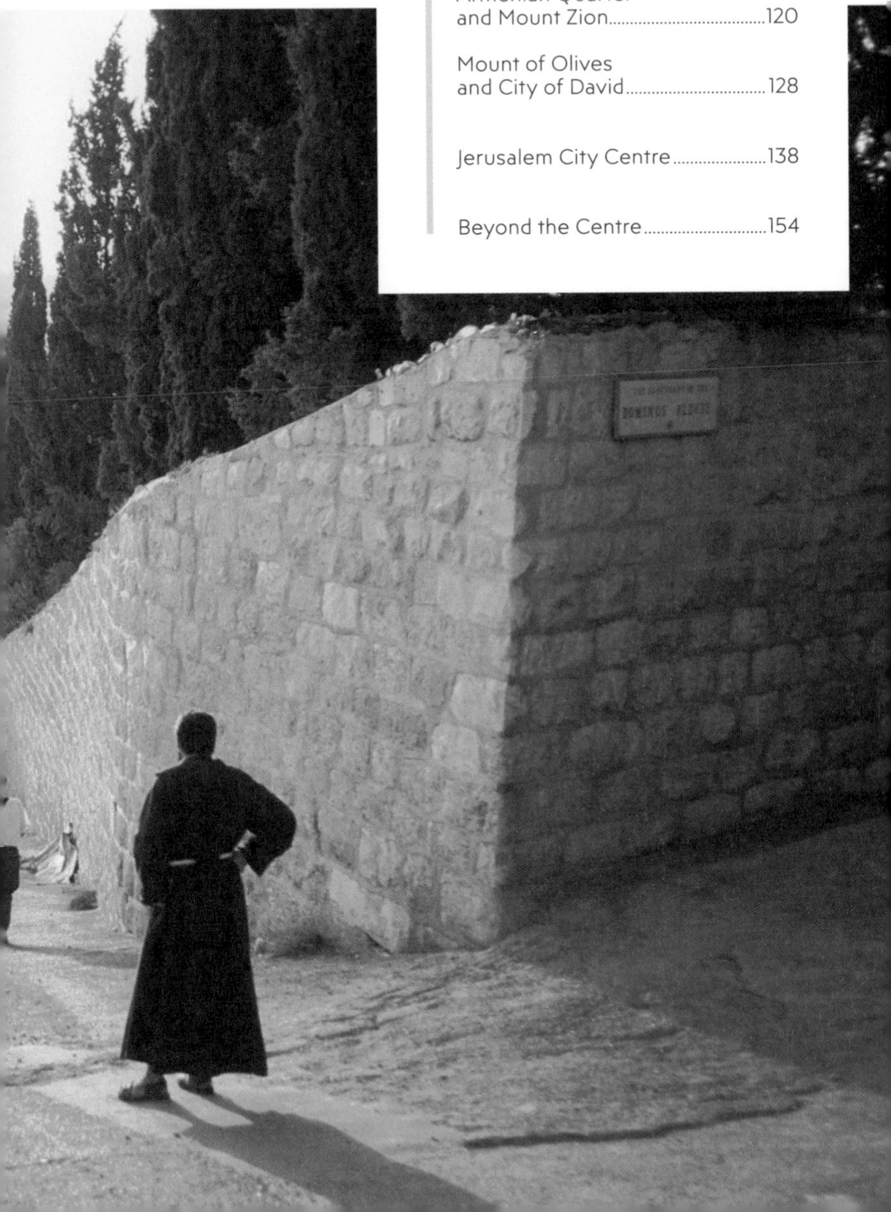

EXPLORE
JERUSALEM

This guide divides Jerusalem into six areas, as shown on this map. Find out more about each area on the following pages. For areas beyond the centre see p154.

GEULA

American Colony Hotel

BEIT YISRAEL

St George's Cathedral

MEA SHE'ARIM

MAHANE YEHUDA

Davidka Square

St Etienne Monastery

JERUSALEM CITY CENTRE
p138

NAKHLA'OT

Zion Square

Russian Compound

MORASHA

Damascus Gate

City Walls

NAKHALAT SHIV'A

Safra Square

Church of the Holy Sepulchre

CHRISTIAN QUARTER
p102

OLD

Mamilla Cemetery

Ha-atsmaut Garden

MAMILLA

Jaffa Gate

The Citadel

DAVID'S VILLAGE

St James's Cathedral

REHAVIA

King David Hotel

City Walls

Zion Gate

YEMIN MOSHE

TALBIYA

Sultan's Pool

ARMENIAN QUARTER AND MOUNT ZION
p120

Liberty Bell Gardens

GERMAN COLONY

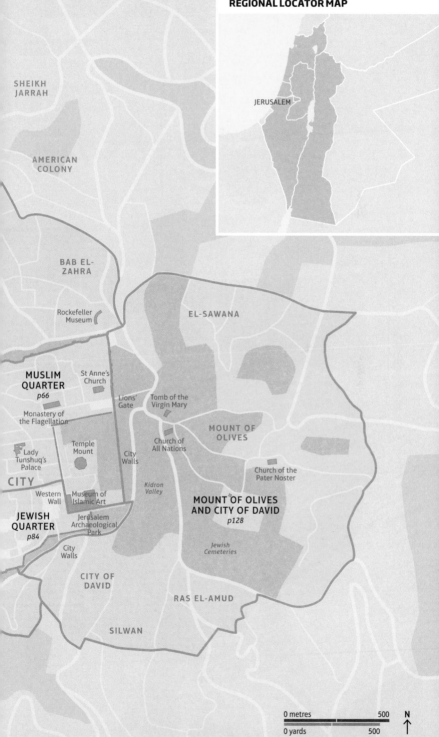

REGIONAL LOCATOR MAP

JERUSALEM

SHEIKH
JARRAH

AMERICAN
COLONY

BAB EL-
ZAHRA

EL-SAWANA

Rockefeller
Museum

MUSLIM
QUARTER
p66

St Anne's
Church

Lions'
Gate

Tomb of the
Virgin Mary

Monastery of
the Flagellation

MOUNT OF
OLIVES

Lady
Tunshuq's
Palace

Temple
Mount

Church of
All Nations

City
Walls

Church of the
Pater Noster

CITY

Western
Wall

Museum of
Islamic Art

*Kidron
Valley*

MOUNT OF OLIVES
AND CITY OF DAVID
p128

JEWISH
QUARTER
p84

Jerusalem
Archaeological
Park

City
Walls

*Jewish
Cemeteries*

CITY OF
DAVID

RAS EL-AMUD

SILWAN

0 metres   500
0 yards   500

N

A bustling street in the Muslim Quarter

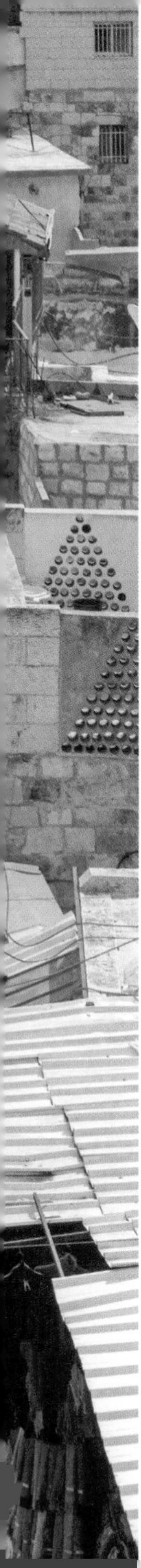

MUSLIM QUARTER

The largest neighbourhood of the Old City, the Muslim Quarter was laid out in its present configuration under the Byzantines. In the 12th century, it was taken over by the Crusaders, who built a wealth of churches and Christian institutions – many of them along the Via Dolorosa, which stretches westward from Lions' Gate. In the 14th and 15th centuries, the Mamelukes rebuilt extensively, especially in areas near the Temple Mount (Al-Haram ash-Sharif), bequeathing the city an architectural legacy of elegant mosques, madrasas and pilgrims' hostels featuring half-dome-shaped entrances, striped masonry and elegant Arabic inscriptions. The monumental Damascus Gate, meanwhile, was constructed in the 1500s on the order of Ottoman sultan Suleyman the Magnificent.

Like the Old City's three other quarters, the Muslim Quarter was given its current religious designation in the 19th century and was religiously mixed until the communal violence of the 1920s and 1930s. Today the most densely populated and poorest neighbourhood of the Old City, the area is linked to the heart of Arab East Jerusalem via its colourful, crowded souks (markets).

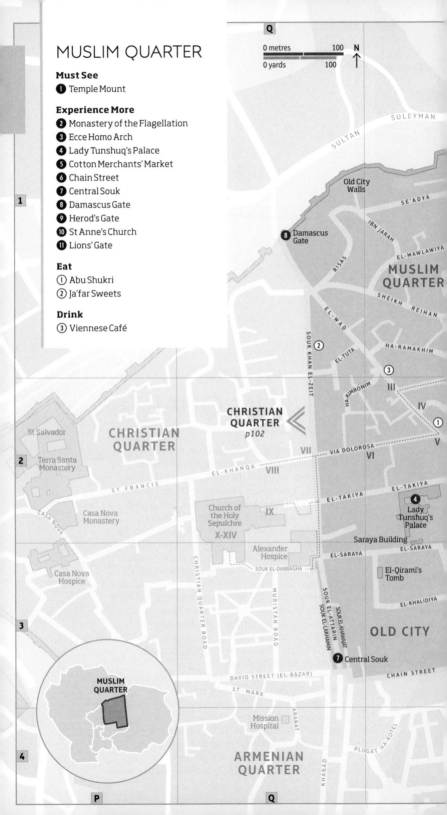

MUSLIM QUARTER

Must See
1 Temple Mount

Experience More
2 Monastery of the Flagellation
3 Ecce Homo Arch
4 Lady Tunshuq's Palace
5 Cotton Merchants' Market
6 Chain Street
7 Central Souk
8 Damascus Gate
9 Herod's Gate
10 St Anne's Church
11 Lions' Gate

Eat
1 Abu Shukri
2 Ja'far Sweets

Drink
3 Viennese Café

0 metres 100
0 yards 100
N

Q

SULEYMAN

SULTAN

Old City Walls

SE'ADYA

IBN JARAH

EL-MAWLAWIYA

8 Damascus Gate

MUSLIM QUARTER

RISAS

EL-WAD

SHEIKH REIHAN

HA-RAMAKHIM

SOUK KHAN EL-ZEIT

2

EL-TUTA

HA-KIMRONIM

3

III

IV

CHRISTIAN QUARTER p102

1

V

St Salvador

CHRISTIAN QUARTER

VII

VIA DOLOROSA

VI

Terra Santa Monastery

EL-KHANQA

VIII

ST FRANCIS

EL-TAKIYA

EL-TAKIYA

Casa Nova Monastery

Church of the Holy Sepulchre

IX

EL-TAKIYA

4 Lady Tunshuq's Palace

CASA NOVA

X-XIV

Saraya Building

Casa Nova Hospice

Alexander Hospice

EL-SARAYA

EL-SARAYA

SOUK EL-DABBAGHA

El-Qirami's Tomb

CHRISTIAN QUARTER ROAD

EL-KHALIDIYA

MURISTAN ROAD

SOUK EL-ATTARIN
SOUK EL-KHAWWAT
SOUK EL-LAKHAMIN

OLD CITY

7 Central Souk

MUSLIM QUARTER

DAVID STREET (EL-BAZAR)

CHAIN STREET

ST MARK

Mission Hospital

ARARAT

ARMENIAN QUARTER

KHABAD

PLUGAT HAKOTEL

P

Q

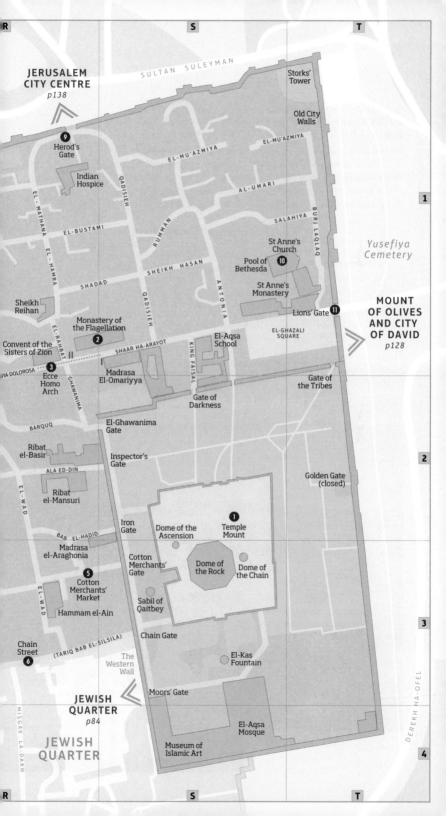

JERUSALEM CITY CENTRE
p138

9 Herod's Gate

Indian Hospice

Old City Walls

Storks' Tower

SULTAN SULEYMAN

EL-MU'AZMIYA

EL-MU'AZMIYA

QADISIEH

RUMMAN

AL-UMARI

SALAHIYA

BURJ LAQLAQ

Yusefiya Cemetery

EL-BUSTAMI

EL - MATHANA

EL - HAMRA

SHADAD

SHEIKH HASAN

QADISIEH

St Anne's Church

Pool of Bethesda

10

St Anne's Monastery

Sheikh Reihan

Monastery of the Flagellation

2

ANTONIA

El-Aqsa School

Lions' Gate

11

MOUNT OF OLIVES AND CITY OF DAVID
p128

EL-RAHBA

Convent of the Sisters of Zion

3 Ecce Homo Arch

VIA DOLOROSA

GHAWANIMA

SHAAR HA-ARAYOT

Madrasa El-Omariyya

KING FAISAL

EL-GHAZALI SQUARE

Gate of Darkness

Gate of the Tribes

BARQUQ

El-Ghawanima Gate

Ribat el-Basir

Inspector's Gate

ALA ED-DIN

Ribat el-Mansuri

EL-WAD

Golden Gate (closed)

BAB EL-HADID

Madrasa el-Araghonia

Iron Gate

Dome of the Ascension

Temple Mount

1

5 Cotton Merchants' Market

Cotton Merchants' Gate

Dome of the Rock

Dome of the Chain

EL-WAD

Hammam el-Ain

Sabil of Qaitbey

Chain Street

6

(TARIQ BAB EL-SILSILA)

Chain Gate

El-Kas Fountain

The Western Wall

DEREKH HA-OFEL

MISGAV LA-DAKH

JEWISH QUARTER
p84

Moors' Gate

JEWISH QUARTER

Museum of Islamic Art

El-Aqsa Mosque

R   S   T

1

2

3

4

❶

TEMPLE MOUNT

📍 S2 **🚪 Entrance for non-Muslims via Moors' Gate only** **🕐 Summer: 7:30–11am & 1:30–2:30pm Sun–Thu; winter: 7:30–10am & 12:30–1:30pm Sun–Thu** **🚫 Fri, Sat, Muslim hols**

Known to Muslims as Al-Haram ash-Sharif (the Noble Sanctuary), this vast rectangular esplanade in the southeastern part of the Old City has been the focal point of Jerusalem for over 3,000 years. Site of the ancient Jewish temples, the modern-day Mount is graced by the glittering Dome of the Rock and other Islamic structures.

📷 **PICTURE PERFECT**
Temple Mount Panorama

For a superb panorama of Temple Mount and the Old City, climb up to the summit of the Mount of Olives (p128) and gaze westward. Arrive early in the morning for the best light on the golden Dome of the Rock.

The First and Second Temples

According to both Jewish and Muslim traditions, Temple Mount is where Abraham offered his son as a sacrifice to God. The site is traditionally believed to be the location of the Jews' First Temple, built by Solomon in the 10th century BC and destroyed by the Babylonians in 587 BC. It was also the location of the Second Temple that later replaced it. The complex was greatly expanded in the 1st century BC by Herod the Great, who nearly doubled the size of the Inner Temple and created the Temple platform by building four walls around a natural hill and filling them in. It is from the Second Temple that Jesus is said to have expelled the merchants and moneychangers. The Temple was destroyed by the Romans after a bitter five-month siege of Jerusalem in AD 70, the culmination of hostilities that began four years earlier with the Jewish Revolt.

Temple Mount, with the Western Wall in the foreground ↑

The main entrance of
El-Aqsa Mosque, which
dates to the 11th century ↑

→
Worshippers relaxing
in the shade of the
complex's courtyard

Islamic Shrine

Left in ruins for more than half a millennium, the site became
an Islamic shrine in AD 691 with the building of the Dome of
the Rock. Construction of the El-Aqsa mosque was begun soon
after, but in the first 60 years of its existence the mosque was
twice razed to the ground by earthquakes. When the Crusaders
captured Jerusalem in 1099, El-Aqsa became the headquarters
of the Templars. Over the centuries other buildings have been
added to the complex, which is the third most important
Islamic religious sanctuary after Mecca and Medina.

Did You Know?

The Jewish holiday of
Chanukah celebrates
the reconsecration
of the Second Temple
in 164 BC.

JERUSALEM AND ISLAM

The Dome of the Rock
and El-Aqsa mosque
represent the first
great religious complex
in the history of Islam.
Although Muslims
venerate many of the
same prophets as the
Jews and Christians, in
particular Abraham,
Jerusalem itself is never
actually mentioned in
the Quran. The choice
of this site was more
likely a political issue.
In constructing his
mosque on the site of
the Temple, the caliph
Abd el-Malik intended
to reinforce the idea
that the new religion
of Islam, and its worldly
empire, was both the
successor and continu-
ation of the Jewish and
Christian religions.

Exploring Temple Mount

Although the undoubted main attraction is the Dome of the Rock, Temple Mount has a great many other features that are worthy of attention. The esplanade acts as a virtual museum of Islamic architecture, beginning with the Dome, which dates back to the Omayyad era and is the earliest structure, and running through the Ayyubid (Grammar College), Mameluke (numerous madrasas) and Ottoman periods. Visitors should be aware that certain parts of the Haram ash-Sharif are out of bounds, notably the area south of the Gate of the Tribes and east of El-Aqsa. Non-Muslims may only access the Temple Mount via Moors' Gate and cannot enter the Dome of the Rock and the El-Aqsa Mosque.

↑ The walls of Temple Mount, with the grey dome of El-Aqsa Mosque behind

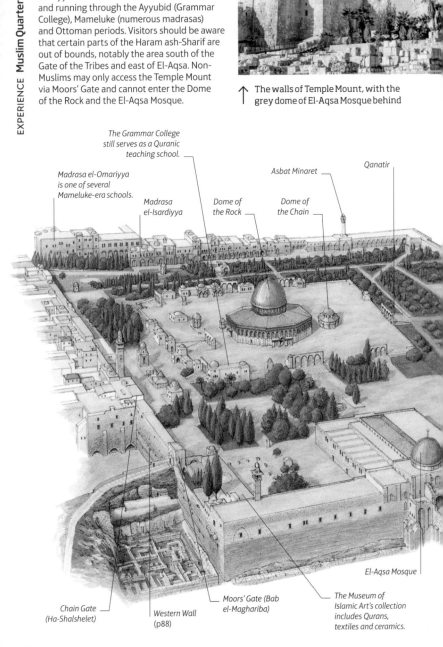

The Grammar College still serves as a Quranic teaching school.

Madrasa el-Omariyya is one of several Mameluke-era schools.

Madrasa el-Isardiyya

Dome of the Rock

Dome of the Chain

Asbat Minaret

Qanatir

Chain Gate (Ha-Shalshelet)

Western Wall (p88)

Moors' Gate (Bab el-Maghariba)

El-Aqsa Mosque

The Museum of Islamic Art's collection includes Qurans, textiles and ceramics.

THE TEMPLE MOUNT IN JEWISH HISTORY

Jews the world over face Jerusalem's Temple Mount when they pray, as it is the holiest site in Judaism. A few synagogues are even decorated with images of the Dome of the Rock (including examples in Safed) because the 7th-century Muslim shrine is believed to stand on the site of the First and the Second Temples. After the Romans destroyed the Second Temple in AD 70, the practice of animal sacrifices ceased and Jewish Sages based in the Galilee reoriented Judaism towards prayer and a written legal code (p56). Today, Jewish religious law prohibits Jews from visiting Temple Mount and Israeli secular law forbids non-Muslims from praying here.

Golden Gate is one of the original city gates but was sealed up by the Muslims in the 16th century. The area is out of bounds.

Did You Know?

The Temple Mount complex covers some 150,000 sq m (1,614,590 sq ft).

↑ The vast courtyard of the Temple Mount, or Al-Haram ash-Sharif

Highlights

El-Aqsa Mosque

▶ El-Aqsa's present form dates from the early 11th century. The interior is dominated by mid-20th-century additions, notably ranks of marble columns donated by Benito Mussolini, and a decorative ceiling paid for by King Farouk of Egypt. Older elements include the mihrab, decorated in 1187 under the patronage of Egyptian sultan Saladin.

Museum of Islamic Art

Housed in the Crusader-era refectory of the Knights Templar, this museum contains objects donated to the Haram ash-Sharif over the centuries, as well as architectural remnants from the site. It is currently closed to the public.

The Qanatirs

◀ Eight short flights of steps lead up to the platform on which the Dome of the Rock sits, each of which date from different periods. The flights are all crowned by a slender arcade known as a *qanatir*.

Dome of the Chain

The most impressive of the Haram's smaller domes is the Dome of the Chain. Its name derives from the legend that a chain once hung from the roof, and whoever told a lie while holding it would be struck dead by lightning.

The Madrasas

Most of the buildings fringing the Haram are *madrasas* - Islamic colleges. Of these, the Ashrafiyya, built in 1482, is a masterpiece of Islamic architecture, while the Uthmaniyya has beautiful decorations.

Golden Gate

▶ This was one of the original Herodian city gates. According to Jewish tradition, the Messiah will enter Jerusalem through this gate.

Dome of the Rock

One of the first and greatest achievements of Islamic architecture, the Dome of the Rock was built in AD 688–91 by the Omayyad caliph Abd el-Malik. Intended to proclaim the superiority of Islam and provide an Islamic focal point in the Holy City, the majestic structure now dominates Jerusalem and has become a symbol of the city. More a shrine than a mosque, the mathematically harmonious building echoes elements of Classical and Byzantine architecture, including the rotunda of the Holy Sepulchre (p106). The dome was originally made of copper but is now covered with gold leaf thanks to the financial support of the late King Hussein of Jordan. Inside, the dazzling cuppola is decorated with elaborate floral motifs.

TILE DECORATION

In the mid-1500s, Ottoman Sultan Suleyman the Magnificent decided to spruce up the Dome of the Rock, whose glass mosaics were showing their age after six centuries of exposure to the elements. He hired ceramic artisans in Iznik, Turkey, to create 45,000 ceramic tiles that were laboriously shipped to Jerusalem. Most of the original 16th-century tiles have been replaced, but a few still adorn parts of the structure protected from the weather.

The text on the interior of the dome commemorates Saladin, who sponsored restoration work on the building.

The exquisitely decorated Dome of the Rock ↓

The drum is decorated with tiles and verses from the Quran which tell of Muhammad's Night Journey.

Green and gold mosaics create a scintillating effect on the walls below the dome.

Outer ambulatory

Quranic verses

Marble panel

Stained-glass window

The octagonal arcade is adorned with an inscription inviting Christians to recognize the truth of Islam.

The Rock is believed to be where Abraham was asked to sacrifice Isaac.

Each outer wall is 20.4 m (67 ft) long. This exactly matches the dome's diameter.

Did You Know?

It took 80 kg (176 lb) of 24-carat gold to re-gild the Dome of the Rock in 1993.

↑ Dome of the Rock, glimpsed through the pillars of the surrounding buildings

EXPERIENCE MORE

❷
Monastery of the Flagellation

🗺 R1 🅰 Via Dolorosa
📞 (02) 627 0444
🕐 Monastery: 7:30am–5pm daily; Studium Museum: 9am–1pm & 4–6pm Tue–Sat (by appt)

Owned by the Franciscans, this complex embraces the simple and striking Chapel of the Flagellation, designed in the 1920s by the Italian architect Antonio Barluzzi, who was also responsible for the Dominus Flevit Chapel on the Mount of Olives (p135). It is located on the site traditionally believed to be where Christ was flogged by Roman soldiers prior to his crucifixion (Matthew 27: 27–30; Mark 15: 16–19).

On the other side of the courtyard is the Chapel of the Condemnation, which also dates from the early 20th century. It is built over the remains of a medieval chapel, on the site popularly identified as where Christ was tried before Pontius Pilate.

The neighbouring monastery buildings house the Studium Biblicum Franciscanum, a prestigious institute of biblical, geographical and archaeological studies. Also part of the complex, the Studium Museum contains objects found by the Franciscans in excavations at Capernaum, Nazareth, Bethlehem and various other sites. The most interesting exhibits are Byzantine and Crusader objects, such as fragments of frescoes from the Church of Gethsemane, precursor of the present-day Church of All Nations (p134), and a 12th-century crozier from the Church of the Nativity in Bethlehem (p232).

❸
Ecce Homo Arch

🗺 R1 🅰 Via Dolorosa

This arch that spans the Via Dolorosa was built by the Romans in AD 70 to support a ramp being laid against the Antonia Fortress, in which Jewish rebels were barricaded.

EAT

Abu Shukri
This tiny, family-run place, opposite the 5th Station of the Cross, serves what some say is Jerusalem's finest hummus, with tahini and fuul (fava beans), chickpeas or pine nuts.

🗺 R2 🅰 63 Al-Wad St
📞 (02) 628 9303

Ja'far Sweets
Renowned for luscious kunafeh: gooey hot cheese and shredded phyllo (filo) soaked in rose-water syrup, with grated pistachios. Very near Damascus Gate.

🗺 Q1 🅰 Khan el-Zeit St
📞 (02) 628 3582

↑ The shaded cloisters of the Franciscan Monastery of the Flagellation on the Via Dolorosa

← Ecce Homo Arch, spanning the Via Dolorosa

Jerusalem some time in the 14th century and had this edifice built for herself. It is one of the loveliest examples of Mameluke architecture in Jerusalem. Unfortunately, the narrow street does not allow for standing back and appreciating the building as a whole, but you can admire the three great doorways with their beautiful inlaid-marble decoration. The upper portion of a window recess also displays some fine stalactite-like decoration, a form known as *muqarnas*. The former palace now serves as an orphanage and is not open to the public.

When Lady Tunshuq died, she was buried in a small tomb across from the palace. The fine decoration on the tomb includes panels of different coloured marble, intricately shaped and slotted together like a jigsaw – this is a typical Mameluke feature known as "joggling".

If you head east and across El-Wad Road, you will enter a narrow alley called Ala ed-Din, which contains more fine Mameluke architecture. Most of the façades are composed of bands of different hues of stone, a strikingly beautiful Mameluke decorative tech-nique known as *ablaq*.

Did You Know?

The exterior of Lady Tunshuq's mausoleum is a miniature version of her palace's façade.

When the Romans rebuilt Jerusalem in AD 135 in the wake of the Second Jewish War *(p49)*, the arch was recon-structed as a monument to victory, with two smaller arches flanking a large central bay. It is the central bay that you see spanning the street.

One of the side arches is also still visible, incorporated into the interior of the neigh-bouring **Convent of the Sisters of Zion**. Built in the 1860s, the convent also contains the remains of the vast Pool of the Sparrow (Struthion), an ancient reservoir which collected rainwater directed from the rooftops. The pool was originally covered with a stone pavement *(lithostrothon)* and it was on this flagstone plaza, according to Christian tradition, that Pilate presen-ted Christ to the crowds and

uttered the words "Ecce homo" ("Behold the man"). However, archaeology refutes this, dating the pavement to the 2nd century AD, long after the time of Christ.

Within a railed section you can see marks scratched into the stone. Historians speculate that they may have been carved by Roman guards as a kind of street game.

Convent of the Sisters of Zion
📞 (02) 627 7292
🕐 8am–5pm daily

4

Lady Tunshuq's Palace

📍R2 🏛 El-Takiya St

Lady Tunshuq, of Mongolian or Turkish origin, was the wife, or mistress, of a Kurdish nobleman. She arrived in

→ Islamic detail, exterior of Lady Tunshuq's Palace

Assorted stalls
in the Cotton ↑
Merchants' Market

5

Cotton Merchants' Market

R3 **Off El-Wad Rd**

Known in Arabic as the Souk el-Qattanin, this is a covered market with next to no natural light but lots of small softly lit shops. It is possibly the most atmospheric street in all the Old City. Its construction was begun by the Crusaders, who intended the market to be a free-standing structure, but later, in the first half of the 14th century, the Mamelukes connected it to the Haram ash-Sharif (p70) via the splendidly ornate Cotton Merchants' Gate facing the Dome of the Rock. (Note, non-Muslims are not permitted to enter the Haram ash-Sharif by this gate, although they are allowed to depart by this route.)

As well as some 50 shop units with living quarters above, the market also has two ornate bathhouses: the Hammam el-Ain, constructed during the 14th century by the Mamelukes, and the Hammam el-Shifa. Both of these have

recently been restored: the former as a spa and the latter as an art gallery. Between the two bathhouses is a former merchants' hostel called Khan Tankiz, which has also undergone restoration.

Less than 50 m (160 ft) south of the Cotton Merchants' Market on El-Wad Road is a small public drinking fountain, or sabil, one of several erected during the reign of Suleyman the Magnificent.

———————————

6

Chain Street

R3

The Arabic name for this street is Tariq Bab el-Silsila, which means "Street of the Gate of the Chain". The name refers to the magnificent entrance gate to the Haram ash-Sharif situated at its eastern end. The street is a continuation of David Street, and together the two streets run the width of the Old City from Jaffa Gate to the Haram ash-Sharif and Dome of the Rock.

Chain Street has several noteworthy buildings that were commissioned by Mameluke rulers in the 14th century. Heading eastwards from David Street, the first that you come to is the Khan el-Sultan caravanserai, a restored travellers' inn. Further along on the right is Tashtamuriyya Madrasa, which features an elegant balcony. It houses the tomb of the emir Tashtamur and is one of a number of final resting places that were built here in the 14th and 15th centuries in order to be close to the Haram ash-Sharif. On the same side of the street is the tomb of the brutal Tartar emir Barka Khan, father-in-law of the Mameluke ruler Baybars, who drove the Crusaders out of the Holy Land. This building, with its intriguing façade decoration, now houses the Khalidi Library, which was established in 1899.

→

Brightly coloured items on display in Jerusalem's historic Central Souk

> **INSIDER TIP**
> **Bargaining in the Old City**
>
> In souks, even after tea and pleasantries, offer half the asking price and ignore the feigned indignation! Look ready to walk away, and the price will plummet.

Opposite the Khalidi Library are two small mausoleums. Of the two, that of emir Kilan stands out for its austere, well-proportioned façade. Further along the street is the tomb of Tartar pilgrim Turkan Khatun, recognizable by the splendid arabesques on its façade. Opposite the Gate of the Chain is the impressive entrance to the 14th-century Tankiziyya Madrasa. In the inscription, three symbols in the shape of a cup show that emir Tankiz, who built the college, held the important office of cupbearer. Nearby, not far from the Cotton Merchants' Market, is a drinking fountain that dates from the reign of Suleyman the Magnificent and combines decorative Roman and Crusader motifs.

The Chain Gate, which leads from Chain Street to Temple Mount

---

7

Central Souk

Q3 **David St/Chain St**
8am–7pm Sat–Thu

The Central Souk consists of three parallel covered streets at the junction of David Street and Chain Street. They once formed part of the Roman Cardo (p94). Today's markets sell mostly clothes and souvenirs, although the section called the Butchers' Market (Souk el-Lakhamin in Arabic), which was restored in the 1970s, still offers all the colour and excitement of a typical eastern bazaar. Be warned, however, that this place is not for the faint-hearted, since the pungent aromas of spices and freshly slaughtered meat can be overwhelming.

8

Damascus Gate

Q1 🚌 **1, 2**

Spotting this gate is easy, not only because it is the most monumental in the Old City, but also because of the perpetual bustle around it.

Arabs call it Bab el-Amud, the Gate of the Column. This could refer to a large column topped with a statue of the emperor Hadrian which, in Roman times, stood just inside the gate. For Jews it is Shaar Shkhem, the gate that leads to the biblical city of Shechem, better known by its Arabic name – Nablus.

The present-day gate was built over the remains of the original Roman gate and parts of the Roman city. Outside the gate, steps lead down to the excavation area. In the first section are remains of a Crusader chapel with frescoes, part of a medieval roadway and an ancient sign marking the presence of the Roman 10th Legion. Further in is surviving arch of the Roman

gate, which provides access to the fascinating **Roman Square Excavations**. The remains of the original Roman plaza, the starting point of the Roman Cardo, include a gaming board engraved in the paving stones. A hologram depicts Hadrian's column in the main plaza. It is possible to explore the upper levels of the gate as part of the ramparts walk *(p100)*.

Roman Square Excavations
🕐 9am–5pm (to 4pm winter) Sat–Thu

9

Herod's Gate

R1

The Arabic and Hebrew names for this gate, Bab el-Zahra and Shaar ha-Prakhim respectively, both mean "Gate of Flowers", referring to the rosette above the arch. It came to be known as Herod's Gate in the 1500s, when Christian pilgrims wrongly thought that the house inside the gate was the palace of Herod the Great's son. It was via the original,

now closed, entrance further east that the Crusaders entered the city and conquered it on 15 July 1099.

10

St Anne's Church

📍 S1 🚌 2 Shaar ha-Arayot St 📞 (02) 628 3285 🕐 8am–noon & 2–6pm daily (to 5pm winter)

This beautiful Crusader church is a superb example of Romanesque architecture. It was constructed between

→ Prayers at the "Virgin Mary's Birthplace", in St Anne's Church

1131 and 1138 to replace a previous Byzantine church, and exists today in more or less its original form. It is traditionally believed that the church stands on the spot where Anne and Joachim, the parents of the Virgin Mary, lived. The supposed remains of their house are in the crypt, which is also noted for its remarkable acoustics.

Shortly after the church was built, it was made larger by moving the façade forwards by several metres. The connection with the original church can still be seen in the first row of columns. In 1192, Saladin turned the church into a Muslim theological school; there is an inscription to this effect above the entrance. Later abandoned, the church fell into ruins, until the Ottomans donated it to France in 1856 and it was restored.

Next to the church are two cisterns that once lay outside the city walls. They were built in the 8th and 3rd centuries BC to collect rainwater. Some time later, under Herod the Great, they were turned into curative baths. Ruins of a Roman temple, thought to have been to the god of medicine, can be seen here, as can those of a later Byzantine church built over the temple. This is also widely believed to be the site of the Pool of Bethesda, described in St John's account of Christ curing a paralysed man (John 5: 1–15).

⑪
Lions' Gate
📍T1

Suleyman the Magnificent built this gate in 1538. Its Arabic name, Bab Sitti Maryam (Gate of the Virgin Mary), refers to the Tomb of the Virgin in the nearby Valley of Jehoshaphat (p136). The Hebrew name, Shaar ha-Arayot, or Lions' Gate, refers to the two emblematic lions situated on either side of the gateway, although one

school of thought insists that they are panthers. There are many different stories to explain the significance of the lions. One is that Suleyman the Magnificent had them carved in honour of the Mameluke emir Baybars and his successful campaign to rid the Holy Land of Crusaders.

Also known as St Stephen's Gate, this name was adopted in the Middle Ages by Christians who believed that the first Christian martyr, St Stephen, was executed here. Prior to that, it was thought that St Stephen had been stoned to death outside Damascus Gate.

The gate is also significant because of its more recent history, as the entrance through which the Arab Legion penetrated the Old City in 1948 (p53) and where Israeli paratroopers entered in 1967 (p54). Today it makes an excellent starting point for the walk along the Via Dolorosa (p110).

Did You Know?

The Muslim Quarter is home to about 27,000 people, almost three-quarters of the Old City's population.

← Historic Damascus Gate, in the wall surrounding Jerusalem's Old City

A SHORT WALK
THE MUSLIM QUARTER

Distance 500 m (1,650 ft) **Nearest bus stop**
Sultan Suleyman Street **Time** 15 minutes

The main routes through this busy quarter are along
the Via Dolorosa and up and down El-Wad. Both
streets are lined with a gaudy array of shops, whose
salesmen eagerly press on visitors all manner of
ornaments and kitsch, from plastic crucifixes to
glass-bowled water pipes. Few people stray from
the main thoroughfares, but those who do are
richly rewarded. The quiet, winding back alleys
contain a wealth of fine medieval Islamic
architecture, much of it dating from the
Mameluke era (1250–1516). Not all of it
is in good condition, but many of
these buildings still perform the
functions for which they were intended.

The **Austrian
Hospice** was built
in 1869 to accommodate
Christian pilgrims.

VIA DOLOROSA

EL-WAD

Crossing the quarter from east to
west, the **Via Dolorosa** (p110)
is revered by Christian pilgrims
as the route taken by Christ as
he was led to his crucifixion.

Abu Shukri
restaurant (p76)

A narrow, stepped street at the
heart of the quarter, **El-Takiya**
contains some of the city's finest
Mameluke architecture.

Lady Tunshuq's Palace (p77)
is typical of the Mameluke
decorative style, with bands
of different coloured stone and
panels of intricate marble inlay.

←
Fresh bread rolls
for sale at a stall
along El-Takiya

The **Convent of the Sisters of Zion**, which runs a pilgrims' hospice, dates from the 19th-century Christian building boom.

The **Ecce Homo Arch** (p76), which spans the Via Dolorosa, is the main section of a Roman triple arch. One of the smaller, flanking arches is incorporated into the structure of the Convent of the Sisters of Zion.

Locator Map
For more detail see p68

MUSLIM QUARTER

Built on the site traditionally associated with the flogging of Christ, the **Monastery of the Flagellation** (p76) complex includes two attractive chapels and the Studium Museum.

▶ START

BARQUA

ALLAH-E-DIN

↑ Bab el-Hadid street, with typical Mameluke-style architectural features

Though badly neglected, **Bab el-Hadid street** has a number of madrasas from the 14th and 15th centuries.

FINISH

BAB — EL-HADID

EL-WAD

Madrasa el-Araghonia (1358)

| 0 metres | 50 |
| 0 yards | 50 |

N ↑

JEWISH QUARTER

In Herodian times, this area abutted the Second Temple enclosure and was occupied by the priestly elite. In the late Roman period, Jews were forbidden from living in Jerusalem, but under the more tolerant Arab rule a small community was re-established here. The district became predominantly Jewish during Ottoman rule, when it acquired its present name. By the 16th century, pilgrimage to the Western Wall – the only surviving remnant of the Temple – had become a strong tradition. After the destruction wrought in the 1948 War and the subsequent years of Jordanian occupation, the Jewish Quarter was liberated by Israeli troops in 1967, and reconstruction work began soon afterwards. A great many ruins from ancient periods were uncovered below more recent buildings. These remains were made accessible to the public, so that the Jewish Quarter of today stands as a fascinating, living mix of more than 3,000 years of Jerusalem Jewry.

JEWISH QUARTER

Must Sees
1. Western Wall
2. Jerusalem Archaeological Park

Experience More
3. The Cardo
4. The Broad Wall
5. Hurva Square
6. Hurva Synagogue
7. Ramban Synagogue
8. Tiferet Yisrael Street
9. Wohl Archaeological Museum
10. Batei Makhase Square
11. The Sephardic Synagogues
12. Old Yishuv Court Museum
13. Ariel Center for Jerusalem in the First Temple Period
14. The Burnt House
15. St Mary of the Germans
16. Dung Gate

Eat
1. Quarter Cafe

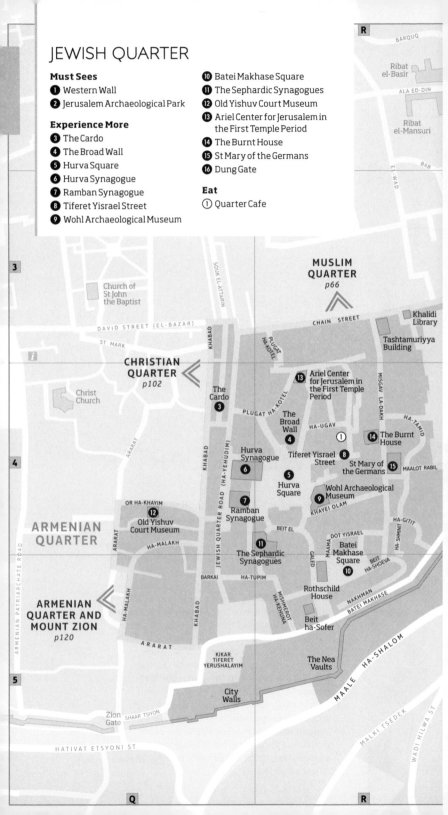

S

T

El-Ghawanima
Gate

Inspector's
Gate

Golden Gate
(closed)

2

Iron Gate

EL-HADID

Temple
Mount

Cotton
Merchants'
Gate

Dome of
the Rock

HA-OFEL

3

Chain Gate

(TARIQ BAB EL-SILSILA)

DEREKH

Beit
Strauss

El-Kas
Fountain

Western Wall ❶

Moors' Gate

WESTERN
WALL
PLAZA

JEWISH
QUARTER

El-Aqsa
Mosque

4

Museum of
Islamic Art

BATEI MAHASE

City
Walls

Davidson
Center

❷
Jerusalem
Archaeological
Park

DEREKH HA-SHILOAKH

⑯ Dung
Gate

DEREKH   HA-OFEL

MOUNT OF OLIVES
AND CITY OF DAVID
p128

MALKI TSEDEK

CITY OF
DAVID

MAALOT IR DAVID

5

JEWISH
QUARTER

0 metres   100
0 yards   100

N

S

T

❶

WESTERN WALL

📍S3 🏠Western Wall Plaza 🌐thekotel.org

A massive, blank wall built of huge stone blocks, the Western Wall (Ha-Kotel in Hebrew) is Judaism's holiest site, and the plaza in front of it is a permanent place of worship. The wall is part of the retaining wall of the Temple Mount and was built by Herod the Great during his expansion of the Temple enclosure (p70).

The Western Wall Plaza functions as a large, open-air synagogue where groups gather to recite the daily, Shabbat (Sabbath) and festival services of the Jewish faith. Special events are also celebrated here, such as the religious coming of age of a boy or girl (bar or bat mitzvah). Some worshippers visit the wall daily to recite the entire Book of Psalms; others, who believe that petitions to God made at the wall are specially effective, insert written prayers into the stones. On Tisha B'Av, the ninth day of the month of Av, which falls in either July or August, a fast is held commemorating the destruction of both Temples (p48).

People sit on the ground reciting the Book of Lamentations and liturgical dirges. Since the plaza is essentially a public space, conflicts arise over such issues as the relative size of the men's and women's sections and the wish of non-Orthodox groups to hold services in which men and women participate together.

> **Others, who believe that petitions to God made at the wall are specially effective, insert written prayers into the stones.**

Did You Know?

The largest of the Western Wall's Herodian-era stones weighs 570 tonnes.

Jewish worshippers at the Western Wall, the sacred remains of the Second Temple ↑

Visiting the Western Wall

Houses covered most of what's now the Western Wall Plaza until relatively recently. When the Israelis gained control of the Old City after the 1967 war, they levelled the neighbouring Arab district. The huge, lower stones of the wall are Herodian, while those higher up date from early Islamic times. During the Ottoman period, the wall became where Jews went to lament the destruction of the Second Temple and for this reason it was for centuries known as the Wailing Wall. Non-Jews can approach the wall, provided they dress appropriately and cover their heads.

At the left-hand corner of the men's prayer section is Wilson's Arch (named after a 19th-century archaeologist). Now contained within a building that functions as a synagogue, it originally carried the Causeway to the Temple.

From the arch, archaeologists have dug the Western Wall Tunnel to explore the wall's foundations. It follows the base of the outside face of the Temple wall

↑ Praying in a covered part of the wall that has been made into a tunnel

along a Herodian street, below today's street level, and emerges on the Via Dolorosa. The Chain of the Generations Centre tells the story of the Jewish people. Access to this and the Western Wall Tunnel is by tour only; book well in advance.

← Women standing in prayer at the women's section of the wall

GENDER EQUALITY AT THE WALL

In the 19th century, the Western Wall was not gender-segregated, but after the 1967 war the Orthodox-run Chief Rabbinate was given control of the Western Wall Plaza and divided it into a men's section and a women's section. In 1968, the Reform Movement demanded that egalitarian (mixed-gender) prayers be permitted, but the issue – championed for decades by Women of the Wall – is still hugely controversial. The Israeli government has made an area for egalitarian prayer available beneath Robinson's Arch, but women have been prevented from bringing Torah scrolls there due to opposition from Orthodox political parties.

The vast Western Wall Plaza, alongside Temple Mount

2 🚲 🚇

JERUSALEM ARCHAEOLOGICAL PARK

📍S4 🏛Batei Makhase St, Jewish Quarter 🕐8am–5pm Sun–Thu, 8am–2pm Fri 🚫Sat & Jewish holidays 🌐archpark.org.il

This small, L-shaped site reveals the entire sweep of the history of Jerusalem, from the days of the First Temple to the Omayyad era. Key remains include the vestiges of Robinson's Arch, a Herodian shopping street, a medieval tower and the Omayyad palaces.

The area south of the Western Wall and Haram ash-Sharif is one of the most important archaeological sites in all Jerusalem. Excavations of the site were begun in the 19th century by biblical scholars such as Edward Robinson, who identified the huge arch that is now named after him. Modern excavations, ongoing here since 1968, have uncovered a wealth of remains that offer fascinating insights into ancient life in the city. Start your visit at the Davidson Center, which provides a multimedia introduction to the site and contextualizes the archaeologists' findings.

Did You Know?

The first serious excavations of the site were made in 1867 by British officer Captain Charles Warren.

ROBINSON'S ARCH

South of the women's section of the Western Wall, high above an area intended for egalitarian Jewish prayer (p89), Robinson's Arch angles out from the surrounding Herodian stones. Built in the late 1st century BC, the arch was once 13 m (43 ft) wide and formed part of a monumental staircase that linked the Temple with the Upper City's market. In AD 70, the structure was destroyed by the Romans; some of the stones that tumbled from the arch still lie where they fell at the moment that the structure collapsed.

The Western Wall is a part of the retaining wall of the Temple Mount, which runs south into the Archaeological Park.

A row of stones projecting from the wall is the remains of Robinson's Arch.

The ritual baths are where worshippers purified themselves before approaching the Temple.

At the base of the Temple Mount is a street dating from the Second Temple era.

The subterranean Davidson Center contains artifacts from the site.

Dung Gate

The remains of the Omayyad Palace,
seen from the corner of Temple Mount ↑

→
Learning about the
history of the site at
the Davidson Center

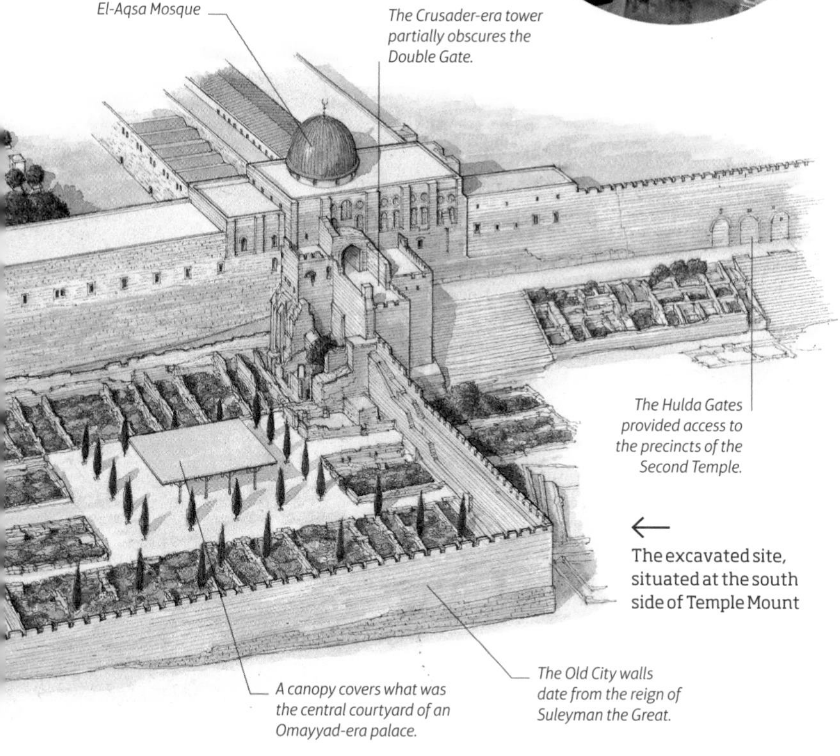

El-Aqsa Mosque

The Crusader-era tower
partially obscures the
Double Gate.

The Hulda Gates
provided access to
the precincts of the
Second Temple.

←
The excavated site,
situated at the south
side of Temple Mount

A canopy covers what was
the central courtyard of an
Omayyad-era palace.

The Old City walls
date from the reign of
Suleyman the Great.

EXPERIENCE MORE

③ The Cardo

📍 Q4

Now in part an exclusive shopping arcade, the Cardo was Jerusalem's main thoroughfare in the Byzantine era. It was originally laid by the Romans, then extended in the 4th century as Christian pilgrims began to flock to Jerusalem and the city expanded accordingly. The Byzantine extension, which remains in evidence today, linked the two major places of worship of the time, the Church of the Holy Sepulchre (p106) in the north and the long-since-vanished Nea Basilica in the south.

The central roadway of the Byzantine Cardo was 12.5 m (41 ft) wide. This was flanked by broad porticoed pavements and lined with shops. You can visit a reconstructed section, which runs for almost 200 m (650 ft) along Jewish Quarter (Ha-Yehudim) Road.

The Cardo's continued importance during the reign of Justinian in the 6th century is apparent from its prominent appearance on the famous Madaba mosaic map (p260) of the Holy Land. Some 500 years later, during the Crusader era, the Cardo was transformed into a covered market.

An exhibition on Jewish Quarter Road entitled "Alone on the Walls" displays photographs that document the fall of the Jewish Quarter to a regiment of the Arab Legion in 1947–8, in which 68 residents lost their lives.

④ The Broad Wall

📍 R1   🏠 Plugat ha-Kotel St

The Jewish Quarter was largely destroyed during the 1948 War (p53) and allowed to deteriorate further under Jordanian occupation.

Following the 1967 Israeli victory, a vast reconstruction programme resulted in many significant archaeological finds. One of these was the unearthing of the foundations of a wall 7 m (22 ft) thick and 65 m (215 ft) long. This was possibly part of fortifications built by King Hezekiah in the 8th century BC to enclose a new quarter outside the previous city wall. The need for expansion was probably brought about by a rush of refugees after the Assyrian invasion of 722 BC.

→

The reconstructed Hurva Synagogue, overlooking the expansive Hurva Square

← Paintings and tapestries for sale in the historic Cardo shopping arcade

On the building next to the exposed wall, a clearly visible line indicates what archaeologists think was the original height of the wall. Also visible are the remains of housing from the same period, demolished to make way for the wall, as described in the Book of Isaiah (22: 10), "And ye have numbered the houses of Jerusalem, and the houses have ye broken down to fortify the wall."

⑤ Hurva Square

📍 R1

This charming square is the social centre of the Jewish Quarter – and, for the devoutly Orthodox families who live nearby, a welcome playground. On the west side are the historic Hurva and Ramban synagogue complexes, as well as the minaret of the long-vanished Mosque of Sidna Omar, which was built in the 14th century under the Mamelukes. The square is surrounded by cafés, souvenir shops and

EAT

Quarter Cafe

A self-service Kosher dairy and fish restaurant operating since 1975 with good value fare and an appetizing view of Temple Mount and Western Wall.

📍 Q4 🏠 11 Tiferet Israel St, Jewish Quarter 📞 (02) 628 7770

a few snack bars that set up open-air tables when the weather is good.

6

Hurva Synagogue

📍 Q4 🏠 Hurva Square 🕐 9am-5pm Sun-Thu, 9am-1pm Fri 🌐 rova-yehudi.org.il

Hurva means "ruin", and the history of this synagogue more than justifies its name. In the 1690s, Jerusalem's

Ashkenazi community rebuilt a long-ruined synagogue here, but two decades later it was burned down by Muslim creditors angered by the community's unpaid debts. From 1857 to 1864, the synagogue was grandly rebuilt in the Neo-Byzantine style, but in 1948, a day before the surrender of the Jewish Quarter, it was blown up by Jordan's Arab Legion.

Although much of the Jewish Quarter was rebuilt in the years after 1967, the Hurva remained a ruin until 2010, when archaeological excavations were followed by reconstruction in the original 19th-century style. There are magnificent city views from the veranda around the base of the dome.

7

Ramban Synagogue

📍 Q4 🏠 Hurva Square 🕐 For morning and evening prayers

When the Spanish rabbi and scholar Moses Ben Nahman (Nahmanides) arrived in Jerusalem in 1267, he was shocked to find only a handful of Jews in the city. Dedicating himself to nurturing a Jewish community, he purchased land near King David's Tomb

↑ The glowing interior of Moses Ben Nahman's Ramban Synagogue

on Mount Zion and built a synagogue. Some time around 1400 it was moved to its present site, perhaps the first time there had been a Jewish presence in this quarter of the Old City since the exile of the Jews in AD 135. The synagogue had to be rebuilt in 1523 after it collapsed. At this time, it was probably the only Jewish place of worship in what was then Ottoman-controlled Jerusalem. In 1587, the authorities banned the Jews from worship in the synagogue and the building became a workshop.

It was not until the Israelis took control of the Old City in 1967 that it was restored as a place of worship.

8
Tiferet Yisrael Street

📍R4

This is one of the busiest streets in the Jewish Quarter, connecting Hurva Square with the stairs down to the Western Wall. Partway along is the shell of the Tiferet Yisrael Synagogue, built from 1857 to 1872 and destroyed by the Jordanians in 1948. The street ends in an attractive, tree-shaded square that has several snack bars and cafés, including the popular Quarter Café, serving kosher food; the terrace offers great views of the Dome of the Rock.

9
Wohl Archaeological Museum

📍R4 🏠1 Ha-Karaim St
📞(02) 626 5906 🕐9am–5pm Sun–Thu, 9am–1pm Fri

In the era of Herod the Great (37–4 BC), the area of the present-day Jewish Quarter was part of a wealthy "Upper City", mostly occupied by the families of important Jewish priests. During post-1967 redevelopment, the remains of several large houses were unearthed. This rediscovered Herodian quarter now lies 3–7 m (10–22 ft) below street level, under a modern building, and houses the Wohl Archaeological Museum.

The museum is remarkable for its vivid evocation of everyday life 2,000 years ago. All the houses had an inner courtyard, ritual baths, and cisterns to collect rain, which was the only source of water at the time. The first part of the museum, the Western House, has a mosaic in the vestibule and a well-preserved ritual bath (mikveh). Beyond this is the Middle Complex, the remains of two separate houses where archaeologists found a maze-pattern mosaic floor covered in burned wood; this, they surmised, was fire damage from the Roman siege of Jerusalem

INSIDER TIP
Two for the Price of One

The entrance fee to the Wohl Archaeological Museum also includes admission to the excavations at the Burnt House (p98).

in AD 70. The most complete of all the Herodian buildings is the Palatial Mansion, with more splendid mosaic floors and ritual baths.

10
Batei Makhase Square

📍R5

This quiet square is named after the so-called Shelter Houses (Batei Makhase), just to the south. They were built in 1862 by Jews from Germany and Holland to house destitute immigrants from central Europe, and restored after severe damage in the 1948 war.

The work brought to light remains of the Nea (New) Basilica, previously known only from the Madaba map (p260) and literary sources. Built by Byzantine emperor Justinian in AD 543, it was at the time the largest basilica in the Holy Land. The remains of one of the apses can be seen near the square's southwest corner. Archaeologists have now traced the full extent of the basilica – an enormous 116 m (380 ft) by 52 m (171 ft). Impressive remains can also be found in the cellar of a house north of the square.

The handsome, arcaded building on the western side of the square was built for the Rothschild family in 1871.

← Remains of ancient houses on show in the Wohl Archaeological Museum

Interior of the Yochanan ben Zakkai Synagogue, one of the Sephardic Synagogues ↑

Standing in front of it are parts of Roman columns, whose original provenance is unknown.

The Sephardic Synagogues

R4 Mishmarot HaKehuna St (02) 628 0592 9am–5pm Sun–Thu, 9am–1pm Fri (call ahead to schedule a visit)

Long the spiritual centre of Jerusalem's Sephardic community, this cluster of synagogues was built below street level because, under Ottoman law, synagogues could not rise higher than nearby mosques. Some of the furnishings were salvaged from Italian synagogues damaged during World War II. The Yochanan ben Zakkai Synagogue, built in the early 1600s, hosts the installation of Israel's Sephardic chief rabbis. Its courtyard was converted into the Middle Synagogue, dating in its present form from the 1830s. The Prophet Elijah Synagogue, once a study hall, was consecrated in 1702. Legend has it that on Yom Kippur, Elijah appeared as the tenth adult male needed for synagogue prayer, hence the name. The Istanbuli Synagogue was built in 1857 by immigrants from Turkey.

Old Yishuv Court Museum

Q4 6 Or ha-Khayim St (02) 627 6319 10am–5pm Sun–Thu (to 3pm winter), 10am–1pm Fri

This small museum is devoted to the city's Jewish community from the mid-19th century to the end of Ottoman rule in 1917. Of Turkish construction, thought to date from the 15th or 16th centuries, it was once part of a private home and contains memorabilia and photographs. Its Ari Synagogue, on the ground floor, used by a Sephardic congregation during the Ottoman period, was badly damaged in the fighting of 1936, and fell into disuse until 1967, when it was restored. On the top floor is the 18th-century Or ha-Khayim Synagogue, used by Ashkenazi Jews in the 19th century. Closed between 1948 and 1967, it is now functioning as a synagogue once more.

ULTRA-ORTHODOX JEWS

Israel's most conservative Jewish communities, ultra-Orthodox Jews – also known as Haredim ("those who tremble before God") – are grounded in rigorous observance of Jewish law and the study of the Torah. Dressed in white shirts, black caftans and black fedoras or homburgs (the men), and long skirts and shirts with long sleeves and high necklines (the women, who, if married, cover their hair), their traditions date back to a 19th-century backlash against most Eastern European Jews' decision to liberate themselves from the confines of the *shtetl* (small Jewish towns or villages). The Haredim reject modern life and, as much as possible, avoid contact with the outside world. More radical groups oppose the use of Hebrew, speaking Yiddish instead, and some do not recognize the State of Israel or its laws.

⓭ ✍️

Ariel Centre for Jerusalem in the First Temple Period

📍 R4 🏠 Bonei Hahomah St
🕘 9am–4pm Sun–Thu (visits must be booked in advance)
🌐 ybz.org.il

The principal and most fascinating exhibit in the Ariel Centre for Jerusalem in the First Temple Period is a model of all the archaeological remains of First Temple Period Jerusalem (around the 8th century BC). The model serves to illustrate the relationships between the different remains, which can be difficult to interpret when they are viewed on the ground, surrounded by various other buildings. It is also interesting to see the original topography of the area around Jerusalem before valleys were filled in and occupation layers were built up. The centre also has an audiovisual show, which describes the city's history from 1000 to 586 BC.

Another display consists of finds from a clandestine dig

A Burnt House stone tablet with Aramaic inscription

that was carried out in 1909–11 by English archaeologist Captain Montague Parker. His team of excavators penetrated underneath the Haram ash-Sharif in search of a chamber that, according to legend, contained King Solomon's treasure. When news of the excavation got out, there were violent demonstrations by both Jews and Muslims, who were united in their angry opposition to the desecration of their holy site. Parker and his excavaters were forced to flee the city.

⓮ ✍️

The Burnt House

📍 R4 🏠 Tiferet Yisrael St
📞 (02) 626 5906 🕘 9am–5pm Sun–Thu, 9am–1pm Fri

In AD 70, the Romans took Jerusalem and destroyed the Temple and Lower City which extended to the south. A month later they rampaged through the wealthy Upper City, setting fire to the houses. The charred walls and a coin dated to AD 69, which were discovered during excavations here in the 1970s, indicate that this was one of those houses.

Artifacts on display include ovens, cooking pots and a spear. A stone weight that was discovered among the debris bears the inscription "son of Kathros", indicating that the house belonged to a wealthy family of high priests. They are also known from a subsequent reference to them in the Babylonian Talmud, which was written between the 3rd and 6th century AD.

The rooms on view, which are introduced by a moving sound-and-light show with commentary, comprise a kitchen, four rooms that may have been bedrooms and a bathroom with a ritual bath. It is believed that these rooms formed part of a considerably larger residence, but it is not possible to carry out further excavations because the remains lie beneath present-day neighbouring houses.

The entrance fee to the house also includes a discount on admission to the Wohl Archaeological Museum (p96), which provides further information on excavations that have been carried out in the city.

JEWISH QUARTER ARCHITECTURE

The Jewish Quarter, heavily damaged during the 1948 War (p53), was systematically razed by the Jordanians, who also expelled all the Jewish residents. Reconstruction began right after the 1967 War, after archaeologists had excavated the site. New houses - deliberately asymmetrical and of varying heights to evoke haphazard historical development - were built along narrow, cobbled streets using traditional Middle Eastern elements such as arches and domes. Many have small courtyards and external stairs.

The Ottoman-era Dung Gate, the main entrance into the Jewish Quarter ↑

⑮
St Mary of the Germans

◎R4 ⚑Misgav la-Dakh St ◷Daily

Lying immediately below the terrace of Tiferet Yisrael's Quarter Café are the original walls of the early 12th-century St Mary of the Germans. This Crusader church was part of a complex that included a pilgrims' hospice (which is no longer in existence) and a hospital. It was built by the Knights Hospitallers and run by their German members. This was in response to the influx of German-speaking pilgrims who were unfamiliar with French, the lingua franca, or Latin, which was the official language of the new Latin Kingdom of Jerusalem.

Activity ceased when Jerusalem was taken by the Muslims in 1187, but the church and the hospital were again used during the brief period between 1229 and 1244 when Jerusalem once more came under Christian Crusader rule.

Today the church is roofless. However, the walls survive to a considerable height, showing clearly the three apses of the typical basilica plan that was so widely used in the Holy Land from early Byzantine times. Beside the church is a flight of steps down to the Western Wall Plaza. These provide wonderful views of the Western Wall, the Dome of the Rock and the Mount of Olives beyond.

⑯
Dung Gate

◎S4

In photographs from the early 20th century, the Dung Gate is no larger than a doorway in the average domestic house. Its name in Hebrew is Shaar ha-Ashpot, and it is mentioned in the Book of Nehemiah (2: 13) in the Old Testament.

The gate's name is probably derived from the ash that used to be taken from the Temple to be deposited outside the city walls. The Arab name is Bab Silwan, because this is the gate that leads to the Arab village of Silwan.

The gate was enlarged by the Jordanians in 1952 to allow vehicles to pass through. It is now the main entrance and exit for the Jewish Quarter, but it nonetheless remains the smallest of all the Old City gates. It still retains its old Ottoman carved arch with a stone flower above.

Did You Know?

The Old City walls are about 12 m (40 ft) tall and 2.5 m (8 ft) thick.

A LONG WALK
OLD CITY WALLS

Distance Jaffa Gate to Lions' Gate 2.5 km (1.5 miles); Jaffa Gate to Dung Gate 1.5 km (1 mile) **Walking time** 60 minutes in total **Nearest station** City Hall Light Rail **Difficulty** Many steep flights of steps

The Old City of Jerusalem may occupy a relatively small area geographically, but its compactness and uneven topography make it a frequently confusing place to explore. One good way to gain an overview is to take to the ramparts and view the crush of alleys, domes and towers from the top of the walls that enclose them. Visitors can walk along two sections of wall: from Jaffa Gate clockwise to Lions' Gate, and from Jaffa Gate anti-clockwise to the Dung Gate. The section between Lions' Gate and the Dung Gate is closed to the public. There is an admission fee to access the ramparts, which are open daily from 9am to 5pm in summer, and from 9am to 4pm (to 2pm Friday) in winter.

Damascus Gate (p80) *features a defensive dogleg entrance tunnel.*

SULTAN

Damascus Gate

SOUK KHAN EL-ZEIT

EL-WAD

New Gate *was added in 1889 to allow pilgrims in compounds outside the walls direct access to the Christian Quarter.*

HA-TSANKHANIM

New Gate

Terra Santa Monastery

ST FRANCIS

College des Frères

Casa Nova Monastery

CHRISTIAN QUARTER

EL-KHANQA

VIA DOLOROSA

Church of the Holy Sepulchre

Alexander Hospice

Muristan

St John the Baptist

DAVID ST (EL-BAZAR)

CHRISTIAN QUARTER ROAD

Start the walk by climbing the steps inside the **Jaffa Gate** *(p116) to the top of the gatehouse and heading north to the first of the walls' 35 watchtowers.*

Jaffa Gate

START

The Citadel

St Mark's Church

Hurva Synagogue

KHABAD

HURVA SQUARE

This section of the ramparts is accessed from outside the city walls, just south of **The Citadel** *(p112). The initial stretch is like a trench, with a high stone wall on either side.*

ARMENIAN QUARTER

Armenian Garden

ARMENIAN PATRIARCHATE

St James's Cathedral

Sephardic Synagogues

Zion Gate

Zion Gate (p125) *is riddled with bullet holes from the fighting in 1948.*

← Damascus Gate, the grandest of all the Old City gates

It was the north wall, just east of **Herod's Gate** (p80), that the Crusader army breached on 15 July 1099 to capture Jerusalem from the Muslims. From here there are views down Salah al-Din, the main street of Arab East Jerusalem.

Locator Map
For more detail see p86

OLD CITY WALLS
JEWISH QUARTER

Storks' Tower

SULEYMAN

At **Storks' Tower**, the wall swings through 90° to run due south. From the ramparts here, you overlook the tombs that cover the Kidron Valley (p134) and the Mount of Olives (p128).

Old City Walls

Herod's Gate

Indian Hospice

EL-MATHANA

QADSIEH

SHADAD

St Anne's Church

Lions' Gate

FINISH

Monastery of the Flagellation

SHAAR HA-ARAYOT

EL-GHAZALI SQUARE

VIA DOLOROSA

This walk ends at **Lions' Gate** (p81), built by Suleyman the Magnificent, where you descend to street level. The beginning of the Via Dolorosa (p110) is just ahead, which, if followed, leads back towards the Jaffa Gate area.

MUSLIM QUARTER

ALA ED-DIN

Lady Tunshuq's Palace

Iron Gate

Temple Mount

Cotton Merchants' Gate

Dome of the Rock

CHAIN STREET

Western Wall

JEWISH QUARTER

WESTERN WALL PLAZA

Museum of Islamic Art

El-Aqsa Mosque

Hulda Gates

0 metres   300
0 yards   300

N
↑

St Mary of the Germans

BATEI MAKHASE SQUARE

Jerusalem Archaeological Park

Dung Gate

MAKHASE

FINISH

BATEI

The final stretch of the walk affords wonderful views of the Arab village of Silwan, before ending at the **Dung Gate** (p99), the smallest of the city gates.

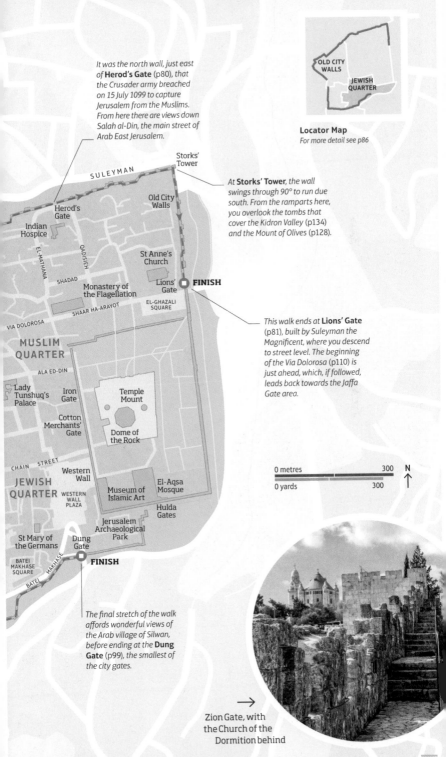

→
Zion Gate, with the Church of the Dormition behind

Frescoes on the ceiling in the Church of the Holy Sepulchre

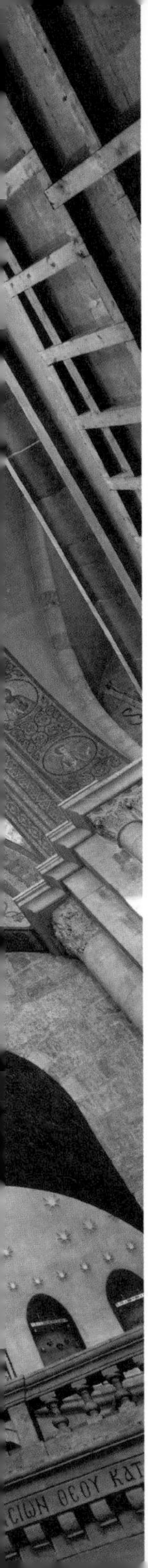

CHRISTIAN QUARTER

Lying north of Jaffa Gate and the Citadel, the Christian Quarter occupies the Old City's northwest corner. Its spiritual heart is the Church of the Holy Sepulchre, identified since at least the 4th century as the site of Jesus's Crucifixion, burial and Resurrection. Over the centuries, the neighbourhood was steadily built up with patriarchates, hospices, churches and other religious institutions, established by a wide variety of Christian denominations. Some of these were built in the late 1800s by European powers such as Austria-Hungary and Germany.

The Old City's most recent gate, New Gate, was created by the Ottomans in 1889 to link the Christian Quarter with Christian institutions located outside the city walls, especially the French-run Notre Dame hospice and the Russian Compound. On the front line after 1948, New Gate was sealed by the Jordanians and reopened by Israel in 1967 following its seizure during the Six-Day War.

CHRISTIAN QUARTER

Must Sees

❶ Church of the Holy Sepulchre
❷ The Citadel

Experience More

❸ Alexander Hospice
❹ Lutheran Church of the Redeemer
❺ Christian Quarter Road
❻ Church of St John the Baptist
❼ Museum of the Greek Orthodox Patriarchate
❽ Jaffa Gate
❾ Omar ibn al-Khattab Square

SAFRA SQUARE

SHIVTEI YISRAEL

Notre Dame de France Hospice

City Hall

JERUSALEM CITY CENTRE *p138*

Mishol Ha-Pninim Garden

HA-TSANKHANIM

St Salvador

CHRISTIAN QUARTER

Former Barclays Bank

New Gate

Terra Santa Monastery

ST FRANCIS

Ha-Leumi Garden

BAB EL-JADID

FRERES

CASA NOVA

Casa Nova Monastery

Museum of the Greek Orthodox Patriarchate **❼**

College des Frères

KHAWALIDA

Casa Nova Hospice

GREEK ORTHODOX PATRIARCHATE

DIMITRIOS

JAFFA ROAD (DEREKH YAFO)

Latin Seminary & Patriarchate

ST PETER

ST PETER

GREEK

Museum of the Greek Catholic Patriarchate

ST GEORGE

MAMILLA

LATIN PATRIARCHATE

CATHOLIC PATRIARCHATE

HA-EMEK

Old City Walls

i

OMAR IBN EL-KHATTAB SQUARE

❽ Jaffa Gate

DAVID'S VILLAGE

❷ The Citadel

❾ Omar ibn al-Khattab Square

SHAMA

PAUL EMILE BOTTA

Khutsot Ha-Yotser

N

P

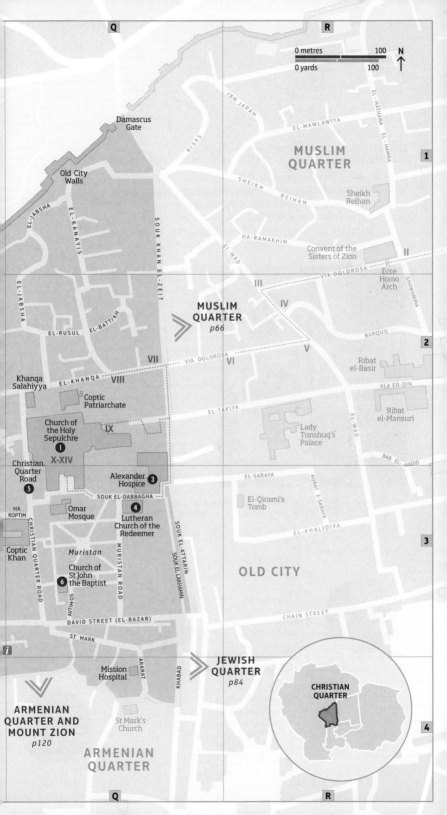

Damascus Gate

Old City Walls

IBN JARAH

EL-MAWLAWIYA

EL-MATHANA

EL-HAMRA

RISAS

**MUSLIM
QUARTER** 1

SHEIKH REIHAN

Sheikh Reihan

HA-RAMAKHIM

EL-JABSHA

EL-KANAYIS

SOUK KHAN EL-ZEIT

EL-WAD

**Convent of the
Sisters of Zion**

II

**Ecce
Homo
Arch**

GHAWANIMA

VIA DOLOROSA

EL-JABSHA

EL-RUSUL

EL-BATTIKH

III

IV

**MUSLIM
QUARTER**
p66

V

BARQUQ

2

**Ribat
el-Basir**

ALA ED-DIN

VII

VIA DOLOROSA

VI

**Khanqa
Salahiyya**

EL-KHANQA

VIII

**Ribat
el-Mansuri**

**Coptic
Patriarchate**

EL-TAKIYA

**Church of
the Holy
Sepulchre**
❶

IX

**Lady
Tunshuq's
Palace**

EL-WAD

BAB EL-HADID

**Christian
Quarter
Road**
❺

X–XIV

**Alexander
Hospice** ❸

EL-SARAYA

SOUK EL-DABBAGHA

HA
KOPTIM

**Omar
Mosque**

CHRISTIAN QUARTER ROAD

**Lutheran
Church of the
Redeemer**
❹

SOUK EL-ATTARIN

SOUK EL-LAKHAMIN

**El-Qirami's
Tomb**

AQBAT E-SARAYA

EL-KHALIDIYA

3

**Coptic
Khan**

Muristan

**Church of
St John
the Baptist**
❻

MURISTAN ROAD

OLD CITY

SOUVIOS

DAVID STREET (EL-BAZAR)

ST MARK

CHAIN STREET

ℹ️

**Mission
Hospital**

ARARAT

KHABAD

**JEWISH
QUARTER**
p84

**CHRISTIAN
QUARTER**

**ARMENIAN
QUARTER AND
MOUNT ZION**
p120

**St Mark's
Church**

**ARMENIAN
QUARTER**

Q

R

4

0 metres   100
0 yards   100

N
↑

Q

R

❶

CHURCH OF THE HOLY SEPULCHRE

📍 Q2 🏠 Entrance from Souk el-Dabbagha 📞 (02) 626 7011
🕐 Summer: 5am–9pm daily (to 8pm Sun); winter: 4am–7pm daily

Built around what is believed to be the site of Christ's crucifixion, burial and Resurrection, this complex church is the most important in Christendom. Tucked away amid a warren of shops, the simple exterior belies the atmospheric chapels within. At the heart of the church, a marble shrine known as the Aedicule encloses the place where Jesus's body is believed to have been laid after his death.

↑ The Stone of Unction, commemorating the anointing and wrapping of Christ's body

The first basilica here was built by Roman emperor Constantine between AD 326 and 335 at the suggestion of his mother, St Helena. It was rebuilt on a smaller scale by Byzantine emperor Constantine Monomachus in the 1040s following its destruction by Fatimid sultan Hakim in 1009, but was much enlarged again by the Crusaders between 1114 and 1170. A disastrous fire in 1808 and an earth-quake in 1927 necessitated extensive repairs. Today, the building is administered by six Christian denominations.

Archaeological evidence that the church rests on a possible site of the Crucifixion is scant, but positive. Excavations show that the site lay outside the city walls until new ones encompassed it in AD 43; that in the early 1st century it was a disused quarry in which an area of cracked rock had been left untouched; and that rock-hewn tombs were in use here in the 1st centuries BC and AD. This all tallies with Gospel accounts of the Crucifixion.

Timeline

1009
The Fatimid sultan Hakim orders the destruction of the Church of the Holy Sepulchre, razing the original 4th-century shrine around the tomb of Christ.

2017
▽ Christ's Tomb is reopened after a US$4 million restoration project, in which a conservation team lifted the covering limestone slab for the first time in almost 500 years.

AD 326

▲ Constantine's builders dig away the hillside to create enough space to build a church around the presumed rock-hewn tomb of Christ.

1555
A marble slab is installed over Christ's Tomb. It is purposely cracked to deter Ottoman looters.

1808
▲ A devastating fire destroys the Stone of Unction and heavily damages the Rotunda.

Did You Know?

Eastern Orthodox Christians call this site the Church of the Resurrection.

The exterior of the church, ↑ crowned by the grey dome over the central nave

Exploring the Church of the Holy Sepulchre

The reconstructions and additions that have shaped this church over the centuries make it a complex building to explore. Its division into chapels and spaces allotted to six different denominations adds a further sense of confusion. The interior is dimly lit, and queues often form at Christ's Tomb, so that the time each person can spend inside the shrine may be limited to just a few minutes. Nonetheless, the experience of standing on Christianity's most hallowed ground inspires many visitors with a deep sense of awe.

The Rotunda, heavily rebuilt after the 1808 fire, is the most majestic part of the church.

Rebuilt after the 1927 earthquake, the Catholikon Dome is decorated with an image of Christ.

The Crusader bell tower was reduced by two storeys in 1719.

For Christians, Christ's Tomb is the most sacred site of all.

The main entrance is early 12th century.

A Stone of Unction has been here since medieval times. The present stone dates from 1810.

Chapel of the Franks

Chapel of Adam

Rock of Golgotha

Golgotha houses the rock venerated as the site of the Crucifixion.

THE STATUS QUO

Fierce disputes, lasting centuries, between Christian creeds (p115) over ownership of the church were largely resolved by an Ottoman decree issued in 1852. Still in force and known as the Status Quo, it divides custody among Armenians, Greeks, Copts, Roman Catholics, Ethiopians and Syrians. Every day, the church is unlocked by a Muslim keyholder acting as a "neutral" intermediary, a task that has been performed by a member of the same family for several generations.

↑ Clergy of the Armenian Apostolic Church celebrating mass in the Chapel of St Helena

Did You Know?

The crack in the Rock of Golgotha is believed to have been caused by an earthquake after the crucifixion.

Highlights

Must See

Golgotha

▷ On the left of Golgotha is the Greek Orthodox chapel, with its altar over the so-called Rock of Golgotha on which the cross of Christ's crucifixion is believed to have stood. To the right is the Roman Catholic chapel, and between them is the Altar of the Stabat Mater, commemorating Mary's sorrow as she stood at the foot of the cross.

Chapel of Adam

▽ Built against the Rock of Golgotha, this chapel is the medieval replacement of a previous Chapel of Adam that was part of Constantine's 4th-century basilica. It was so called because tradition told that Christ was crucified over the burial place of Adam's skull.

Christ's Tomb

The present-day shrine around the tomb of Christ was built in 1809–10, after the fire of 1808. The outer Chapel of the Angel has a low pilaster using a piece of the stone said to have been rolled from the mouth of Christ's Tomb by angels. A low door leads to the inner Chapel of the Holy Sepulchre, in which a marble slab covers the place where Christ's body was supposedly laid.

Rotunda and Syrian Chapel

▷ The Rotunda is built in classical Roman style. The 11th-century dome was replaced after the 1808 fire, as was the colonnade. In the back wall is the chapel used by the Syrians, which contains Jewish rock tombs (c 100 BC–AD 100).

Chapels of St Helena and the Finding of the Cross

The side walls of St Helena's Chapel are foundations of the 4th-century basilica. Below is the Finding of the Cross Chapel, a former cistern in which St Helena is said to have found the True Cross.

Ethiopian Monastery

This simple monastery occupies a series of small buildings on the roof of St Helena's Chapel. The Ethiopians of Jerusalem were forced here in the 17th century, when, unable to pay Ottoman taxes, they lost ownership of their chapels in the main church to other communities.

A cluster of small buildings on the roof of the Chapel of St Helena is inhabited by a community of Ethiopian monks.

The Chapel of St Helena is now dedicated to St Gregory the Illuminator, patron of the Armenians.

Stairs to the Inventio Crucis Chapel

↑ The Church of the Holy Sepulchre, with its numerous chapels

VIA DOLOROSA

The Via Dolorosa in Jerusalem traditionally traces the last steps of Jesus Christ, from where he was tried to Calvary, where he was crucified, and the tomb in the Church of the Holy Sepulchre, where he is said to have been buried. There is no historical basis for the route, which has changed over the centuries. However, the tradition is so strong that countless pilgrims walk the route, identifying with Jesus's suffering as they stop at the 14 Stations of the Cross. On Fridays, the Franciscans lead a procession along the route. The walk is not done the week after Easter or Christmas.

ORIGINAL ROUTE

The more probable route for the original Via Dolorosa begins at the Citadel, the Jerusalem residence of Pontius Pilate and thus a likely location for the trial of Christ. The condemned would probably have been led out of the city via what is now David Street and the Central Souk.

↑ The Church of the Holy Sepulchre lit by "holy fire" during Easter ceremonies

Seventh Station *Jesus falls for the second time. A large Roman column in a Franciscan chapel indicates this station.*

Sixth Station *A woman known as Veronica wipes away Jesus's blood and sweat, and her handkerchief reveals an impression of his face.*

Tenth to Thirteenth Stations *These four stations are all in the place identified as Golgotha (Calvary) within the Church of the Holy Sepulchre (p106).*

Fourteenth Station *The last Station of the Cross is the Holy Sepulchre itself.*

Eighth Station *Jesus consoles the women of Jerusalem.*

Ninth Station *Jesus falls for the third time. The place is marked by part of the shaft of a Roman column.*

← The marble relief above the door to the chapel at the Third Station

Second Station *Jesus takes up the cross after being flogged and crowned with thorns. This station is in front of the Franciscan Monastery of the Flagellation (p76).*

First Station *Jesus is condemned to death. The traditional site of the Roman fortress where this took place lies inside a Muslim college, the Madrasa el-Omariyya.*

Third Station *Jesus falls beneath the weight of the cross for the first time. This is commemorated by a small chapel with a marble relief.*

Fourth Station *Jesus meets his mother Mary. This is in front of the Armenian Church of Our Lady of the Spasm.*

Fifth Station *Simon of Cyrene is ordered by the Roman soldiers to help Jesus carry the cross (Mark 15: 21). This is the start of the ascent to Calvary.*

→ A procession of pilgrims tracing the footsteps of Jesus along the route

2 ✎ 🅜 🖵 🛍

THE CITADEL

📍P1 🚪Jaffa Gate 🕐Sep-Jul: 9am–4pm Sat-Thu (to 2pm Fri);
Aug: 9am–5pm Sat-Thu (to 4pm Fri) 🌐tod.org.il

This imposing fortress, also known as the Tower of David, dominates
Jaffa Gate. Inside, the Tower of David Museum uses multimedia to
present 4,000 years of Jerusalem's history, while a walk around the
ramparts offers spectacular views over the city.

The present-day structure of the Citadel dates mainly from the
Middle Ages and includes additions made in 1532 by Suleyman
the Magnificent. However, excavations have revealed remains
dating back to the 2nd century BC, and indicate that there
were fortifications here from Herodian times. Some believe
this supports the view that this is the most likely site of Christ's
trial and condemnation. On certain evenings (check website for
details), the Citadel is illuminated with the Night Spectacular.
This sound-and-light show allows spectators to immerse
themselves in the history of Jerusalem as the streets come
alive with images and music.

> **Spectators can immerse
> themselves in the history of
> Jerusalem as the streets come
> alive with images and music.**

*The name "Tower of David"
is also applied to this
minaret, added in 1655.*

*The mosque
was built by the
Mamelukes above
a Crusader hall.*

*Southeast
Tower*

←
Verrochio's *David*,
a gift to Jerusalem
from the city of
Florence in Italy

*Base of
an early
Islamic tower*

💬 INSIDER TIP
Herodian Stone

To identify limestone
blocks carved in the
1st century BC by the
masons of Herod the
Great, look for large
square-cut stones with
indented borders like
those at the base of
the Western Wall.

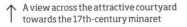
↑ A view across the attractive courtyard
towards the 17th-century minaret

EXPLORING THE TOWER OF DAVID MUSEUM

There is a lot to see in the Citadel's Tower of David Museum. To help the visitor, there are three well-signposted routes: the Observation Route runs along the ramparts for the best panoramic views of the city, both Old and New; the Excavation Route concentrates on the archaeological remains in the courtyard; and the Exhibition Route takes visitors through a series of rooms tracing the history of the city. This takes the form of displays, dioramas and models, rather than a collection of historical artifacts. Visitors can join a free English tour of the route departing at 11am Sunday to Friday, and lasting 90 minutes.

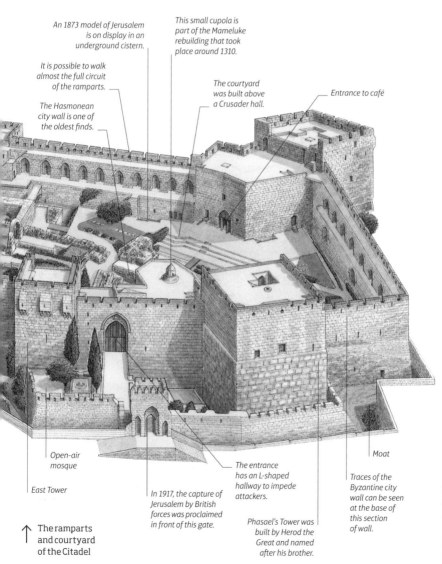

An 1873 model of Jerusalem is on display in an underground cistern.

This small cupola is part of the Mameluke rebuilding that took place around 1310.

It is possible to walk almost the full circuit of the ramparts.

The courtyard was built above a Crusader hall.

Entrance to café

The Hasmonean city wall is one of the oldest finds.

Open-air mosque

East Tower

In 1917, the capture of Jerusalem by British forces was proclaimed in front of this gate.

The entrance has an L-shaped hallway to impede attackers.

Phasael's Tower was built by Herod the Great and named after his brother.

Moat

Traces of the Byzantine city wall can be seen at the base of this section of wall.

↑ The ramparts and courtyard of the Citadel

EXPERIENCE MORE

3

Alexander Hospice

📍 Q3 🏠 Souk el-Dabbagha 📞 (02) 627 4952 🕐 Excavations: 9am-6pm daily

Home to St Alexander's Church, the central place of worship for Jerusalem's Russian Orthodox community, the Alexander Hospice also houses some important excavations. When founded in 1859, the site was already known to contain ruins of the original church of the Holy Sepulchre, built in AD 335. However, in 1882, excavations revealed remains of a Herodian city wall, proving that the site of the Holy Sepulchre church was outside the ancient city walls and adding credence to the claim that it was on the true site of Christ's crucifixion (p106). Also preserved here are remnants of a colonnaded street and, in the church, part of a triumphal arch from Hadrian's forum, begun in AD 135. The excavations are open to the public, but only parts of the church can be visited.

4

Lutheran Church of the Redeemer

📍 Q3 🏠 24 Muristan Rd 📞 (02) 626 6800 🕐 10am-5pm Mon-Sat (to 4pm winter) 🌐 elcjhl.org

This Neo-Romanesque church was built for the German Kaiser Wilhelm II, and completed in 1898. Renewed interest in the Holy Land by Europe during the late 19th century had ushered in a period of restoration and church building, with many nations wanting a religious presence in Jerusalem. The Lutheran Church of the Redeemer was constructed over the remains of the 11th-century church of St Mary of the Latins, built by wealthy merchants from Amalfi in Italy. An even earlier church is thought to have existed on the site from the 5th century. Many details from the medieval church have been incorporated into the new building, and the entrance way, decorated with the signs of the zodiac and symbols of the months, is largely original. The attractive cloister, inside the adjacent Lutheran hospice, has two tiers of galleries and dates from the 13th–14th centuries. Perhaps the most interesting part of the church is the bell tower. After climbing the 177 steps, visitors are rewarded with great views from the highest point in the Old City.

1889

The year the newest of the Old City's gates, New Gate, was created by the Ottomans.

5

Christian Quarter Road

📍 Q3

Together with David Street, which runs from Jaffa Gate towards the Muristan, Christian Quarter Road is one of the main thoroughfares in the Christian Quarter. Marking off the Muristan zone, it passes the western side of the Holy Sepulchre, and runs parallel to Souk Khan el-Zeit. It is lined with shops selling

Religious items, crafts, and antiques for sale along Christian Quarter Road

antiques, Palestinian handicrafts (embroidery, leather goods and Hebron glass) and religious articles (icons, carved olive-wood crucifixes and rosaries).

Midway up the road on the right, down an alley signposted for the Holy Sepulchre, a short stairway descends to the modest Omar Mosque, with a distinctive square minaret. Its name commemorates the caliph Omar, the person generally credited with saving the Holy Sepulchre from Muslim control after Jerusalem came under Muslim dominion in 638. Asked to go and pray in the church, which would almost certainly have led to it being converted into a mosque, he instead prayed on the steps outside, ensuring it remained a Christian site. The Omar mosque was built in 1193, by Saladin's son Aphdal Ali, beside the old Hospital of the Knights of St John.

The unassuming Khanqa Salahiyya is at the top of Christian Quarter Road. Built by Saladin between 1187 and 1189 as a monastery for Sufi mystics, it is on the site of

←

The Lutheran Church of the Redeemer, retaining some medieval elements

the old Crusader Patriarchate of Jerusalem. It is not open to non-Muslims. Along the north side of the mosque is El-Khanqa Street, an attractive, old, stepped street with interesting shops.

6

Church of St John the Baptist

🚇 Q3 🏛 Christian Quarter Rd

The silvery dome of the Church of St John the Baptist is clearly visible above the rooftops of the Muristan, but the entrance is harder to spot among the hordes of people along busy Christian Quarter Road. A small doorway leads into a courtyard, which in turn gives access to the neighbouring Greek Orthodox monastery and the church (which is closed to the public).

Founded in the 5th century, this is one of the most ancient churches in Jerusalem. After falling into ruin, it was extensively rebuilt in the 11th century, and apart from the two bell towers which are a later addition, the modern church is little changed.

In 1099, many Christian knights who had been wounded during the siege

of Jerusalem were taken care of in this church. After their recovery they decided to dedicate themselves to helping the sick and protecting pilgrims visiting Jerusalem. Founding the Knights of the Hospital of St John, they later developed into the military order of the Hospitallers and played a key role in the defence of the Holy Land during the Crusades.

CHRISTIANITY IN THE HOLY LAND

Jerusalem is the only place in the world where most Christian denominations maintain a presence. The largest are the Melchite Greek Catholic and the Greek Orthodox. The Russian Orthodox Church also has an important presence. Oriental Orthodox churches include the Armenian, Ethiopian, Coptic and Syriac. The Holy Land's oldest Protestant denomination is the Anglican Church. About 2 per cent of the population of Israel and the West Bank is Christian.

7

Museum of the Greek Orthodox Patriarchate

📍P2 🏛Greek Orthodox Patriarchate Rd ☎(02) 627 4941

Tucked away in the back alleys of the Christian Quarter, this museum (currently closed for restoration) houses a collection of ecclesiastical items that includes icons, embroidered vestments, mitres, chalices and filigree objects. It also has a fine array of archaeological finds.

The most interesting relics are two white-stone sarcophagi found at the end of the 19th century in a tomb near the present-day King David Hotel (*p142*). They are considered to belong to the family of Herod the Great, and are covered in wonderfully elaborate floral decoration, which represents

some of the finest Herodian-era funerary art ever found. The museum also displays Crusader objects, including a 12th-century carved capital from Nazareth, and artifacts found in the tomb of Baldwin I (King of Jerusalem, 1100–18) in the Church of the Holy Sepulchre. Other treasures include a 12th-century mitre carved from rock crystal, with bands of copper around the base and set with gems, which may once have contained relics of the Holy Cross. Among a collection of historical firmans (imperial edicts), is one that purports to have been issued by the caliph Omar in AD 638, granting the Greek Orthodox Church custody of Jerusalem's holy places.

8

Jaffa Gate

📍P3

This is the busiest of the seven Old City gates. It is the main gate for traffic and pedestrians coming from modern West Jerusalem via

Mamilla. Despite the great size of the gate, the entrance tunnel is narrow; it is also L-shaped – both of these measures were designed to thwart the advance of attackers. It was constructed during the reign of Suleyman the Magnificent – an exact date of 1538 is given in a dedication within the arch on the outside of the gate. The breach in the wall through which cars now pass was

---

CHRISTIAN INFORMATION CENTER

Run by the Franciscans, this information centre facing the Citadel (Tower of David) can provide details on Christian communities, worship services, churches, holy places and shrines all over the Holy Land. Its website (*www.cicts.org*) has useful contacts. From 1859 to 1917, the CIC's building served as Jerusalem's Austrian Imperial Post Office.

↓ Local vendor offering bread for sale outside the historic Jaffa Gate

← Bustling Omar ibn al-Khattab Square, leading to the Jaffa Gate

made in 1898, in order to allow the visiting Kaiser Wilhelm II of Germany to enter the city in his carriage.

Immediately inside the gate, set into the wall behind some railings on the left, are two graves. Tour guides often tell how these belong to Suleyman's architects, executed because they failed to incorporate Mount Zion within the city walls. An alternative legend has it that they were killed to prevent them ever building such grand walls for anyone else. In actual fact, they are the graves of a prominent citizen and his wife.

Jaffa Gate is one of the places where visitors can access the ramparts to walk along the city walls (p100). To the Arabs this gate is known as Bab el-Khalil, from the Arabic name for Hebron (El-Khalil), after the old road to the town that started here.

❾ Omar ibn al-Khattab Square

⌖ P4

Not so much a square as a widening of the road as it passes around the Citadel, this bustling area just inside Jaffa Gate is a focal point of Old City life. Located at the junction of the Christian, Muslim and Armenian quarters, the square takes its name from the caliph Omar, who captured Jerusalem for Islam in AD 638. The Muslim name for the plaza is somewhat misleading, as most of the surrounding property is owned by the Greek Orthodox Patriarchate.

In the late 19th century, the Patriarchate built the hotels and shops on the north side, including the Neo-Classical New Imperial Hotel.

At a street junction behind the hotel is a Roman column, erected around AD 200 in honour of the prefect of Judaea and commander of the 10th Legion. This was one of the legions that participated in the recapture of Jerusalem and destruction of the Second Temple in AD 70 (p48), and was subsequently quartered in the city. The column now supports a street light.

Several cafés with pavement tables fringe the east side of the square. Next to the cafés is the Christian Information Centre, and, opposite the entrance to the Citadel, the Anglican Christ Church compound. Its Neo-Gothic church (1849) was the first Protestant building in the Holy Land.

> **Located at the junction of the Christian, Muslim and Armenian quarters, the square takes its name from the caliph Omar who captured Jerusalem for Islam.**

A SHORT WALK
THE CHRISTIAN QUARTER

Distance 500 m (1,650 ft) **Nearest bus stop** HaKishle/Armenian Patriarchy **Time** 15 minutes

The most visited part of the Old City, the Christian Quarter is a head-on collision between commerce and spirituality. At its heart is the Church of the Holy Sepulchre, the most sacred of all Christian sites. It is surrounded by such a clutter of churches and hospices that all one can see of its exterior are the domes and entrance façade. The nearby streets are filled with shops and stalls that thrive on the pilgrim trade. Respite from the crowds can be found in the cafés of Muristan Road.

Did You Know?

Zalatimo's houses the remains of the doorway of the original 4th-century Holy Sepulchre church.

Omar Mosque
Along with David Street, **Christian Quarter Road** (p114) *is the area's main shopping thoroughfare.*
The founding of the Crusader Knights Hospitallers is connected with the small **Church of St John the Baptist** (p115).
CHRISTIAN QUARTER ROAD
START
From the Jaffa Gate area, **David Street** *is the main route down through the Old City. This cramped, stepped alley doubles as a busy tourist bazaar.*
DAVID STREET
MURISTAN ROAD
The intersecting avenues of the **Muristan** *were created when the Greek Orthodox Church redeveloped the area in 1903.*
0 metres 30
0 yards 30
N

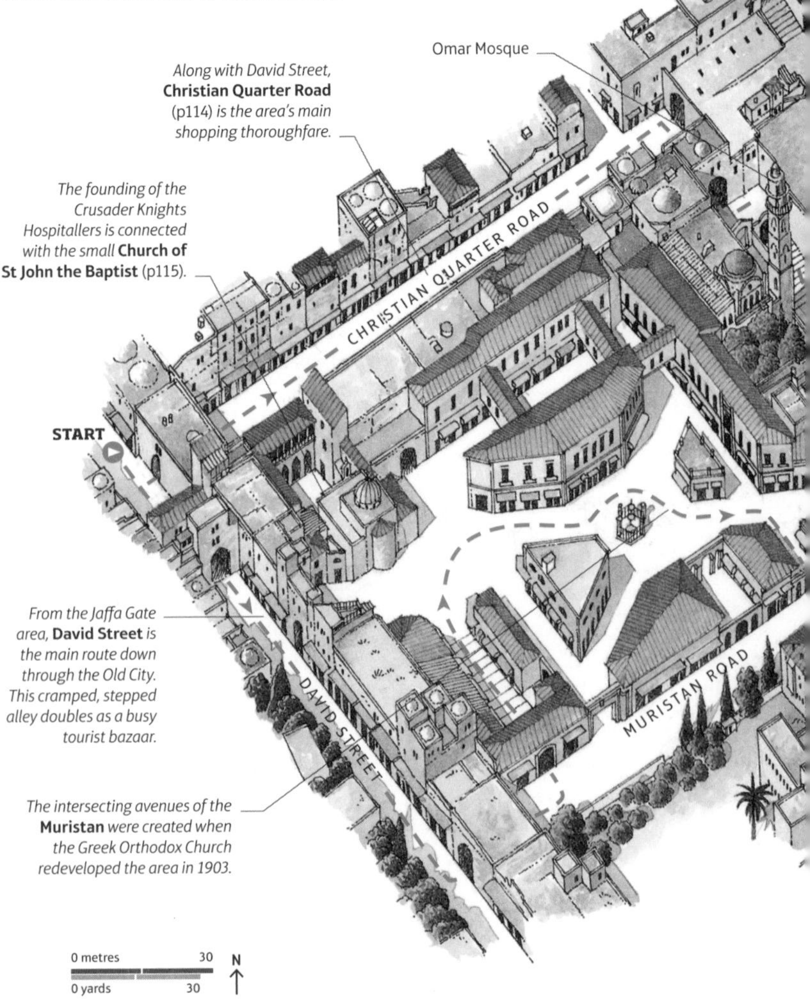

*The Stabat Mater Altar is one of numerous chapels and shrines that fill the **Church of the Holy Sepulchre** (p106), which commemorates the Crucifixion and burial of Christ.*

Khanqa Salahiyya

Locator Map
For more detail see p104

CHRISTIAN QUARTER

↑ The entrance gate to one of the avenues of the Muristan

FINISH

Ethiopian Monastery (p109)

Zalatimo's *is a famed confectionery shop.*

Pillars of original Byzantine Holy Sepulchre church (p106)

The **Alexander Hospice** (p114) *is built over the ruins of the early Holy Sepulchre church.*

SOUK EL-DABBAGHA

SOUK KHAN EL-ZEIT

The shops in the **Souk el-Dabbagha** *sell an array of religious souvenirs.*

The **Lutheran Church of the Redeemer** (p114) *has a lovely medieval cloister.*

→ View from the tower of the Lutheran Church of the Redeemer

ARMENIAN QUARTER AND MOUNT ZION

Armenian Christians have lived in Jerusalem since shortly after AD 301, when their country became the world's first Christian state. The Cathedral of St James was constructed during Crusader rule on the site of a 5th-century Armenian church, and became the focal point around which the neighbourhood evolved over the subsequent centuries. It still serves as the spiritual centre of Jerusalem's Armenian community.

Accessed from the Armenian Quarter through the Zion Gate, Mount Zion is identified in Jewish tradition as the site of King David's tomb. It is also associated with Jesus's Last Supper by Christians, who began worshipping here after Christ's death. Originally located inside the Old City, Mount Zion was left on Jerusalem's outskirts when the city walls were rebuilt by Suleyman the Magnificent in the 1530s – legend has it that this was a mistake on the part of his engineers. Following the division of Jerusalem after the 1948 war, Mount Zion was the closest Jews could get to the Jordanian-controlled Western Wall. This lasted until 1967, when the city was reunified after the Six-Day War.

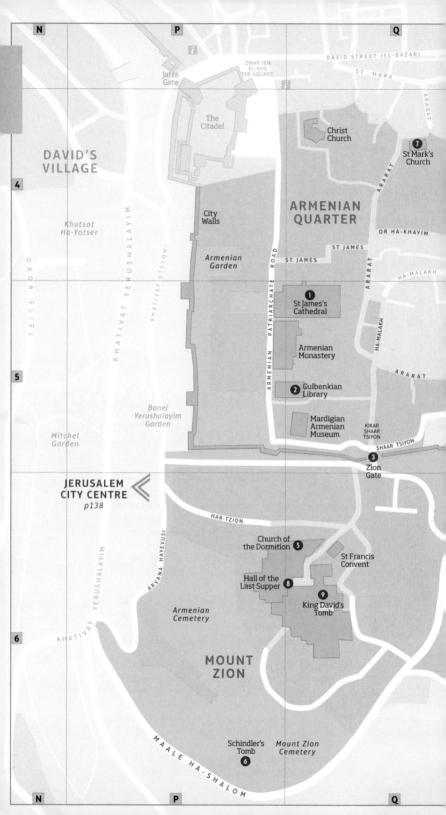

N

P

Q

DAVID STREET (EL-BAZAR)

ST MARK

OMAR IBN
EL-KHA
TAB SQUARE

Jaffa
Gate

ARARAT

The Citadel

Christ
Church

St Mark's
Church ❼

DAVID'S
VILLAGE

Khutsot
Ha-Yotser

ARMENIAN
QUARTER

City
Walls

OR HA-KHAYIM

4

DROR ELIEL

KHATIVAT ETSYONI

KHATIVAT YERUSHALAYIM

Armenian
Garden

ST JAMES

ARARAT

HA-MALAKH

ST JAMES

ST JAMES

St James's
Cathedral ❶

ARMENIAN PATRIARCHATE ROAD

HA-MALAKH

5

Bonei
Yerushalayim
Garden

Armenian
Monastery

Mitchel
Garden

ARARAT

Gulbenkian
Library ❷

Mardigian
Armenian
Museum

KIKAR
SHAAR
TSIYON

SHAAR TSIYON

Zion
Gate ❸

JERUSALEM
CITY CENTRE
p138

HAR-TZION

Church of
the Dormition ❺

ARVANA HAYEVUSI

St Francis
Convent

Hall of the
Last Supper ❽

King David's
Tomb ❾

KHATIVAT YERUSHALAYIM

Armenian
Cemetery

6

MOUNT
ZION

MAALE HA-SHALOM

Schindler's
Tomb ❻

Mount Zion
Cemetery

N

P

Q

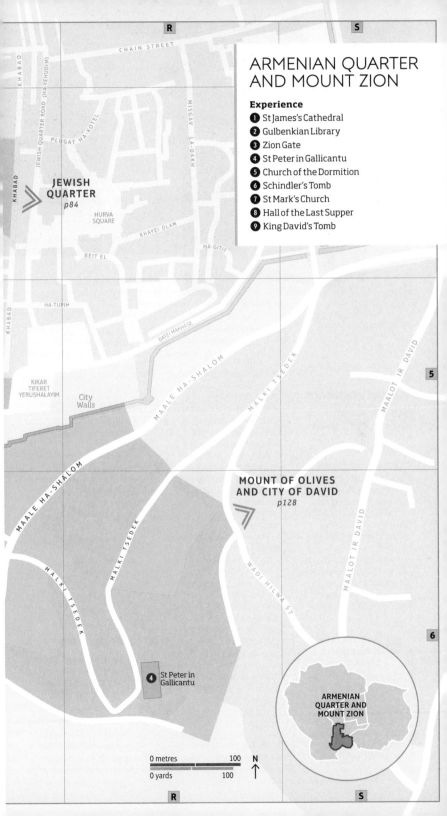

ARMENIAN QUARTER AND MOUNT ZION

Experience

1. St James's Cathedral
2. Gulbenkian Library
3. Zion Gate
4. St Peter in Gallicantu
5. Church of the Dormition
6. Schindler's Tomb
7. St Mark's Church
8. Hall of the Last Supper
9. King David's Tomb

CHAIN STREET

KHABAD

JEWISH QUARTER ROAD (HAYEHUDIM)

PLUGAT HA-KOTEL

MISGAV LA-DAKH

KHABAD

JEWISH QUARTER
p84

HURVA SQUARE

KHAYEI OLAM

BEIT EL

HA-GITIT

HA-TUPIM

KHABAD

BATEI MAKHASE

KIKAR TIFERET YERUSHALAYIM

City Walls

MAALE HA-SHALOM

MALKI TSEDEK

MAALOT IR DAVID

5

MOUNT OF OLIVES AND CITY OF DAVID
p128

MAALE HA-SHALOM

MALKI TSEDEK

MALKI TSEDEK

WADI HILWA ST

MAALOT IR DAVID

6

4 St Peter in Gallicantu

ARMENIAN QUARTER AND MOUNT ZION

0 metres   100
0 yards   100

N

R

S

↑ St James's Cathedral, the focal point of Jerusalem's Armenian Christian community

EXPERIENCE

①

St James's Cathedral

❑ Q5 **⌂** Armenian Patriarchate Rd **☎** (02) 628 2331 **🕐** 6–7:30am & 3–3:30pm daily

The Armenian Cathedral is one of the most beautiful of all Jerusalem's sacred buildings. It was originally constructed in the 11th and 12th centuries over the reputed tomb of St James the Great, the Apostle executed by Herod Agrippa I (AD 37–44). Many alterations and additions have subsequently been made to the building, most notably in

---

INSIDER TIP
Armenian Ceramics

Lovely Armenian-style ceramics are made at several workshops around Jerusalem's Old City, including Garo Sandrouni (*www.garo sandrouni.com*) in the Armenian Quarter.

---

the 18th century, when much of the decoration we see today was added.

Entrance to the cathedral is via a small courtyard with a 19th-century fountain. On the western wall are inscriptions in Armenian, one of which dates from 1151. Hanging in the vaulted porch are wooden bars. Each afternoon a priest strikes these with a wooden mallet known as a *nakus*, to signal the start of the service.

The enchanting cathedral interior is only dimly illuminated by a forest of oil lamps hung from the ceiling. There are no seats; instead the floors are laid with precious rugs. Four great square piers divide the main space into three aisles. These piers, along with the walls, are covered in blue-and-white tiles with floral and abstract patterns. In the apses at the end of each of the three aisles are altars, separated from the rest of the church by the iconostasis screen. Two thrones stand in the choir; the one nearest the pier is said to be that of St James the Less, traditionally held to have been a step-brother of Christ

and the first bishop of Jerusalem. It is used only once a year, in January, on the occasion of his feast day. The other throne is the one normally used by the patriarch.

The cathedral contains many small shrines and chapels. The third on the left as you enter is the most important: it supposedly holds the head of St James the Great. Off to the right, the Etchmiadzin Chapel has some beautiful tiling.

When planning a visit, bear in mind the very limited opening hours.

---

②

Gulbenkian Library

❑ Q5 **⌂** Armenian Patriarchate Rd **☎** (02) 628 2331 **🚌** 38 **🕐** 2–6pm Mon–Fri **🌐** armenian-patriarchate.com/gulbenkian

Located within the complex of St James's Cathedral, the Gulbenkian Library is one of the largest and most important resource centres dedicated to the history and culture of the Armenian people. It first opened in 1932 and has a growing collection of more than 100,000 works, both historical and contemporary, a large number of which are in Armenian. The library also contains the third largest collection of Armenian newspapers, along with an extensive stock of periodicals and magazines.

A separate room houses rare and early imprints. Significant among these is a copy of the inaugural issue of the official publication of the Armenian Patriarchate. Other interesting objects are examples of the first books printed in the very first print shop in Jerusalem, which has been active since 1833 and is located inside the Armenian monastery.

The Patriarchate also curates an extraordinary collection of 4,000 ancient manuscripts, housed in the Church of St Toros, close to the library.

> St Peter in Gallicantu looks modern, but in the crypt are ancient caves where, it is said, Christ spent the night before being taken to Pontius Pilate.

→

The church of St Peter in Gallicantu, on the reputed site of Peter's denial of Christ

❸
Zion Gate

🔲 Q5

Zion Gate was constructed by Suleyman the Magnificent's engineers in 1540. It allowed direct access from the city to the holy sites on Mount Zion. Fighting was particularly fierce here in 1948, when Israeli soldiers were desperate to breach the walls to relieve the Jewish Quarter, under siege by the Jordanians. The gate's exterior is terribly pock-marked by bullet holes. A short distance to the west there is conspicuous damage to the base of the wall where soldiers tried to blast their way through with explosives.

In Arabic, the gate is known as Bab el-Nabi Daud (Gate of the Prophet David), because of its proximity to the place traditionally known as King David's Tomb (p127).

———

❹ 🚶
St Peter in Gallicantu

🔲 R6 🏠 Malki Tsedek Rd
📞 (02) 673 1739 🚌 38
🕐 9am–5pm Mon–Sat

To the east of Mount Zion, on the slopes overlooking the City of David (p132) and the Kidron Valley, this church commemorates the

traditional site of St Peter's reported denial of Christ, fulfilling the prophecy, "Before the cock crows twice, thou shalt deny me thrice" (Mark 14: 72). Built in 1931, the church looks modern, but in the crypt are ancient caves where, it is said, Christ spent the night before being taken to Pontius Pilate. Herodian remains have been found under the church and the garden contains part of a Hasmonean stairway, in use in Christ's time. Mosaics from a previous 5th- to 6th-century Byzantine church and monastery have also been unearthed here.

5

Church of the Dormition

Q6 🅰 **Mount Zion**
📞 **(02) 565 5330** 🚌 **38, 20**
🕐 **9am–5pm Mon–Sat, 11:30am–5pm Sun (closed noon–1pm for prayer)**

Crowned by a tall bell tower and a dome with four small corner turrets, the Neo-Romanesque Benedictine Church of the Dormition dominates the Mount Zion hilltop. The large, airy, white-stone church stands on the site where the Virgin Mary is said to have fallen into an "eternal sleep". After Christ's death, according to Christian tradition, his mother lived on Mount Zion until she died.

The hill soon became a holy site, and there may have been a church here as early as the 4th century AD. It is certain that around the 6th century a large basilica was built on the site, which later fell into ruins. When the Crusaders came, they too erected a church with chapels to the Dormition of the Virgin and the Last Supper.

Today's church includes the Chapel of the Dormition and Dormition Abbey, built in the early 20th century for Kaiser Wilhelm II and inspired by the cathedral in Aachen, Germany.

During the 1948 and 1967 wars, the church was a strategic outpost of Israeli soldiers and was damaged in several battles. The main part of the church boasts a fine mosaic floor featuring zodiac symbols and the names of saints and prophets. In the crypt is a wood and ivory sculpture of the "sleeping" Virgin, while the walls are adorned with images of Old Testament women, including Eve, Judith, Ruth and Esther. On the mezzanine are remains of previous churches.

6

Schindler's Tomb

P6 🅰 **Mount Zion** 🚌 **1, 2**

Downhill from Zion Gate, the path forks left past the Chamber of the Holocaust, a small museum remembering the thousands of Jewish communities wiped out by the Nazis. Across the road at the end of the path is a Christian cemetery, where the grave of German-born Oskar Schindler is located.

During World War II, this industrialist went out of his way to use Jewish prisoners as labourers in his factory, thus saving over 1,000 people from the death camps. He became a symbol of the fight against the Holocaust and asked to be buried in Jerusalem. He died in 1974. His courageous stand against the Nazis was retold in Steven Spielberg's Oscar-winning 1993 film, *Schindler's List*.

7

St Mark's Church

Q4 🅰 **5 Ararat St** 📞 **(02) 628 3304** 🕐 **9am–1pm & 3–5pm Mon–Sat (to 4pm winter)**

This small church is the centre of the Syrian Orthodox

> ### VALLEY OF HINNOM
> The valley below Mount Zion has been associated with fire and death since at least the time of the Prophet Jeremiah (late 7th century BC), who railed against the sacrifice of children here by the pagan cult of Moloch. In the New Testament, the valley is portrayed as a place of "unquenchable fire" in which unbelievers will suffer for eternity. Thus it is the source of many Jewish and Christian concepts of hell.

Church of the Dormition, bathed in the golden glow of sunset community in Jerusalem and is rich in biblical associations, albeit of suspect authenticity. According to tradition, the church was built on the site of the house of Mary, mother of St Mark the Evangelist. A stone font in the church is supposedly that in which the Virgin Mary was baptized, and the church also has a painting on parchment of the Virgin and Child often attributed to St Luke. Historians identify it as dating from a much later period. Some scholars do believe, however, that a small cellar room here was the true site of the Last Supper, not Mount Zion.

8
Hall of the Last Supper

📍 Q6 ⬛ Mount Zion
🕐 8am–6pm daily

Located on Mount Zion, the Hall of the Last Supper is on the first floor of a Gothic building that is all that remains of the large church built by the Crusaders to commemorate Mary's Dormition. Christian tradition maintains that it is on the site of Christ's last meal with his Disciples. The room is unadorned apart from the Gothic arches dividing it.

In the Middle Ages the hall became part of the adjacent

Franciscan monastery, while in the 15th century it was turned into a mosque by the Turks, who added a mihrab and some stained-glass.

9
King David's Tomb

📍 Q6 ⬛ Mount Zion 📞 (02) 581 1911 🚌 1, 3 🕐 8am–9pm Sat–Thu & hols, 8am–2pm Fri (to 1pm winter)

Beneath the Hall of the Last Supper, on the lower floor, are small chambers venerated as King David's Tomb. The main chamber is bare apart from a cenotaph covered by a drape. The site was first identified as David's tomb in the 11th century AD, and in the 15th century was incorporated into a mosque by the Muslims, who consider David a true prophet. In spite of doubts about the tomb's authenticity, it is one of the most revered Jewish holy sites. It was particularly so between 1948 and 1967,

↑ The Islamic Mihrab inside the Hall of the Last Supper

when the Old City was under Jordanian control and the Western Wall was inaccessible to Jews, so they came here to pray. Today, the entrance hall is still used as a synagogue, with separate seating for men and women. From the 4th to the 15th centuries, the tomb was associated with Pentecost and the death of the Virgin, and, according to tradition, it was here that Christ washed his Disciples' feet after the Last Supper (John 13: 1–17).

→ Statue of King David playing the harp, at the entrance to King David's Tomb

The Jewish cemetery on the Mount of Olives

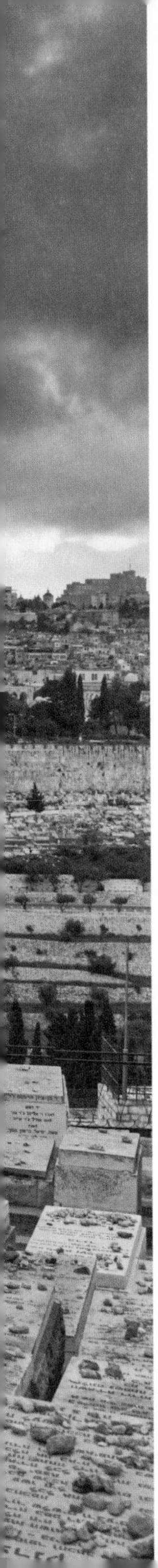

MOUNT OF OLIVES AND CITY OF DAVID

According to the Bible, King David conquered Jerusalem from the Jebusites around 1000 BC. During the First Temple period, the core of the Israelite capital of Jerusalem was situated south of Mount Moriah (the Temple Mount) on a sloping ridge now known as the City of David. The city was captured by the Babylonians in 586 BC and has lain in ruins ever since. Today, the site is excavated by archaeologists seeking to determine whether it was the fortified capital of a strong, centralized kingdom, as described in the Bible, or a small mountain town ruled by a local chieftain whose authority was embellished by the biblical text.

Across the Kidron Valley, the ridge known as the Mount of Olives (Olivet) has served as a Jewish burial site since biblical times, in part because an ancient rabbinic tradition holds that in the Messianic Era the resurrection of the dead will start here. According to the New Testament, Jesus visited the Mount of Olives three times during the week before his Crucifixion. In AD 70, the Romans' infamous Legio X Fretensis (10th Legion) camped here during the bloody siege of Jerusalem.

MOUNT OF OLIVES AND CITY OF DAVID

Must See

❶ City of David

Experience More

❷ Kidron Valley
❸ Garden of Gethsemane
❹ Church of All Nations
❺ Dominus Flevit Sanctuary
❻ Church of St Mary Magdalene
❼ Tomb of the Virgin Mary
❽ Jewish Cemeteries
❾ Mosque of the Ascension
❿ Russian Church of the Ascension
⓫ Church of the Pater Noster

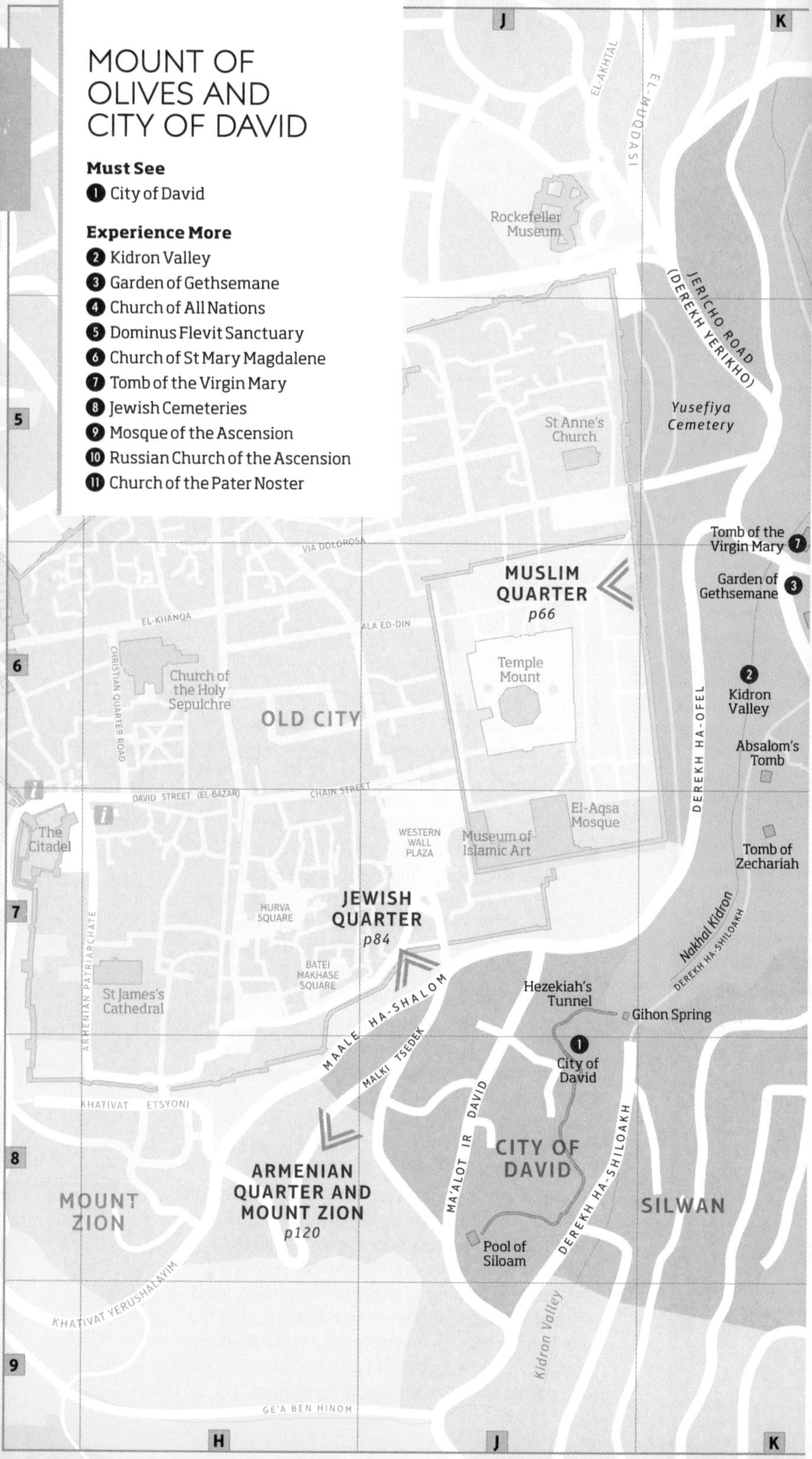

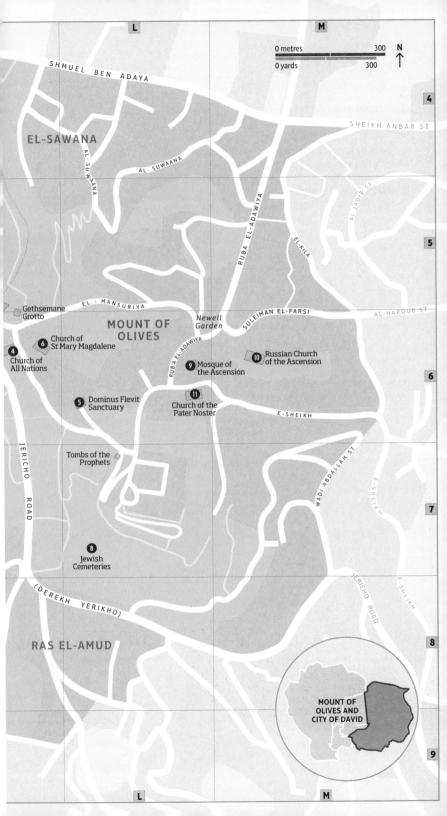

L

M

0 metres   300

0 yards   300

N

4

SHMUEL BEN ADAYA

SHEIKH ANBAR ST

EL-SAWANA

AL-SUWAANA

AL-SUWAANA

RUBA EL-ADAWIYA

EL-KILA

AL-JADID ST

5

EL-MANSURIYA

Newell Garden

SULEIMAN EL-FARSI

AL-HARDUB ST

Gethsemane Grotto

MOUNT OF OLIVES

6 Church of St Mary Magdalene

RUBA EL-ADAWIYA

10 Russian Church of the Ascension

4 Church of All Nations

9 Mosque of the Ascension

6

5 Dominus Flevit Sanctuary

11 Church of the Pater Noster

E-SHEIKH

Tombs of the Prophets

WADI ABDALLAH ST

E-SHEIKH

JERICHO ROAD

7

8 Jewish Cemeteries

(DEREKH YERIKHO)

JERICHO ROAD

E-SHEIKH

8

RAS EL-AMUD

MOUNT OF OLIVES AND CITY OF DAVID

9

L

M

❶ 🖼️ 🗺️

CITY OF DAVID

📍 J8 🏛️ Maalot Ir David 🕐 Winter: 8am–5pm Sun–Thu, 8am–2pm Fri & holiday eves; summer: 8am–7pm Sun–Thu, 8am–4pm Fri & holiday eves
🌐 cityofdavid.org.il

Believed by archaeologists to be the location of King David's capital, this site has turned up finds that include houses from as far back as the 10th century BC. Underneath the city lies a fascinating system of water supply channels – the exciting walk in thigh-deep water through Hezekiah's Tunnel is not to be missed.

South of the Temple Mount, or Haram ash-Sharif (p70), a rocky ridge runs beside the Kidron Valley. Its summit was already settled by the Jebusites, a Canaanite people, in the 20th century BC, making this the oldest part of Jerusalem. It was from them that David supposedly took the city for his capital in about 1000 BC (2 Samuel 5: 6–17). On the site are remains of buildings up to the city's capture by the Babylonians in 586 BC. They include 13th-century-BC walls belonging to the Jebusite acropolis, fragments of a palace attributed to David and houses burned in the Babylonian attack. Excavations have also revealed an impressive water supply system carved into the rock beneath the city, designed to ensure that the population could withstand sieges during times of war.

↑ Exploring the underground excavations at the ancient city

↑ The northern part of the City of David, lying to the south of Temple Mount

City of David Highlights

THE HISTORIC CITY OF KING DAVID

Archaeologists have long debated whether a United Monarchy under Kings David and Solomon, described in the Bible, is a historical fact or a folk tale. Was King David's Jerusalem a resplendent, fortified capital governed by a powerful king, or was it a backwater village ruled by a local chieftain? Sceptics argue that no monumental fortifications from the 10th century BC have been found in Jerusalem, but in 2018 archaeologists announced that excavations and carbon-dating at Tel 'Eton in the Hebron Hills indicate a high degree of social complexity and sophistication, thereby bolstering the United Monarchy thesis.

Hezekiah's Tunnel and Pool of Siloam

▷ In the 10th century BC, a tunnel, later attributed to Solomon, was dug to take water from the Gihon Spring to fields in the Kidron Valley. In the face of Assyrian invasion in about 700 BC, King Hezekiah had a new tunnel built to bring the spring water right into the city, so concealing the source of the supply. Hezekiah's Tunnel ran 533 m (1,750 ft) from the spring to a large, new storage pool - the Pool of Siloam - in the south of the city. The pool is now smaller than it was originally and was rebuilt after the Romans sacked Jerusalem in AD 70. Visitors can wade through the tunnel from the Gihon Spring - wear shoes and bring a flashlight with you.

Warren's Shaft

▽ Warren's Shaft is named after Charles Warren, its 19th-century English discoverer. At the bottom of the vertical shaft is a pool fed by the Gihon Spring. Nearby is the Jebusites' 18th-century-BC city wall, identified by the large, uncut stone blocks used in its construction. It was sited to bring the entrance to Warren's Shaft within the confines of the city.

Royal Quarter

Archaeologists digging in the Royal Quarter found 51 First Temple-era bullae (seal impressions on clay). One bears the name of Gemaryahu ben Shafan, mentioned in the biblical Book of Jeremiah as a scribe of Yehoyakim (Jehoiakim), King of Judah.

Cistern

Discovered in 1998, this 15-m- (50-ft-) wide underground reservoir from the First Temple era could store 250,000 litres (5,500 gal) of water. It is lined with waterproof plaster, on which the handprints of the builders can still be seen.

Canaanite Tunnel

Apparently excavated around 1800 BC by the Canaanites, this now-dry tunnel once transported water for use in agriculture. Exploring it is a good option if you'd prefer not to get your feet wet in nearby Hezekiah's Tunnel.

↑ Ancient rock-cut tombs in the Kidron Valley, dating from the Jewish Second Temple period

EXPERIENCE MORE

❷ Kidron Valley

◎ K6

The Kidron Valley is between the Old City and the Mount of Olives. According to the Hebrew prophet Joel, its middle section – the Valley of Jehoshaphat ("God shall judge") – is where the nations will be tried on the Day of Judgement (Joel 3: 2-3). The area has several impressive tombs hewn out of solid bedrock

MOUNT SCOPUS

On the next hill north of the Mount of Olives, the main campus of the Hebrew University of Jerusalem *(new.huji. ac.il)* was inaugurated in 1925. Members of its first board of directors included Martin Buber, Sigmund Freud and Albert Einstein. Nearby, the Jerusalem War Cemetery *(www. cwgc.org)* contains the graves of 2,515 British, Australian and New Zealand forces killed in World War II.

during the Second Temple Period. Absalom's Tomb, its roof like an inverted funnel, was ascribed in medieval times to King David's rebellious son, Absalom. Behind it, the so-called Tomb of Jehoshaphat (the 9th century BC king of Judah) features a carved frieze. The pyramid-topped Tomb of Zechariah is actually the monument of the adjacent mausoleum of the priestly B'nei Hezir family. It is also known as the Grotto of St James because St James supposedly hid here while Jesus was arrested.

❸ Garden of Gethsemane

◎ K6 ⌂ Church of All Nations, Mount of Olives ⊞ 236, 257 ◷ 8:30am-noon & 12:30-4pm 🖳 gethsemane-en. custodia.org

On the grounds of the Church of All Nations, this quiet grove of ancient olive trees is where Jesus is believed to have prayed on the night of his betrayal and arrest (Mark 14: 32–50). Some of the largest trees have been carbon-dated

Did You Know?

The Mount of Olives is home to more than 150,000 Jewish graves.

to the 12th century, and DNA tests have revealed that eight of them grew from cuttings from the same mother tree – perhaps taken by Christians who believed the tree to have witnessed Jesus's agony.

❹ Church of All Nations

◎ K6 ⌂ Jericho Rd ☎ (02) 626 6444 ◷ 8am-noon & 2-5pm daily (to 6pm in summer)

The Church of All Nations is also known as the Basilica of the Agony, for the rock in the

→

The beautiful ceiling and façade *(inset)* of the Church of All Nations

Garden of Gethsemane on which it is believed Christ prayed the night before he was arrested. A 4th-century church here was destroyed in an earthquake in 747. The Crusaders built a new one, aligned to cover three outcrops of rock, recalling Christ's three prayers during the night. It was consecrated in 1170, but fell into disuse after 1345.

After excavations in the early 20th century, the present church was designed by Antonio Barluzzi and built in 1924 with funds contributed by 12 nations, hence the name and the 12 domes bearing national coats of arms. In the centre of the nave, ringed by a wrought-iron crown of thorns, is the rock of the Byzantine church. The mosaic in the apse represents Christ's Agony, while others depicting his arrest and Judas's kiss are at the sides. The plan of the Byzantine church is traced in black marble on the floor, and sections of Byzantine mosaic pavement can also be seen. Outside, the gilded mosaic scene on the pediment also depicts the Agony.

⑤ Dominus Flevit Sanctuary

◉ L6 ⌂ Mount of Olives ☎ (02) 626 6450 ⏰ 8–11:45am & 2:30–5pm daily

This chapel stands where medieval pilgrims identified a rock as the one on which Jesus sat when he wept over the fate of Jerusalem – the name of the chapel means "The Lord Wept".

Designed in the shape of a teardrop by Italian architect Antonio Barluzzi, it was built in 1955 over a 7th-century chapel, with part of the original apse preserved. The view of the Dome of the Rock from the altar window is justly famous.

A mosaic floor, which was preserved in situ outside, is from a 5th-century monastery. The graves on view nearby show the types found in the 1950s in a vast cemetery here, in use periodically from 1600 BC to AD 70. Also on show are some carved stone ossuaries.

⑥ Church of St Mary Magdalene

◉ K6 ⌂ Mount of Olives ☎ (02) 628 4371 ⏰ 10am–noon Tue & Thu

In 1885, Tsar Alexander III had this Russian Orthodox church built in memory of his mother, Maria Alexandrovna. Set amid trees, its seven gilded onion domes are among the most striking features of the sky-line seen from the Old City. These and other architectural features are in 16th- to 17th-century Muscovite style.

It was consecrated in 1888 in the presence of Grand Duke Sergei Alexandrovich (Tsar Alexander III's brother) and his wife, Grand Duchess Elizabeth Feodorovna, who is buried here.

The interior of the Tomb of the Virgin Mary, decorated with icons and ornaments ↑

7

Tomb of the Virgin Mary

📍K6 🚌Jericho Rd ☎(02) 628 4054 ⏰6am–12:30pm & 2:30–6pm daily

Believed to be where the Disciples entombed the Virgin Mary, this underground sanctuary in the Valley of Jehoshaphat is one of the most intimate holy places in Jerusalem. The façade, the impressive flight of 47 steps and the royal Christian tombs in side niches halfway down, all date from the 12th century. The tomb on the right, going down, is venerated as that of St Anne and St Joachim, Mary's parents. The first tomb was cut in the hillside here in the 1st century AD. The cruciform crypt as seen today, much

of it cut into solid rock, is Byzantine. The Tomb of Mary stands in the eastern branch of the crypt, which is decorated with icons and ornaments. Religious services are held here by Armenian Greek, Coptic and Syrian Christians. The site was sanctified by Muslims because, according to the 15th-century scholar Mujir al-Din, Muhammad saw a light over the tomb of his "sister Mary" during his Night Journey to Jerusalem. Outside, to the right of the façade, is the Cave of Gethsemane, or Cave of the Betrayal, the traditional location of Judas's betrayal.

> Some Jews believe that in the End of Days, when the Messiah comes, the Resurrection of the Dead will begin on the Mount of Olives.

cemetery in the world. The first burials took place here in caves about 3,000 years ago, during the time of the First Temple. Some Jews believe that in the End of Days, when the Messiah comes, the Resurrection of the Dead will begin on the Mount of Olives – a big upside, therefore, of being buried here. Famous graves include those of Eliezer ben Yehuda, the "Father of Modern Hebrew"; S Y Agnon, winner of the Nobel Prize for Literature; and Israeli Prime Minister Menahem Begin.

🏔 **GREAT VIEW**
Old City

Standing just over 800 m (2,625 ft) tall, the Mount of Olives is famed for its views of the Old City, which encompass the Church of the Holy Sepulchre, the Dome of the Rock and the Hurva Synagogue.

8

Jewish Cemeteries

📍L7 🚌52 Jericho Rd, Mount of Olives 🚍236 ☎(02) 627 5050 🌐mountofolives.co.il

The western slopes of the Mount of Olives are home to the oldest and largest Jewish

9

Mosque of the Ascension

📍L6 🚌Off Ruba el-Adawiya St, Mount of Olives ⏰8am–5pm daily (to 2:30pm in winter); if closed, ring bell

A Christian noblewoman built the first chapel here around AD 380 to commemorate Christ's Ascension. It had

⑩ Russian Church of the Ascension

🗺 M6 🏠 Off Ruba el-Adawiya St, Mount of Olives 📞 (02) 628 4373 🕐 Summer: 9am–noon Tue & Thu; winter: 10am–1pm Tue & Thu

This church of a still active Russian Orthodox convent was built between 1870 and 1887. The bell tower, a prominent landmark, was built high enough for pilgrims too infirm to walk to the River Jordan to see it from afar. The 8,000-kg (8-tonne) bell was hauled from Jaffa by Russian pilgrims.

Two 5th-century Armenian mosaics were found during construction. A small museum was built over one, which is fragmentary; the other is in the Chapel of the Head of John the Baptist, inside the church. An iron cage on the floor shows where John's decapitated head was supposedly found.

THE RUSSIANS IN JERUSALEM

In the 19th century, Europe competed for a stake in the Holy Land, which was then ruled by the Ottoman Empire. The Russian Orthodox Church, seeing itself as the successor to the Byzantine Empire, bought Jerusalem land on a grand scale, and some 200,000 Russian pilgrims a year visited the city. In World War I, the Ottomans expelled Russians and seized their holdings.

⑪ 🚫 🚫 Church of the Pater Noster

🗺 L6 🏠 Mount of Olives 📞 (02) 626 4904 🕐 8:30am–noon & 2:30–5pm Mon–Sat

This church stands next to the partly restored ruins of one commissioned by the emperor Constantine, who sent his mother, St Helena, to supervise construction in AD 326. It was above a grotto where the Ascension was commemorated. By Crusader times, the grotto was known as the place where Christ had taught the Disciples the Pater Noster (meaning "Our Father"), or Lord's Prayer (Matthew 6:9).

The present church and a Carmelite monastery were built between 1868 and 1872 by the French Princesse de la Tour d'Auvergne. Today, the church and its cloister are famous for the tiled panels inscribed with the Pater Noster in over 100 languages.

three porticoes around an uncovered space, where it is said that dust miraculously formed the image of Christ's footprints. The Crusaders rebuilt the chapel as an octagon and the column bases of their portico are still visible.

The chapel became a Muslim shrine after Saladin's conquest in 1187. The minaret and mosque are 17th century.

→ The peaceful cloister of the Church of the Pater Noster

JERUSALEM CITY CENTRE

By the 1860s, Jerusalem's Old City was not only bursting at the seams but was also critically unhygienic, giving rise to the establishment of extra-muros Jewish neighbourhoods like Mishkenot Sha'ananim, Yemin Moshe, Nakhalat Shiv'a and Mea She'arim. Around the same time, European national churches constructed a number of Christian institutions outside the city walls, intended to cater to pilgrims. They each brought with them their own architectural styles: the buildings of the Russian Compound, for instance, have a distinctly Muscovite spirit. At first, living outside the Old City – whose gates were locked tight each night – was seen as recklessly dangerous, but because of population pressures the New City continued to grow. During the British Mandate, construction of new areas, including the city centre around Ben Yehuda Street, continued apace. Today, over 95 per cent of Jerusalem's population lives outside the Old City and downtown commerce is concentrated on and around Jaffa Street, between Mamilla and the bustling Mahane Yehuda food market.

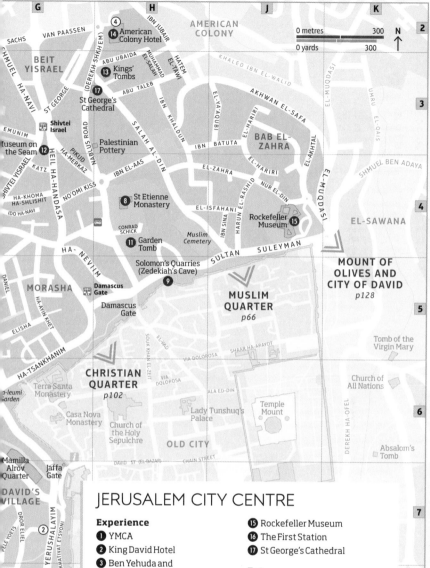

JERUSALEM CITY CENTRE

Experience

1. YMCA
2. King David Hotel
3. Ben Yehuda and Nakhalat Shiv'a
4. Italian Synagogue
5. Ticho House
6. Ha-Neviim Street
7. Russian Compound
8. St Etienne Monastery
9. Solomon's Quarries (Zedekiah's Cave)
10. Mea She'arim
11. Garden Tomb
12. Museum on the Seam
13. Kings' Tombs
14. American Colony Hotel
15. Rockefeller Museum
16. The First Station
17. St George's Cathedral

Eat

1. Chakra
2. The Eucalyptus
3. Mona

Stay

4. American Colony Hotel
5. YMCA Three Arches Hotel
6. Abraham Hostel

Shop

7. Azoulay Art
8. Cadim Ceramics Gallery
9. Baltinester Brothers

EXPERIENCE

1

YMCA

📍 F7 🏠 26 King David St 🚌 7, 30, 38 🕐 Tower: 8am–8pm daily 🌐 ymca.org.il

Built in 1926–33 by Arthur Loomis Harmon, who also created New York's Empire State Building, Jerusalem's YMCA is one of the city's best-known landmarks. It has three sections: the central body, with a bell tower offering extraordinary views (for a fee), and two side wings. The decorative elements on the exterior – including the 5-m (16.5-ft) bas-relief of one of the six-winged seraphim described in the Old Testament (Isaiah 6: 2–3) – reflect a stylized form of Oriental Byzantine design, combined with elements of Romanesque and Islamic art.

Yet the exterior, splendid as it is, does not prepare the visitor for the fabulously elaborate decor on the inside. Here, design elements from three different cultures are woven through with symbols from the three main monotheistic religions. In the concert hall, the dome's 12 windows represent the 12 Tribes of Israel, the 12 Disciples of Christ and the 12 Followers of Muhammad, while depicted on the chandelier are the Cross, Crescent and Star of David. The entire decor has a kind of Art Deco gloss, while the ethos of its eclectic design is one of peace and tolerance between faiths and cultures.

2

King David Hotel

📍 F7 🏠 23 King David St 🚌 13, 18 🌐 danhotels.com

This legendary hotel, hosting prime ministers, presidents and kings, was built by a consortium of Egyptian-Jewish businessmen and opened in 1930, from when provisions were brought daily from Cairo by train. A gem of Mandate-era architecture, its spacious lobbies and luxurious public areas were designed to resemble palaces of the Biblical Kings David and Solomon – look for decorative elements inspired by Assyrian, Hittite, Phoenician and ancient Greek architecture. In 1946, the Irgun (Etzel), a right-wing Zionist paramilitary group led by Menahem Begin, blew up the hotel's southern wing, housing the civilian and military headquarters of the British administration, killing 91 people. The damage wasn't repaired until 1961; more floors were added in 1969. Famous guest have included Winston Churchill, Eleanor Roosevelt, Ethiopian Emperor Haile Selasie, Anwar Sadat (during his landmark 1977 visit to Israel), Jordan's King Hussein, Britian's Prince Charles and seven serving US presidents.

Did You Know?

Mark Twain visited Jerusalem in 1867. He described his travels in the best-selling *The Innocents Abroad*.

3

Ben Yehuda and Nakhalat Shiv'a

📍 E5 🚌 20, 23, 27 🚊 Jaffa Center

At the heart of western Jerusalem is the triangle formed by Jaffa Road, King George V Street and traffic-free Ben Yehuda Street. This area was long a stronghold of secular Jewish culture and nightlife, in marked contrast to the ultra-Orthodox neighbourhoods to the north, though this is changing as the city becomes more religious.

← The YMCA building, dominated by its central tower observation point

↑ Lively, pedestrianized Ben Yehuda Street, with shops and street vendors

Built in the early 1920s, Ben Yehuda Street, known as the Midrachov ("pedestrian mall"), is lined with eateries, cafés, souvenir shops and street musicians, and stays animated until very late. At the end is Zion Square, from which the stone houses of Nahalat Shiv'a, connected by hidden courtyards, stretch southward. The name, which means "Estate of the Seven", refers to the seven Jewish families who established the neighbourhood in the 1860s. Today, it is known for boutiques with top-quality Judaica, jewellery and art.

4

Italian Synagogue

📍E5 🚌27 Hillel St 🚍18, 21, 22, 30 🕐10:30am–4:30pm Sun-Wed, noon-7pm Thu 🌐ijamuseum.org

Originally a German college constructed in the late 19th century, this building now houses an 18th-century synagogue from Conegliano Veneto, near Venice in Italy. By the early 20th century, the synagogue had fallen into disuse, and in 1952 it was decided to dismantle the interior and bring it to Jerusalem. It is arguably the most beautiful synagogue in Israel, and on Saturdays and Jewish holidays the Italian-Jewish community worships here.

The building also houses the Museum of Italian-Jewish Art, which has some fascinating items, such as medieval ritual objects. On the lower floor is the Centre of Studies on Italian Judaism and a library on the same subject.

→ An exhibit in the Museum of Italian Jewish Art in the Italian Synagogue

←

Entrance of Ticho House, which houses a collection of Anna Ticho's art

⑤ 🏛

Ticho House

📍E4 🏠9 Ha-Rav Kook St 📞(02) 645 3746 🚌13, 18, 20
🕐Noon-8pm Sun-Thu 🚫Jewish hols

Built in the 19th century as the luxurious residence of a wealthy Jerusalem family, this is one of the city's loveliest examples of an Arab mansion. Its large central drawing room is the focal point of both the architecture and the social life of the building. In the early 20th century, it was bought by Dr Abraham Ticho, a famous Jewish ophthalmologist who gave the poor free treatment, irrespective of their ethnic origin or religion. Dr Ticho's wife, Anna, who grew up and studied in Vienna, was an artist. By day the house was a clinic and by night it was the centre of Jerusalem's social and intellectual life. Nowadays the house is administered by the Israel Museum (p156), to which Anna Ticho left more than 2,000 watercolours and drawings. Some of these are exhibited here. The house also has a charming restaurant overlooking a lovely garden.

⑥

Ha-Neviim Street

📍F4 🚌1

One of the oldest streets found outside the Old City, Ha-Neviim (Street of the Prophets) marks the dividing line between the religious and secular halves of modern Jerusalem (ultra-Orthodox Mea Shearim lies just to the north; the drinking and dining scene of the Russian Compound is to the south). Once a prestigious address, Ha-Neviim is lined with some grand buildings. At No 58 is Thabor House, the self-designed home of Conrad Schick, a German who arrived in the Holy Land a Protestant missionary and became the city's most renowned architect of the late 19th century. The house now belongs to the Swedish Theological Institute, but visitors can admire the eccentric fortress-like main

Did You Know?

The Pre-Raphaelite painter William Holman Hunt once lived at 64 Ha-Neviim Street.

gate. Someone will usually answer the bell and admit the curious into the courtyard to admire the building's façade, complete with embedded archaeological finds.

A couple of minutes' walk to the north, along narrow, leafy Etyopya Street, is Ben Yehuda House, named after the man responsible for reviving popular usage of the Hebrew language. This was his residence in the early years of the 20th century.

A little further up the lane is the striking, round form of the Ethiopian Church, which sits in beautifully tended gardens. It was built between 1873 and 1911 and is modelled after churches in Ethiopia, with its sanctuary clearly separated from the main body of the church. Just five minutes' walk away, back on Ha-Neviim Street, the Ethiopians also have their consulate. It is notable for a vivid blue and gold mosaic on the façade depicting the Lion of Judah.

⑦ 🏛

Russian Compound

📍F5 🏠1 Mishol Hagevura St 🚌13, 18, 20

The Russians were among the first people to settle outside the Old City in the 19th century (p137). The process began around 1860 when a few acres of land were acquired a short distance outside the city walls. The Russians built a self-contained compound to provide lodgings for the city's growing number of Russian pilgrims, and also erected a cathedral for services. Consecrated in 1864, the **Cathedral of the Holy Trinity** is fashioned in

The Cathedral of the Holy Trinity is fashioned in a distinctly Muscovite style, with eight drums topped by green domes.

a distinctly Muscovite style, with eight drums topped by green domes. Across the plaza, under a pavement grille, is what is known as Herod's Column, a 12-m (40-ft) stone pillar, which historians believe is from the Byzantine period or was intended for the Second Temple before it cracked and was abandoned.

These days the Russians own only the cathedral, as many of the other buildings belonging to the compound were sold to the Israeli government by the Soviet Union in 1964, in exchange for shipments of Israeli oranges.

The building with the crenellated tower – the grandest of the former pilgrims' hostels – is now home to the Agriculture Ministry. The street on which it stands, Heleni ha-Malka, is one of the city's nightlife centres, filled with bars and cafés. The former women's hostel, behind the cathedral, now houses the **Underground Prisoners' Museum 1917–48**, which is dedicated to Jewish underground movements,

some members of which were jailed here during the British Mandate *(p51)*.

Cathedral of the Holy Trinity
🕐 9am–1pm Tue–Fri, 9am–noon Sat & Sun

Underground Prisoners' Museum 1917–48
📞 (02) 623 3166 🕐 9am–5pm Sun–Thu

EAT

Chakra
Renowned for creative Israeli cuisine, including vegetarian dishes, made with the finest ingredients. It also boasts classy décor and a fabulous patio.

📍 E6 🏠 41 King George St 🕐 6pm–1am Sun–Fri, 12:30pm–1am Sat 🌐 chakra-rest.com

₪ ₪ ₪

The Eucalyptus
On a beautiful stone courtyard, this place serves food inspired by scenes from the Bible.

📍 G7 🏠 14 Khativat Yerushalayim St, Hutzot HaYotzer 🕐 5–11pm Sun–Thu, 8:15–11pm Sat 🌐 the-eucalyptus.com

₪ ₪ ₪

Mona
Outstanding French-style food, beautifully and professionally presented. A great place for a romantic evening.

📍 D6 🏠 Artists' House, 12 Shmuel Ha-nagid St 🕐 6:30pm–1am Sun–Thu, 12:30–4:30pm & 6pm–1am Fri, 12:30pm–1am Sat 🌐 monarest.co.il

₪ ₪ ₪

↑ Mass at the beautiful Holy Trinity Cathedral in the Russian Compound

↑ Visitors at the atmospheric Solomon's Quarries (Zedekiah's Cave) in the Old City

8

St Etienne Monastery

📍H4 🏛Nablus Rd 📞(02) 626 4468 🚌17 🕐8am-noon & 12:30-6pm Mon-Sat

The name of this site relates to the belief that in AD 439 Cyril of Alexandria interred the remains of St Stephen (St Etienne in French), the first Christian martyr, in a basilica built on this spot. The basilica was destroyed by the Persians in AD 614, and a subsequent 7th-century chapel on the same site was also destroyed, this time by the Crusaders holding Jerusalem, who feared Saladin would use it as a base for assaults on the city. The present monastery was built between 1891 and 1901 by the French Dominicans. Its eclectic design includes an Oriental tower, Romanesque walls and Neo-Gothic flying buttresses. Within are remains of the mosaic floor of the original Byzantine church, as well as the Ecole Biblique, the Holy Land's first school of biblical archaeology.

9

Solomon's Quarries (Zedekiah's Cave)

📍H5 🏛Sultan Suleyman St 📞(02) 627 7550 🚌1 🕐9am-5pm Sat-Thu (to 4pm winter) 🚫Fri

This is an enormous empty cave stretching under the Old City, with its entrance at the foot of the wall between Damascus and Herod's gates. Carved out by labourers over thousands of years, it was rediscovered in 1854 by American missionary James Turner Barclay. Despite the popular name, historians are not convinced that the cave has any connection with Solomon, but it is likely that Herod took stone from here for his many building projects, including his modification of the Second Temple. The quarry is also known as Zedekiah's Cave, after the last king of Judaea who, legend has it, hid here during the Babylonian conquest of Jerusalem in 586 BC.

10

Mea She'arim

📍F4 🚌1, 9, 13, 34

The heart of ultra-Orthodox (Haredi) Jerusalem, Mea She'arim, founded in 1874, is home to some of the most conservative and insular Jewish communities in the world. The stone-built alleyways, communal courtyards and dwellings – both low-rise and high-density – provide a refuge for Hasidic and Lithuanian (Misnaged) traditionalists, who seek to keep contact with modern ideas and the outside world to an absolute minimum. Dress is traditional in the extreme, and married women keep their hair (or, for the especially modest, their shaved heads) covered beneath a snood (wigs are considered immodest here).

← The soaring interior of the 19th-century basilica in St Etienne Monastery

Visitors should dress very modestly, too, with women in skirts that reach below the knee and men in long trousers and shirts with long sleeves. The locals here do not like being stared at, so be very respectful of local customs and avoid taking photographs.

11

Garden Tomb

☉ H4 **△** Conrad Schick St **🚌** 1, 3 **🕐** 8am-7pm Mon-Fri, 8am-6pm Sat **🌐** garden tomb.org

Towards the end of the 19th century, the British general Charles Gordon, of Khartoum fame, was visiting Jerusalem and started a dispute among archaeologists. He argued that this skull-shaped hill was the Golgotha referred to in the New Testament (Mark 15: 22) and that the real burial site of Jesus Christ was here and not at the Holy Sepulchre *(p106)*. Excavations carried out in 1883 did in fact unearth some ancient tombs, but further study found them to date back only to the 9th–7th century BC, with an entirely

different configuration from those in use in Christ's time. Today, the tomb is run by a nondenominational NGO, and is popular with Protestants, particularly Anglicans.

12

Museum on the Seam

☉ G3 **△** 4 Chel Ha-Handasa St **🚇** Shivtei Israel **🕐** 10am-5pm Mon, Wed & Thu, 2-8pm Tue, 10am-2pm Fri **🕐** Sat & Sun **🌐** mots.org.il

This museum is situated right on Jerusalem's "seam" – the heavily fortified dividing line between the Israeli- and Jordanian-controlled parts of the city from 1948 to 1967. The unique institution describes itself as a "socio-political museum of contemporary art", with the explicit goal of "raising controversial social issues for public discussion". The museum hosts temporary exhibitions by artists from around the world, which unflinchingly explore both the local and universal implications of national, ethnic and

economic fault lines. The building that it occupies was owned by a Christian Arab family before the 1948 War *(p53)*; during the conflict it served as a front-line IDF position and sustained serious damage to the exterior that is still visible.

TOP 3 **JERUSALEM FOR CHILDREN**

Israel Museum
The museum's Youth Wing is packed with creative, hands-on exhibits and activities for kids *(p156)*.

Bloomfield Science Museum
🌐 mada.org.il
Has fun, kid-oriented exhibits and demonstrations about science and technology.

Train Theater
🌐 traintheater.co.uk
This repertory puppet theatre has been staging much-beloved productions for children since 1981.

→ The Museum on the Seam, a unique socio-political art gallery

SHOP

Azoulay Art
Specializes in delicate, colourful *ketubahs* (marriage contracts) made using traditional paper-cutting techniques, plus beautiful Judaica.

📍E5 🏠5 Yoel Moshe Salomon St 🌐ketubah azoulayart.com

Cadim Ceramics Gallery
Cooperative gallery showcasing the work of about a dozen virtuoso ceramists using various techniques and styles.

📍E5 🏠4 Yoel Moshe Salomon St 📞(02) 623 4869

Baltinester Brothers
Made-to-order silver and gold jewellery with your name in Hebrew letters; also carries decorated Kiddish cups.

📍F5 🏠31 Jaffa St 🌐baltinester jewelry.com

13 Kings' Tombs

📍H3 🏠Salah al-Din St 🚌23

Despite the name, this single but elaborate tomb is thought to have been that of Queen Helena of Adiabene. In the 1st century AD, she converted to Judaism and moved to Jerusalem from her kingdom in Mesopotamia. The tomb was named by early explorers who believed that it housed members of the dynasty of David. A small entrance, an easily missed plain door in a wall, leads down into a dimly lit maze of chambers with stone doors.

The tomb is currently closed to the public.

14 American Colony Hotel

📍H2 🏠23 Nablus Rd 📞(02) 627 9777 🚌17

This elegant hotel, built in 1865–76, has long been a favourite of diplomats and journalists. It started life as

> Despite the name, the single but elaborate Kings' Tomb is thought to have been that of Queen Helena of Adiabene.

the home of a rich Turkish merchant. The name American Colony came about in the late 19th century, when Anna and Horatio Spafford of Chicago bought the building and made it the centre of an American religious community dedicated to good works. When the community broke up in the early 20th century, Baron Ustinov, related to the actor Peter Ustinov, suggested converting the building to accommodate pilgrims to the Holy Land. Soon after, it was turned into a beautiful hotel, which it remains today.

If the cost of staying here overnight proves to be prohibitive, it is definitely worth coming for lunch, which can be taken out in the lovely tree-shaded courtyard.

The flower-decked courtyard of the American Colony Hotel ↑

↑ Part of the fascinating historic collection housed in the Rockefeller Museum

Rockefeller Museum

📍 J4 🏠 27 Sultan Suleyman St 🚌 1, 3, 51 🕐 10am–3pm Mon, Wed, Thu & Sun, 10am–2pm Sat 🌐 imj.org.il/en/wings/archaeology/rockefeller-archaeological-museum

This museum was made possible by a substantial financial gift made in 1927 by the American oil magnate John D. Rockefeller. British architect Austin Harrison designed the white-stone building along Neo-Gothic lines, with Byzantine- and Islamic-style decorative motifs and a central courtyard. It was once one of the most important museums in the Middle East and the first to make a systematic collection of finds from the Holy Land. These days, it is a branch of the Israel Museum (p156), with an impressive collection.

Among many remarkable objects are the stuccowork from Hisham's Palace in Jericho, beams from the Holy Sepulchre church and wooden panels from El-Aqsa mosque. Other exhibits worth seeing include a fascinating portrait modelled on an 8,000-year-old cranium discovered in Jericho; a lovely Bronze Age bull's head; a Canaanite vase in the shape of a human head; sculptures from the time of the Crusades; and finds from Judaean Desert caves.

The First Station

📍 G9 🏠 David Remez St 🚌 7, 38, 74, 75 🕐 Daily 🌐 firststation.co.il

Inaugurated in 1892, the train line from Jaffa to the holy city of Jerusalem ended at this Ottoman-era station, about 1 km (0.5 miles) south of Jaffa Gate. Rail service stopped in 1998 but the complex has found new life as a bustling and atmospheric dining, shopping, entertainment and cultural centre. A dozen restaurants serve hummus, sandwiches, crêpes, pasta, meat, fish and ice cream, with snacks and meals suitable for all budgets. Cultural events range from chess marathons to salsa nights to qigong. Kids are well catered for, with activities galore.

___

St George's Cathedral

📍 H3 🏠 30 Nablus Rd 📞 (02) 627 1670 🚌 17

This archetypal Middle England-style Anglican cathedral, with its pretty, cloistered courtyard, stands in startling contrast to the other buildings that line the bustling streets of the surrounding East Jerusalem neighbourhood.

The cathedral dates from 1910 and is named for the patron saint of England, who was actually a Palestinian conscript in the Roman army occupying Britain. He was executed in AD 303 for tearing up a copy of the emperor Diocletian's decree forbidding Christianity. He is supposedly buried at Lod (ancient Lydda), now better known as the site of Ben Gurion airport.

During World War I, the cathedral was the local headquarters of the Turkish army, and the 1917 truce sanctioning British presence in Palestine was signed in the bishop's quarters. The cathedral is not usally open for visitors so it is best to call ahead.

→ The Anglican St George's Cathedral, seat of the Bishop of Jerusalem

A LONG WALK
WEST JERUSALEM

Distance 4 km (2.5 miles) **Walking time** 60 minutes **Nearest Station** City Hall Light Rail **Difficulty** Relatively flat

The heart of West Jerusalem, centred on Jaffa Road, was largely developed during the years of the British Mandate (1917–48). So, while it is nowhere near as ancient as the Old City, it does carry a weight of modern history related to the founding of the Jewish state of Israel. Aside from the scattering of historic buildings and monuments, this is also the heart of the modern city, with pedestrianized streets of cafés, restaurants and shops, cultural centres and busy markets. The food stalls around Mahane Yehuda Market make an excellent place for a refreshment break, as do the cafés at the junction of Heleni-Ha-Malka and Jaffa Road, and the many more food and drink establishments in Nakhlat Shiva. It is a highly rewarding area to explore, but avoid doing this walk on Friday afternoon or Saturday as everything is closed.

*The small monument here of a mortar on a plinth is a **Davidka**, a weapon that played a large role in the 1948 War.*

Mahane Yehuda Market
(p163) *is the city's prime source of fresh produce, from fruit and vegetables to fish and meat.*

0 metres   300
0 yards   300

N ↑

Agrippas Street *has traditionally been a poor area with cheap rents that have attracted immigrants, hence all the signs in Cyrillic.*

↑ A stall selling fresh fruit and vegetables at Mahane Yehuda Market

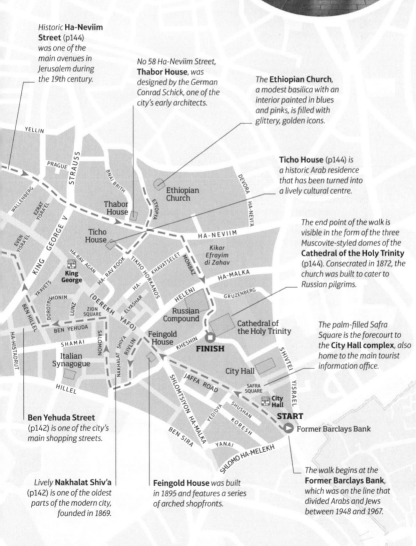

Bustling Ben Yehuda Street, a popular spot for shopping

JERUSALEM CITY CENTRE
WEST JERUSALEM

Locator Map
For more detail see p140

Historic **Ha-Neviim Street** (p144) *was one of the main avenues in Jerusalem during the 19th century.*

No 58 Ha-Neviim Street, **Thabor House,** *was designed by the German Conrad Schick, one of the city's early architects.*

The **Ethiopian Church,** *a modest basilica with an interior painted in blues and pinks, is filled with glittery, golden icons.*

The end point of the walk is visible in the form of the three Muscovite-styled domes of the **Cathedral of the Holy Trinity** *(p144). Consecrated in 1872, the church was built to cater to Russian pilgrims.*

Ticho House (p144) *is a historic Arab residence that has been turned into a lively cultural centre.*

The palm-filled Safra Square is the forecourt to the **City Hall complex,** *also home to the main tourist information office.*

Ben Yehuda Street (p142) *is one of the city's main shopping streets.*

Ben Yehuda Street (p142) is one of the city's main shopping streets.

Lively **Nakhalat Shiv'a** *(p142) is one of the oldest parts of the modern city, founded in 1869.*

Feingold House *was built in 1895 and features a series of arched shopfronts.*

The walk begins at the **Former Barclays Bank,** *which was on the line that divided Arabs and Jews between 1948 and 1967.*

YELLIN
PRAGUE
STRAUSS
BNAI BRITH
WALLENBERG
EZRAT YISRAEL
EVEN YISRAEL
KING GEORGE V
HA-RAV AGAN
HA-RAV KOOK
TIKHO HA-HORRANOS
KHAVATSELET
MONBAZ
EYOPYA
DEVORA
HA-NEVIA
Thabor House
Ethiopian Church
Ticho House
King George
HA-NEVIIM
Kikar Efrayim di Zahav
HA-MALKA
(DEREKH YAFO)
ELYASHAR
HELENI
GRUZENBERG
YAAVETS
DOROTSHONIM
LUNZ
ZION SQUARE
BEN HILLEL
BEN YEHUDA
SHAMAI
HILLEL
HA-HISTADRUT
SHALOMON
NAKHALAT SHIVA
RIVLIN
KHESHIN
Feingold House
Russian Compound
Cathedral of the Holy Trinity
FINISH
SHUVTEI
YISRAEL
Italian Synagogue
JAFFA ROAD
City Hall
SAFRA SQUARE
City Hall
SHLOMTSIYON HA-MALKA
YEDIDYA
SHUSHAN
KORESH
START
Former Barclays Bank
BEN SIRA
YANAI
SHLOMO HA-MELEKH

151

A LONG WALK
EAST JERUSALEM

Distance 2.5 km (1.5 miles) **Walking time** 45 minutes
Nearest station Damascus Gate Light Rail stop
Difficulty Mostly flat

East Jerusalem is the Palestinian Arab part of the city. It lies north of the Old City and east of the main north–south road Derekh Ha-Shalom, swelling over the Mount of Olives and down the other side. The main street is Salah al-Din Street, which is visited as part of this walk. High-profile tourist sights are few, but it is a vibrant area with many points of interest, including Christian pilgrimage sights. It is also home to the Holy Land's most atmospheric old hotel, the American Colony Hotel, whose beautiful courtyard café and welcoming cellar bar make excellent refreshment stops.

*The **American Colony Hotel** (p148) was originally built as a home for a wealthy 19th-century Arab merchant, but was subsequently sold to pilgrims from Chicago, hence the name.*

*The admirably restrained interior of **St George's Cathedral** (p149) contains the royal arms formerly displayed in Government House during the time of British rule.*

the **Palestinian Pottery** *was founded back in 1922 by the Balians, one of three Armenian families brought over by the British authorities from Turkey to renovate the tiles on the Dome of the Rock (p74).*

*Claims for the **Garden Tomb** (p147) as the burial place of Jesus have been dismissed by archaeologists, but it still attracts numerous pilgrims.*

Schmidt's Girls' College *is designed in fine Germanic style by the same architect behind Mount Zion's Church of the Dormition (p126).*

Orient House, an elegant 1897 villa, was the headquarters of the Palestinian Authority in Jerusalem until it was shut down by the Israeli government in 2001.

DALMAN
DEREKH SHKHEM
IBN
American Colony Hotel
VAN PAASSEN
ABU UBAIDA
Orient House
ST GEORGE
Kings' Tombs
ABU TALEB
SALAH AL-DIN
St George's Cathedral
NABLUS ROAD
Shivtei Israel
Palestinian Pottery
KHEIL HA-HANDASA
PIKUD HA-MERKAZ
IBN EL-AAS
NO'OMI KISS
St Etienne Monastery
(DEREKH
Garden Tomb
SHKHEM)
HA-NEVI'IM
Damascus Gate
Damascus Gate
START

*The walk starts at **Damascus Gate** (p80), the largest and one of the busiest of the Old City gates.*

↑ A mosaic in St George's Cathedral showing the Resurrection of Jesus

↑ The attractive courtyard
of the Rockefeller Museum

Locator Map
For more detail see p140

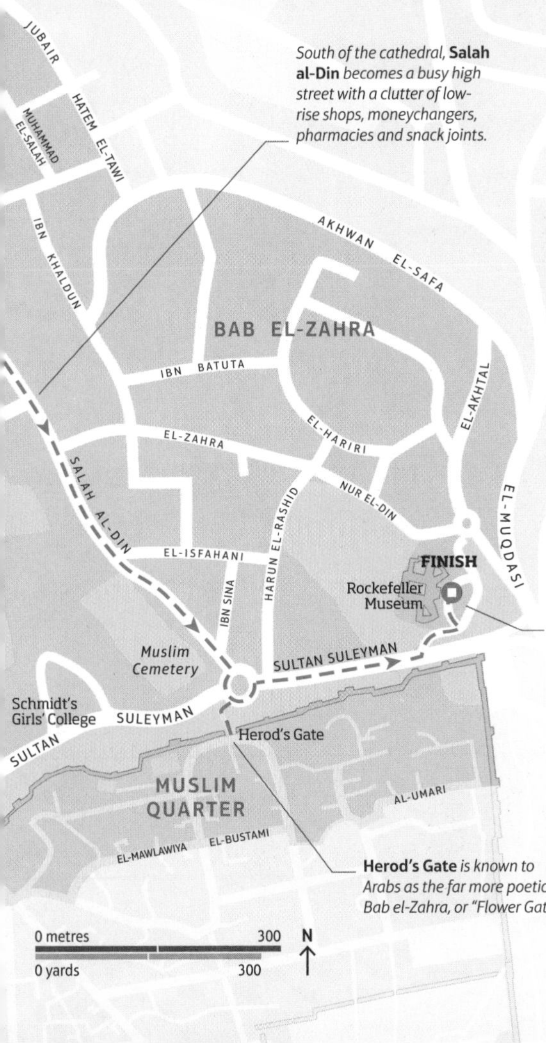

EAST
JERUSALEM

JERUSALEM
CITY CENTRE

JUBAIR

HATEM EL-TAWI

MUHAMMAD EL-SALAH

IBN KHALDOUN

*South of the cathedral, **Salah al-Din** becomes a busy high street with a clutter of low-rise shops, moneychangers, pharmacies and snack joints.*

AKHWAN EL-SAFA

Did You Know?

In 1917, an American Colony Hotel sheet was used as a white flag by the Ottomans to surrender to the British.

BAB EL-ZAHRA

IBN BATUTA

EL-ZAHRA

EL-HARIRI

EL-AKHTAL

SALAH AL-DIN

HARUN EL-RASHID

NUR EL-DIN

EL-ISFAHANI

IBN SINA

EL-MUQDASI

FINISH

Rockefeller
Museum

*End the walk at the **Rockefeller Museum** (p149), which is worth a visit for its fascinating collection of archaeological finds from the Holy Land.*

*Muslim
Cemetery*

SULTAN SULEYMAN

Schmidt's
Girls' College

SULEYMAN

SULTAN

Herod's Gate

MUSLIM QUARTER

AL-UMARI

EL-MAWLAWIYA

EL-BUSTAMI

Herod's Gate *is known to Arabs as the far more poetic Bab el-Zahra, or "Flower Gate".*

0 metres	300
0 yards	300

N ↑

Must See

❶ Israel Museum

Experience More

❷ LA Mayer Museum
   of Islamic Art
❸ Monastery of the Cross
❹ Bible Lands Museum
❺ Knesset
❻ Yad Vashem
❼ Biblical Zoo
❽ Supreme Court
❾ Mahane Yehuda
   and Nakhla'ot
❿ Mount Herzl and
   Herzl Museum
⓫ Ein Kerem
⓬ Chagall Stained Glass
   at Hadassah Hospital
⓭ Abu Ghosh

BEYOND THE CENTRE

Since the creation of the state of Israel in 1948, the boundaries of Jerusalem have greatly expanded in all directions, with what were not too long ago small isolated villages evolving into suburbs of the city. They have not, however, lost their character. Places such as Ein Kerem, nestled in the valley below Mount Herzl, and Abu Ghosh, further to the northwest, have a great deal of rural charm, as well as several attractive religious buildings linked with biblical events. The city has also been endowed with many significant modern buildings, including the Israel Museum and the Knesset, both of which were built in the 1960s.

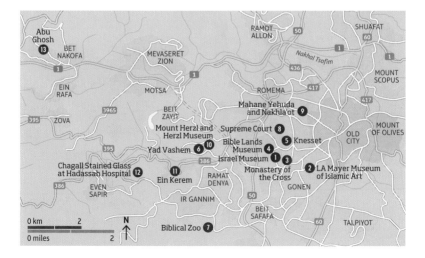

❶ 🛝 🎨 🍴 ☕ 🛍️

ISRAEL MUSEUM

🏠 11 Ruppin Rd, Givat Ram 🚌 7, 9, 14, 35 🕐 10:30am–4pm
Sat–Mon, Wed, Thu & hols, 4–9pm Tue, 10am–2pm Fri &
holiday eves 🚫 Yom Kippur 🌐 imj.org.il

One of the world's leading museums of art and archaeology, the Israel Museum has a breathtaking collection representing human material culture from prehistory to 21st-century Israeli artworks. Highlights include the Dead Sea Scrolls, artifacts found at Masada, centuries-old synagogues and superb European paintings.

Built in 1965 on a ridge overlooking West Jerusalem, the Israel Museum was designed by Israeli architects Alfred Mansfeld and Dora Gad as a modernist reference to traditional Arab hilltop villages. Thanks to its wide variety of sources, the collection is extraordinarily eclectic. Its core was inherited from the Bezalel School and Museum (Israel's first arts academy) and the Israel Antiquities Authority, and this has been supplemented by gifts, loans and acquisitions from around the globe. The Jewish Art and Life Wing presents the culture and art of the Jewish diaspora, the Archaeology Wing provides a chronological journey through the Holy Land and the Fine Arts Wing features masterpieces from some of art's most famous names. The biggest draw for most visitors is the Shrine of the Book, which houses some of the world-famous Dead Sea Scrolls (p159). The museum also houses a model of Jerusalem in the Second Temple period, the Ruth Youth Wing for Art Education, with interactive art activities, and the Billy Rose Art Garden, which blends Western sculpture and Japanese zen gardens.

↑ Admiring some of the works on display in the Fine Arts Wing

→ Anish Kapoor's *Turning the World Upside Down* (2010) in the Billy Rose Art Garden

500,000
—
Objects are contained within the Israel Museum's collection.

↑ The Shrine of the Book, with its contrasting white dome and black basalt wall

The biggest draw for most visitors is the Shrine of the Book, which houses some of the world-famous Dead Sea Scrolls.

DESIGN OF THE SHRINE OF THE BOOK

Inspired by the lids of the jars in which the scrolls were found, the Shrine of the Book is a landmark in design. The white dome and black basalt wall reference the battle between the Sons of Darkness and the Sons of Light described in the War Scroll, while jets of water symbolize the ritual purity of the community that wrote the scrolls.

↑ Examining Judaica from around the world in the Jewish Art and Life Wing

JEWISH ART AND LIFE WING

The museum's collection of Jewish Ethnography and Judaica spans the period from the Middle Ages to the present, and has exhibits from as far afield as Spain and China. Five main sections integrate the sacred and secular dimensions of Jewish life from different cultures. Among the most precious objects are the medieval illuminated manuscripts. These include a 14th-century German *Haggadah* (the story read at Passover of the Israelites' liberation from Egypt) and the Rothschild Miscellany, a 15th-century collection of biblical, legal and other pieces. Elaborate silverwork includes *hadassim* (spiceboxes used during the ceremony of separation between the Sabbath and the start of the week) and the *rimonim* (pomegranates that decorate Torah scrolls in the synagogue). Another highlight is the large collection of *Hannukkiot* – the oil lamps that are lit for Hanukkah. There are also four beautiful, complete synagogue interiors. The daily life of Jewish communities around the world is represented in textiles, jewellery, reconstructions of rooms and ritual articles connected with life events such as birth and marriage.

> 🔍 HIDDEN GEM
> ### The Nuremberg Mahzor
> This large, illuminated Hebrew prayer book contains the Ashkenazi yearly cycle of prayers, with commentaries, and a rare collection of liturgical poems.

FINE ARTS WING

The museum's art collections cover a wide range of periods and artistic disciplines. The modern art collection has international works from the 1890s to the 1960s, including paintings by Gauguin, Chagall and Modigliani. Other rooms are devoted to design, architecture and contemporary art.

The large collection of Israeli art begins with paintings and drawings produced in the 19th century, at the beginning of Jewish resettlement. The 1920s and 30s are represented by figurative pieces by artists such as Reuven Rubin and Yitzhak Danziger.

Other rooms are devoted to prints and drawings, Old Master paintings, Islamic and East Asian art, and the art of Africa, the Americas and Oceania. Pieces from the Levine Photography Collection are incorporated into the other exhibitions in this wing and build on the museum's long history of collecting photographs.

← *Portrait of Jeanne Hebuterne, Seated* (1918) by Amedeo Modigliani

ARCHAEOLOGY WING

The Archaeology Wing is the largest section of the museum. Most pieces are on loan from the Israel Antiquities Authority and come from excavations carried out all over the country. The digs cover a vast period of history – from as far back as 1.5 million BC – and have revealed artifacts from an impressive number of civilizations. Visitors will require at least two hours to fully explore the exhibits.

The artifacts are arranged chronologically. Objects to look out for in the Dawn of Civilization section include the jewellery and sculpted figures of the Natufian culture and the elegant copperware of the so-called Judaean Desert Treasure. Highlights from the Canaanite Period are the sophisticated gold jewellery and the anthropoid sarcophagi found at Deir el-Balah in the Gaza Strip.

The Israelite Period (1200–586 BC) spans the rise of the Israelites to the destruction of Solomon's Temple. Look out for the ivory pomegranate inscribed with ancient Hebrew and the priestly benediction written on a tiny silver amulet – the earliest known fragment of biblical text.

Finds from the next 300 years are relatively scarce but the Hellenistic, Roman and Byzantine periods (332 BC–AD 636) offer fascinating objects, such as the sarcophagi and ossuaries from Jewish catacombs and beautiful mosaics. The last room focuses on "Muslims and Crusaders" and

↑ A selection of ancient artifacts on display in the Archaeology Wing

"Neighbouring Cultures", with artifacts from Egypt, Assyria, Babylonia, Greece and Rome. This wing also houses exhibitions on glass, early Hebrew writing and coins.

DEAD SEA SCROLLS

In 1947, a Bedouin shepherd discovered jars containing seven ancient scrolls. Over the next two decades, fragments of some 800 more were found in 11 caves, and the nearby settlement of Qumran (p218) was uncovered. The scrolls date to between the 3rd century BC and AD 68, and some contain the oldest existing versions of biblical scriptures.

SHRINE OF THE BOOK

Built to house the Dead Sea Scrolls and other important artifacts, the intriguingly shaped Shrine of the Book has become a symbol of the whole museum. Inside, a long passageway – designed to evoke the catacomb-like environment in which the scrolls were found – has a permanent exhibition on life in Qumran at the time the scrolls were written. It leads into the main chamber under the dome, which contains a facsimile of the Great Isaiah Scroll, the only biblical book that survived in its entirety. Its 66 chapters were written on strips of parchment, which were then sewn together to a length of more than 7 m (23 ft). One of the surrounding display cases contains part of the real scroll.

On the Shrine's lower level are 2nd-century-AD articles, such as keys and baskets. Also on display here is the 10th-century Aleppo Codex – not one of the Dead Sea Scrolls, but the oldest complete Bible in Hebrew.

Adjacent to the Shrine of the Book is a Second Temple-era model of Jerusalem. This large-scale model offers visitors a three-dimensional view of the topography and architecture of Jerusalem during the 1st century.

←

The facsimile of the Great Isaiah Scroll at the heart of the Shrine of the Book

EXPERIENCE MORE

2
LA Mayer Museum of Islamic Art

📍 2 Ha-Palmakh St
🚌 13 ⏱ 10am-3pm Mon-Wed, 10am-7pm Thu, 10am-2pm Fri & Sat
🌐 islamicart.co.il

This gem of a museum presents the artistic brilliance of Islamic civilization with illuminated manuscripts, ceramics, metalwork and jewellery from the Arab world, Moorish Spain, Turkey, Iran and India. Another highlight, if an incongruous one, is one of the world's premier collections of clocks and watches, including an extraordinary timepiece

> **Another highlight of the LA Mayer Museum of Islamic Art, if an incongruous one, is one of the world's premier collections of clocks and watches.**

made by Abraham-Louis Breguet for an admirer of Marie Antoinette. Known as the Queen, it was stolen in 1983 in a mysterious break-in and eventually recovered in 2006.

3
Monastery of the Cross

📍 Hayim Hazaz Ave
🚌 32 ⏱ 10am-4pm Mon-Sat (to 6pm in summer) 🌐 jerusalem-patriarchate.info

Surrounded by high stone walls supported by massive buttresses, this fortified monastery spent the first few centuries of its existence dangerously far from the walls of the city (today it's just a stone's throw from the Knesset). The complex is believed to stand on the spot where the tree used by the Romans to make Jesus's cross grew. A Byzantine church that stood here in the 6th century was destroyed by the Persians in AD 614,

> ### Did You Know?
> The Knesset, Israel's parliament, has 30 members elected in a districtless nation-wide ballot.

but part of its mosaic floor can be seen on one side of the church's main altar.

The present-day complex was built in the 11th century by Georgian monks; it was later ransacked several times but never destroyed. During Crusader rule, the monastery flourished and Georgia's national poet, Shota Rustaveli, lived here, but by 1685 the Georgians' fortunes had declined and the complex was sold to the Greek Orthodox Patriarchate. Today, the monastery's frescoes show an unusual combination of Christian, pagan and worldly images. Particularly evocative of monastic life are the refectory on the upper floor and the kitchen.

↑ Exhibits in the Bible Lands Museum illustrating the contexts of Bible stories

④

Bible Lands Museum

⌂ 25 Avraham Granot St, Givat Ram 🚌 7, 9, 14, 35, 66 🕙 9:30am-5:30pm Sun-Tue & Thu, 9:30am-9:30pm Wed, 10am-2pm Fri, Sat & eves of Jewish hols ⛔ Jewish hols 🌐 blmj.org

The exhibits in this rather unremarkable building opposite the Israel Museum (p156) are displayed in a way that enables the visitor to build a clear and illuminating picture of the cultural context in which the biblical texts were written. The items are arranged according to both chronology and region. The result is a clear illustration of the way in which different cultures influenced each other and new societies evolved.

The outstanding collection of archaeological finds reflects the cultures of the Holy Land region in biblical times. The museum was inaugurated in 1992 with the private collection of Elie Borowski, a passionate scholar of ancient Middle Eastern civilizations. The collection

←

Interior of the Monastery of the Cross, with sturdy stone walls and sacred art

features many finely crafted objects from ancient Egypt, Syria, Anatolia, Mesopotamia and Persia. A great number of the artifacts shed light on the culture of the Mesopotamian region in the millennia before the Christian era. They include ancient inscriptions, jewellery, mosaics, seals, ivory carvings and scarabs.

---

⑤ 🕳

Knesset

⌂ 1 Kaplan, Givat Ram 📞 (02) 675 3333 🚌 14, 35, 66 🕙 8:30am-2pm Sun & Thu

The seat of the Israeli Parliament takes its name from the Knesset ha-Gedola (Great Assembly) of 120 men that governed the political and civic life of Jews in the Second Temple period. The building, opened in 1966, was designed by architect Joseph Klarwin and inspired by the Parthenon in Athens and reconstructions of the Temple.

Opposite the entrance is a large menorah (candelabrum), symbol of the State of Israel. It is the work of British sculptor Benno Elkan and was a gift from the British parliament. The relief work depicts crucial moments in Jewish history, with biblical quotations. A nearby monument with an

eternal flame commemorates the dead of the Holocaust and Israel's wars. The Knesset's reception area was designed by Russian-Jewish artist Marc Chagall. It is adorned with his mosaics and a triple tapestry of the creation, the exodus of the Israelites from Egypt and the city of Jerusalem. The main chamber ends in a stone wall – a very clear reference to the Western Wall (p88).

Tours are available for visitors: call or email (tours@knesset.gov.il) well in advance to book. Bring your passport and dress modestly.

↑ The Knesset Menorah, in front of the Knesset in the Park of Roses

→
The intensely moving
Yad Vashem Holocaust
memorial and museum

 6

Yad Vashem

🏠 Mount Herzl 🚌 10, 16,
20, 23, 27 🕐 8:30am-6pm
Sun-Wed, 8:30am-8pm
Thu, 8:30am-2pm Fri & hols
🌐 yadvashem.org

Yad Vashem, meaning "a
memorial and a name" (from
Isaiah 56: 5), is an archive,
research institute, museum
and, above all, a monument
to perpetuate the memory
of the more than six million
Jews who were killed in the
Holocaust. More than 20
moving monuments occupy
this hillside site.

Entrance to Yad Vashem
is along the Avenue of the
Righteous Among Nations,
which is lined with plaques
bearing the names of Gentiles
who helped Jews and, in doing
so, put their own lives at risk.
Some 23,000 people are
recognized, including Oskar
Schindler (p126). The avenue
leads down to the Historical
Museum, which was designed
by Jewish architect Moshe
Safdie. The museum is one
long corridor, carved into the
mountain, with ten exhibition
halls. Exhibits include some
2,500 personal items donated

by survivors, adding a harrow-
ing first-person dimension
to the horrors that began
with the rise of the Nazis in
1933 and culminated in the
death camps.

The Hall of Remembrance
beside the museum is a stark,
tomb-like chamber that bears
the names of 21 of the main
camps on flat, black basalt
slabs. At its centre is a casket
of ashes from the cremation
ovens; above it is an eternal
flame. The Hall of Names
inside the Historical Museum
records the names of all those
Jews who perished, along with
as much biographical detail

as possible. Yad Vashem also
has a museum of Jewish art
and a visual centre where
films related to the Holocaust
may be viewed. Visitors must
dress appropriately – no
shorts or miniskirts.

 7

Biblical Zoo

🏠 Manahat 🚌 26A, 33
🕐 9am-5pm Sun-Thu
(to 7pm Jun-Aug), 9am-
4:30pm Fri, 10am-5pm
Sat (to 6pm Jun-Aug)
🌐 jerusalemzoo.org

The Jerusalem Biblical Zoo,
also known as the Tisch
Family Zoological Gardens,
is famous for its collection of
wildlife featured in the Bible,
many of which are no longer
naturally present in the Holy
Land. There are bears, lions,
Nile crocodiles and Arabian
oryx, plus other endangered
species from around the world.
The attractive site is in the
southwestern suburbs.

←
South African giraffe
calves at the Biblical Zoo
in Jerusalem

5,000
—
Jewish communities destroyed in the Holocaust are listed in Yad Vashem's Valley of the Communities.

8

Supreme Court

🏠 Shaarei Mishpat St, Givat Ram 📞 (02) 675 9612 🚌 14, 66 🕐 8:30am–2:30pm Sun-Thu

In the absence of a formal constitution, Israel's Supreme Court plays a pivotal role in the lives of ordinary citizens. Its significance is reflected in the building's design, which manages to depict the concept of justice. The two copper pyramids on the roof are powerful symbols of the immutable nature of the principles of law. The long sweeping stairway seems to represent the accessibility of the law to ordinary people, and at the top it offers an all-embracing view of Jerusalem.

Motifs from the past, such as Islamic elements in the inner courtyard and a Byzantine-era mosaic by the entrance, recall Israel's cultural and historical influences. They are given a modern context to link the past with the present and reflect the universality of justice.

EAT

Mamlechet HaHalva
The "Kingdom of Halva" offers over 100 varieties of *halva*, a sweet, crumbly paste made from sesame seeds.

🏠 A12 Etz Chaim St

₪ ₪ ₪

Shimshon Pickles Center
Shimshon specializes in olives, pickles, marinated hot peppers, salads and goat cheese.

🏠 19 Mahane Yuhuda St

₪ ₪ ₪

9

Mahane Yehuda and Nakhla'ot

🏠 Between Jaffa Rd and Betzalel St 🚌 6, 7, 8, 13, 14, 18, 21, 74, 75 🚊 Mahane Yehuda 🌐 machne.co.il

Lying northwest of the city centre triangle, Mahane Yehuda, or "the shuk", is Jerusalem's main food, fruit and vegetable bazaar. It is a maze of covered alleyways lined with tables piled high with fresh produce, pungent spices and local delicacies, where stall owners call out to passers-by in sing-song cadences. After dark the market is transformed into the heart of the city's nightlife with bars, music venues, cafés and top quality eateries.

To the south, across Agripas Street, lies Nachla'ot, where two-storey stone buildings, built around courtyards, are linked by narrow lanes. Established in the late 1800s (around the same time as Mahane Yehuda), the area has long been home to Jews of North African and Middle Eastern origin. Nachla'ot is famous for its scores of small synagogues, each following liturgical and musical traditions brought from places such as the Greek island of Ioannina, Melilla (Spanish Morocco), Aleppo (Syria) and Shiraz (Iran).

Did You Know?

Ein Kerem's Spring of the Virgin is named for Mary, mother of Jesus, who reputedly once drank from it.

10 ♿ 🏛

Mount Herzl and Herzl Museum

📍 Mount Herzl 🚌 10, 16, 20, 23, 27 🕒 8:30am–6pm Sun–Thu, 8:30am–1:30pm Fri; call ahead 🌐 herzl.org.il

Mount Herzl (in Hebrew *Har Hertzel*) is a high hill north of central Jerusalem, named after Theodor Herzl, the man considered to be the founder of Zionism (*p51*). The slopes serve as a large cemetery, with Herzl's tomb at the top of the hill. The site is the burial place of Israel's presidents and three of its prime ministers, and also houses the country's main military cemetery. The Herzl Museum, at the site entrance, offers a crash course in Zionist history, with audiovisuals and re-creations of Herzl's study and library.

11

Ein Kerem

📍 7 km (4 miles) W of central Jerusalem 🚌 28, 184

John the Baptist, according to Christian tradition, was born and lived in Ein Kerem ("the vineyard spring"). The picturesque village contains several fine churches and monasteries connected with his life. Recognizable by its tall, thin tower, the Franciscan Church of St John the Baptist dates from the 17th century, but is built over the ruins of earlier Byzantine and Crusader structures. Steps inside the church lead down into a natural cave, the Grotto of the Nativity of St John, which tradition connects with the birth of the Baptist.

The other church of note is the two-tiered Church of the Visitation, completed in 1955 to a design by Antonio Barluzzi, architect of the Dominus Flevit Sanctuary (*p135*) and the Chapel of the Flagellation (*p76*).

It commemorates the Virgin Mary's visit to Elizabeth, mother of John the Baptist, who was then pregnant, an episode depicted in mosaic on the church's façade. Within is a natural grotto, in front of which are the remains of Roman-era houses. According to tradition, the grotto is where Elizabeth hid with her infant son to escape from the Massacre of the Innocents (the killing of all first-born sons, ordered by King Herod). The courtyard walls are lined with tiled panels inscribed with the *Magnificat* (Luke 1: 46–55), Mary's hymn of thanks, in 42 languages.

At the bottom of the hill below the church is a small, abandoned mosque. Beside it surfaces the spring (popularly known as the Spring of the Virgin) from which the village takes its name.

One of the other pleasures of Ein Kerem is its tranquil, wooded, valley setting. This is best appreciated on a scenic walk that starts beside the sculpture at the beginning of the access road to Yad Vashem.

> The picturesque village of Ein Kerem contains several fine churches and monasteries connected with the life of John the Baptist.

↑ Marc Chagall's colourful stained-glass windows at the Hadassah Hospital

EAT

Machneyuda

A magnet for foodies from all over Israel, drawn by the virtuoso dishes and raucous market atmosphere.

🏠 10 Beit Ya'akov St
🕐 12:30-4pm & 6:30pm-midnight daily
🌐 machneyuda.co.il

₪₪₪

Nagy (Naji)

Renowned for its kebabs, this place also serves excellent hummus, salads and labneh, with plenty of choice for vegetarians.

🏠 4 Mahmou Rashid St 📞 (02) 533 6520 🕐 8am-midnight daily

₪₪₪

Sultan Sweets and Café

This little coffee shop has first-rate *kunafeh* (a sweet, gooey cheese pastry), baklava, home-made *halva* and strong Arab coffee.

🏠 29 HaShalom St
📞 (02) 579 7044
🕐 9am-8pm Mon-Sat

₪₪₪

Chagall Stained Glass at Hadassah Hospital

🏠 Ein Kerem 📞 (02) 677 6271 🚌 19, 27 🕐 8:30am-3:30pm Sun-Thu (call ahead to arrange a visit)

A splendid cycle of 12 stained-glass windows decorates the synagogue at the otherwise unremarkable Hadassah Hospital. They were created in 1960–61 by the Russian-Jewish artist Marc Chagall, and then installed the following year for the building's inauguration. Each window represents one of the 12 tribes of Israel. Tradition associates each of the tribes with a symbol, a precious stone and a social role, and these elements are all represented in Chagall's imagery and choice of colour.

←

Statue of Our Lady meeting Elizabeth at Ein Kerem's Church of the Visitation

13

Abu Ghosh

🏠 13 km (8 miles) W of central Jerusalem
🚌 185, 195

This Arab town, in the Judean Hills just north of the main Jerusalem–Tel Aviv road, has long maintained friendly relations with its Jewish neighbours. Named after a family from the Caucasus that settled here in the 16th century, it is famed for its rival hummus restaurants and its biannual vocal music festival.

The Crusaders believed this to be the site of Emmaus, where Jesus appeared to two of His disciples in the days after the Resurrection. The beautiful, Romanesque-style Church of the Resurrection, built in the mid-1100s by the Knights Hospitallers, is remarkably well preserved.

On the hill above the village stands Our Lady of the Ark of the Covenant Church, built in 1924 over the remains of a 5th-century church; some of the original church's mosaics can still be seen. The site is said to be the location of the house of Avinadav, where the Ark of the Covenant was kept after being liberated from Philistine captivity before it was taken to Jerusalem by David (1 Samuel 7: 1–2).

The town's huge, Caucasian-style mosque, inaugurated in 2014, was funded by the government of the Russian republic of Chechnya.

EXPERIENCE
ISRAEL AND THE
PALESTINIAN TERRITORIES

Salt crystals floating on the Dead Sea

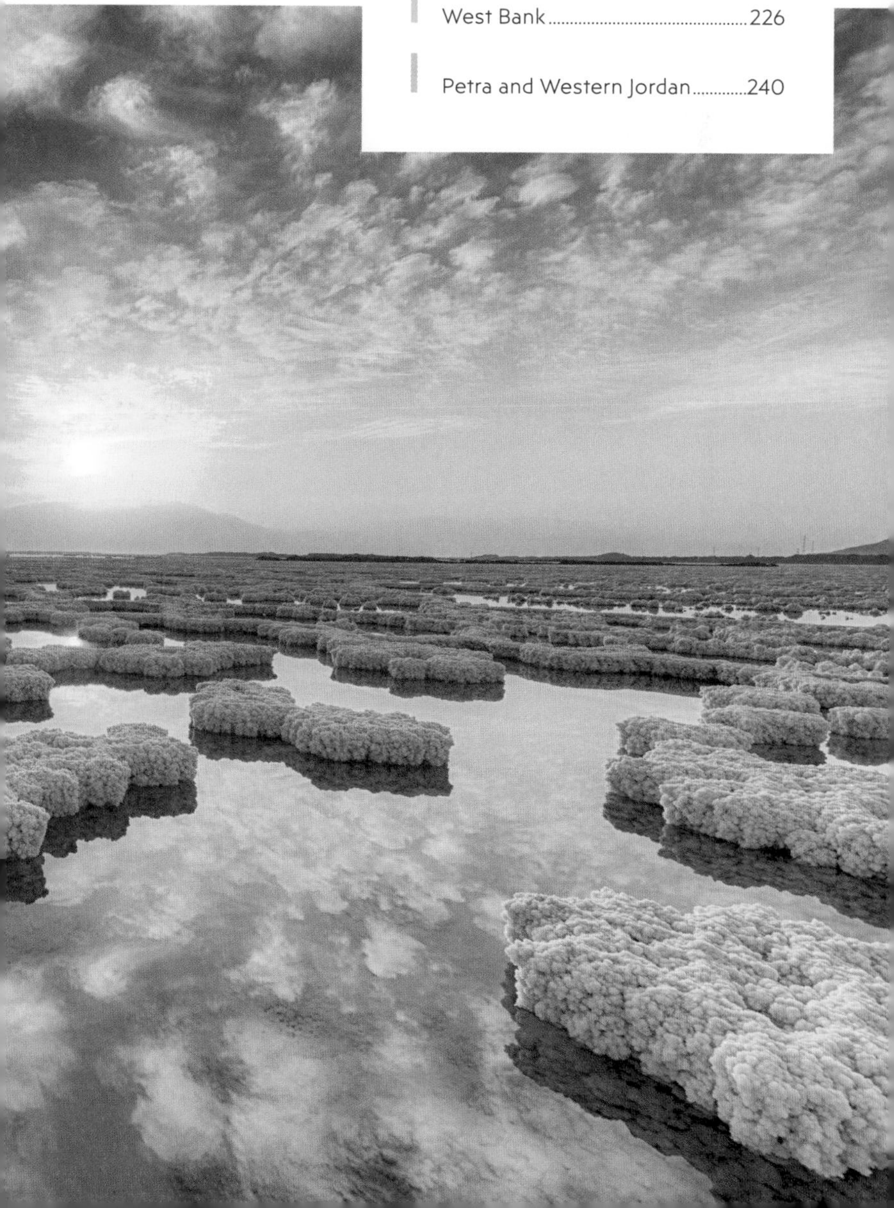

TEL AVIV

The port city of Jaffa (Joppa) was mentioned in Egyptian documents as early as the 15th century BC. According to the Hebrew Bible, the cedars of Lebanon used to build the First Temple were brought ashore here, and it was from Jaffa that Jonah set sail shortly before being swallowed by the whale. The New Testament tells of St Peter's sojourn in the city, which later in the 1st century AD was destroyed by the Romans after it served as a centre of Jewish resistance during the Great Revolt (AD 66–70). The Crusaders conquered Jaffa in 1099 and, except for a brief interlude, ruled it for the next 169 years. The city returned to Muslim rule, although Napoleon made a brief appearance in 1799, when his soldiers destroyed the city and massacred its Ottoman garrison. A short-lived "American Colony" was founded in 1865 by American Christians, who were followed by the Templers, German Christians who established the settlements of Valhalla (1869) and Sarona (1871). The "garden city" of Tel Aviv was founded on the dunes north of Jaffa in 1909, and its population quickly swelled with Jews fleeing persecution in both Palestine and Europe. Over the 20th century, it became established as a vibrant, cosmopolitan city, and today is home to the most dynamic start-up ecosystem outside of the United States.

TEL AVIV

Must Sees
1 Tel Aviv Museum of Art
2 Rothschild Boulevard

Experience More
3 Rabin Square
4 Dizengoff Street
5 Dubnov Garden
6 Tel Aviv Performing Arts Center
7 Ben-Gurion Boulevard
8 Tel Aviv Port
9 Charles Clore Park
10 Tel Aviv Beachfront
11 Tel Aviv Marina
12 Metzitzim Beach
13 Neve Tzedek
14 Sheinkin Street
15 Bialik Street
16 Carmel Market
17 ANU – Museum of the Jewish People
18 Meir Garden
19 Eretz Israel Museum
20 Nachalat Binyamin

Eat
① Pastel
② Alena
③ Kitchen Market
④ 416
⑤ HaBasta

Stay
⑥ Hotel Montefiore
⑦ Arbel Suites Hotel
⑧ Tal by the Beach
⑨ Abraham Hostel

Shop
⑩ Nachalat Binyamin Arts and Crafts Fair

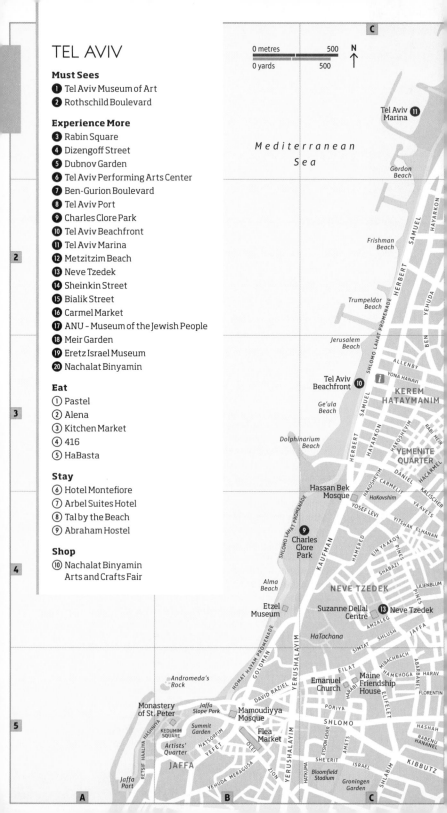

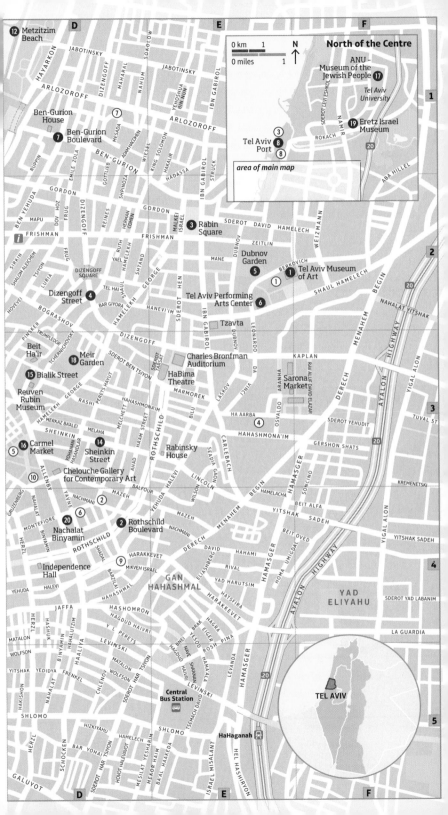

TEL AVIV MUSEUM OF ART

📍 E2 🏠 27 Ha-Melekh Shaul Blvd 🕐 10am–6pm Mon, Wed & Sat, 10am–9pm Tue & Thu, 10am–2pm Fri 🌐 tamuseum.org.il

Israel's premier museum of modern and contemporary art brings together works by international superstars such as Van Gogh and Picasso, with outstanding exhibitions featuring thought-provoking – and often provocative – Israeli art.

The museum was founded in 1932 by Meir Dizengoff, the first mayor of Tel Aviv. Beginning with just a few dozen works, the collection has steadily grown to become the finest in Israel. The pieces on display span the 17th century to the present day, and cover the major movements in late 19th- and 20th-century European and American art – from Impressionism and Cubism to Abstract Expressionism and Pop Art – with works by numerous world-famous names such as Monet, Degas, Rothko and Pollock. The collection is split between the Brutalist main building, which opened in 1971, and the newer Herta and Paul Amir Building, an arresting, angular structure that was inaugurated in 2011. There is also a lovely sculpture garden and performance spaces. Temporary exhibitions can be seen in the Helena Rubenstein Pavilion, a striking modernist pavilion opened in 1959 that's 1 km (half a mile) southwest of the main building.

A mural by Roy Lichtenstein in the museum lobby ↑

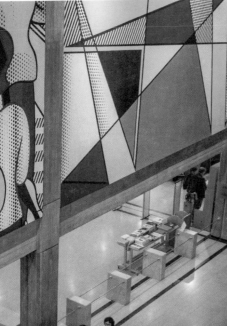

1 The eye-catching Herta and Paul Amir Building opened in 2011 and houses five floors of galleries.

2 Sculptures of birds and human figures by Israeli artist Zadok Ben Daviv are on display in front of the museum.

3 *The Shepherdess* (1889) by Vincent van Gogh was painted during the artist's voluntary hospitalization in an asylum.

ISRAELI ART

The Tel Aviv Museum of Art is known for its pioneering solo exhibitions featuring Israeli artists. Modern Israeli art has often focused on issues of identity and conflict, as well as the complex relationships between the local and the universal, the periphery versus the centre, and east versus west.

Enjoying a coffee break at one of the kiosks that line the delightful thoroughfare ↑

❷
ROTHSCHILD BOULEVARD

📍 D4

Walkers, cyclists and scooter riders flock to this elegant thoroughfare, which lies at the heart of Bauhaus Tel Aviv. Its ficus-shaded central strip shelters an appealing array of drink and food kiosks and environmental sculptures, with plenty of benches for people watching.

Lined with palm trees and Eclectic- and Bauhaus-style buildings from the 1920s and 1930s, as well as the modern skyscrapers of Tel Aviv's financial district, Rothschild Boulevard stretches for 1.5 km (1 mile) from flowery HaBima Square – home of the world-class HaBima Theater and the Charles Bronfman Auditorium concert hall – southwest of Neve Tzedek. The Haganah Museum at No 23 tells the history of the clandestine pre-state military organization that later became the Israel Defense Forces, while across the street, at No 16, stands Independence Hall (undergoing renovations until 2023). It was here, on 14 May 1948, where Israel's Declaration of Independence was made. Nearby real estate, among the city's priciest, is home to top restaurants and classy boutique hotels.

↑ Patrons relaxing at one of the many restaurants that line the boulevard

> **Nearby real estate, among the city's priciest, is home to top restaurants and classy boutique hotels.**

TEL AVIV'S BAUHAUS ARCHITECTURE

The world's largest assemblage of buildings in the International Modern style, also known as Bauhaus, is in Tel Aviv. Altogether there are some 4,000 examples within the city. These buildings, largely erected in the 1930s and 1940s, were designed by immigrant architects trained in Europe, particularly in Germany, home of the modernist Bauhaus School. The simplicity and functionality of the style, which aimed to unify art with technology, was considered highly appropriate to the socialist ideals of Zionism that underpinned the founding of the new city.

EXPERIENCE MORE

❸
Rabin Square

⊙E2 🚌 10, 12, 24, 25

Tel Aviv's largest public square is often the venue for large-scale political, cultural and sporting events.

On 4 November 1995, at the end of a huge peace rally, Prime Minister Yizhak Rabin was assassinated here by a right-wing Jew; a memorial, situated on Ibn Gabirol Street, between the 14-storey city hall and Gan Halr shopping mall, marks the spot.

The massive, rust-coloured sculpture, shaped like a Star of David when seen from above, is a memorial for the victims of the Holocaust, designed by Yigal Tumarkin.

Much of the square currently looks like a construction site, however, due to works on a new underground station.

---

❹
Dizengoff Street

⊙D2 🚌 5, 22, 72

Tel Aviv's most stylish shopping area back in the 1960s, Dizengoff Street runs north to south and links the Dizengoff Center, Israel's first (and still-flourishing) shopping centre, with the Tel Aviv Port, a distance of 3 km (2 miles).

Two blocks north of the Dizengoff Center is Dizengoff Square. It was named in honour not of Meir Dizengoff, the city's first mayor, but rather his wife, Tzina. In 2019 the square was restored to its original, mid-1930s layout, with a street-level fountain roundabout in the middle.

The square is surrounded by Bauhaus-style buildings, including the Cinema Hotel. Built as a movie theatre in 1939, it has ribbons of horizontal windows, over-hanging ledges and curved balconies; take the elevator up to the roof terrace for some fine city views. The city's Bauhaus heritage is celebrated at the **Bauhaus Center**, which hosts exhibitions, offers architectural walking tours and sells Bauhaus-themed books and souvenirs.

Bauhaus Center

🅰🅿🆎🆑 🏠77 Dizengoff St
🕐10am-7pm Sun-Thu, 10am-2:30pm Fri, 10am-7:30pm Sat
🌐bauhaus-center.com

---

❺
Dubnov Garden

⊙E2 🏠Dubnov St
🚌9, 18

Situated behind the Tel Aviv Peforming Arts Center, a block east of Ibn Gabirol Street, this island of green is one of dozens of small parks scattered around the city's residential areas. It has two play areas for children, one of them shaded, as well as grass, benches and a water fountain designed to refresh both humans and dogs.

---

6 🔲

Tel Aviv Performing Arts Center

📍 E2 🏛 19 Shaul HaMelech Blvd 🚌 9, 14 🕐 For performances 🌐 Israeli Opera: israel-opera.co.il; Cameri Theater: cameri.co.il

Part of a cultural campus that includes the Tel Aviv Museum of Art and Beit Ariela (the city's central public library), the Tel Aviv Performing Arts Center is home to several arts organizations and venues. The Israeli Opera has a home here, and their performance spaces also host international dance troupes.

The Cameri Theater is Tel Aviv's municipal theatre company, which features works by Israeli playwrights. The two institutions share a long, glass-enclosed lobby.

Opened in 1994, the complex is architecturally interesting too. Postmodern in inspiration, it combines curved and angular elements that create an asymmetrical façade and skyline; patrons arriving on foot enter from Shaul HaMelech Boulevard, passing through a towering modern arch.

7

Ben-Gurion Boulevard

📍 D1 🚌 4, 10, 13

This animated boulevard, with a tree-shaded pedestrian promenade and a bicycle path

← The Holocaust Memorial, by Yigal Tumarkin, on Tel Aviv's Rabin Square

↑ Fresh juice for sale along bustling Ben-Gurion Boulevard

running down the middle, links Rabin Square with the beach, a distance of 1.3 km (0.8 mile). Locals come here to stroll with their pushchairs or dogs (or both) and to sip freshly squeezed juices or coffee, purchased from little kiosks. It is named for David Ben-Gurion (1886–1973), Israel's first prime minister, who lived at No 17 for much of the time between 1931 and 1973. His home is now a museum, the **Ben-Gurion House**, whose exhibits and décor – virtually unchanged in half-a-century – offer fascinating insights into his life and times.

Ben-Gurion House

🏛 17 Ben-Gurion Blvd 🕐 8am–3pm Sun & Tue–Thu, 8am–5pm Mon, 8am–1pm Fri, 11am–2pm Sat 🌐 bg-house.org

---

Did You Know?

David Ben-Gurion left his house to the State of Israel, to be used for "reading, study and research".

STAY

Hotel Montefiore
Eclectic-style 1920s hotel with very high standards.

📍 D4 🏛 36 Montefiore St 🌐 hotelmonte fiore.co.il

💲💲💲

Arbel Suites Hotel
Spotless modern suites with kitchenettes; some have a balcony.

📍 D1 🏛 11 Hulda St 📞 (03) 522 5450

💲💲💲

Tal by the Beach
Stylish boutique hotel near Metzitzim Beach.

📍 F1 🏛 287 HaYarkon St 🌐 atlas.co.il

💲💲💲

Abraham Hostel
Dorm beds and private rooms, plus rooftop patio.

📍 D4 🏛 21 Levontin St 🌐 abraham hostels.com

💲💲💲

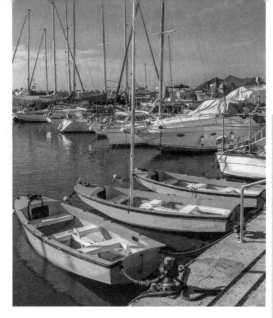

← Yachts and rowing boats berthed at the watersports hub of Tel Aviv Marina

Across the street from the park stands Hassan Bek Mosque, built – using forced labour – in 1916 by the eponymous Ottoman military governor of Jaffa. During the 1948 War, Arab soldiers used the mosque's minaret as a firing position. Manshiye was severely damaged during the fighting and was demolished in the 1960s – a fate that was also planned for Neve Tzedek (*p180*). Charles Clore Park stands on the rubble that demolition contractors bulldozed into the sea.

The park hosts major outdoor events such as Gay Pride (the parade ends here) and the Tel Aviv EAT food festival. The shell of the old Dophinarium complex, site of a horrific suicide bombing in 2001, was demolished in 2018 and is scheduled to be replaced by an uninterrupted seafront promenade.

⑧ Tel Aviv Port

🗺 F1 🚌 4, 6, 9, 11, 72
🌐 namal.co.il

Tel Aviv's cargo port, which was established in 1936 and closed in 1965, was transformed into the city's favourite strolling, shopping, dining, drinking and clubbing precinct in the early 2000s after decades of dereliction. Old warehouses became industrial-chic commercial spaces, restaurants, bars and cafés, and an undulating wooden boardwalk – lashed by waves when the surf's up – was constructed along the waterfront. The romantic Mandate-era Wauchope Bridge across the Yarkon River estuary was rebuilt, creative play areas for children were added, and on the water-cargo ships were replaced by yachts and other pleasure craft.

On Shabbat, some of the only shopping in town can be found here.

⑨ Charles Clore Park

🗺 C4 🚏 Kaufmann St

A few hundred metres north of Old Jaffa, grassy Charles Clore Park – named for a British businessman and philanthropist – stretches along the waterfront. Within the park sits a black glass cube, constructed inside the ruins of the only remaining building from the pre-1948, majority-Arab neighbourhood of Manshiye. It houses the Etzel 1948 Museum, which looks at the battle fought here in April 1948 from a right-wing Israeli perspective.

⑩ Tel Aviv Beachfront

🗺 C4 🚏 HaYarkon St
🚌 11

Tel Aviv's seafront stretches for 13.5 km (9 miles) from Herzliya to Bat Yam. The 13 official swimming beaches

→ *A Woman Against the Wind* (1972) by Ilana Goor, in Charles Clore Park

TOP 5 TEL AVIV BEACHES

Metzitzim
Shallow water and ice cream nearby draw families here.

Hilton Beach
Part unofficial gay beach; part good for surfing; part for dogs.

Gordon Beach
A popular spot with European tourists.

Frishman Beach
A family favourite, with a statue of David Ben-Gurion doing a headstand (he used to do yoga here).

Jerusalem Beach
Be prepared for energetic games of *matkot* (beach raquetball) here.

offer all the delights of the Mediterranean – warm water (31° C/88° F in August), gentle waves (usually) – along with pergolas, open-air showers, deckchairs and parasols for rent, fitness and exercise equipment, cafés, toilets, changing rooms and, of course, lifeguards on duty (mid-April to early October).

A seafront promenade, for walkers, scooter riders and cyclists, links Reading Park – just north of the Yarkon River, near Reading power station and the, now defunct, Sde Dov airport – to Jaffa's port, passing through the Tel Aviv Port. It parallels kilometres of glorious, fine-grained sand, washed onto these shores by sea currents from the Nile River.

Even in winter it's often warm enough to sunbathe here, and all the beaches face west so this is a good place to be at sunset.

⓫ Tel Aviv Marina

🅟 C1 🅐 Shlomo Lahat Promenade 🚌 4, 10, 13, 100 🌐 telaviv-marina.com

Picturesque Tel Aviv Marina houses 320 yacht berths for yachts up to 20 m (66 ft) long and is encircled by a seawall that's accessible to pedestrians. Unfortunately, the approach to the marina from Ben Gurion Boulevard is obscured by Atarim Square, an early-70s, Brutalist monstrosity that blocks sight lines and access to the beach. The city has been trying to replace the complex for decades, and construction should soon begin on a more aesthetic seafront development.

Between the square and the marina sits the Olympic-sized Gordon Pool, founded in 1956. An institution among local swimmers, it is famously filled with crystal-clear, mineral-rich saline groundwater that's changed daily, pumped up from a depth of 150 m (nearly 500 ft). There are separate pools for children and toddlers, and sunbeds, chairs and parasols for lounging between laps.

⓬
Metzitzim Beach

🅟 D1 🅐 Havakuk HaNavi St 🚌 11, 55, 100

The iconic Israeli film *Metzitzim* was shot on location here in 1972, giving this family-friendly beach its name. Its facilities include changing rooms, shade-giving pergolas, dry-land access to the sea-wall and close proximity to the snacks, drinks and food available at the Tel Aviv Port.

Except on Shabbat, adjacent Nordau Beach is gender-segregated (Sunday, Tuesday and Thursday for women; Monday, Wednesday and Friday for men).

1909

The year that Tel Aviv was founded on the sand dunes north of Jaffa.

An open-air-café in the lively shopping area of Sheinkin Street ↑

⓭ Neve Tzedek

📍 C4

Jaffa's first Jewish suburb, Neve Tzedek ("abode of justice") was founded in 1887 by well-off families seeking fresh air and an escape from the overcrowding of Jaffa's Old City. It found itself on the front line in 1948 and subsequently became a slum, housing Jewish immigrants and refugees from the Middle East and North Africa. The area's low-rise houses and narrow lanes began to be gentrified during the 1980s, and today it is one of the most expensive parts of the city, with a number of classy boutiques.

Located at the heart of the neighbourhood is the **Suzanne Dellal Center**, one of the world's most important institutions dedicated to modern dance. Its delightful courtyard, peppered with orange trees, is a popular place for people to meet and relax.

The small **Rokach House Museum** occupies the one-time home of Shimon Rokach, one of the founders of Neveh Tzedek. Displays in the house illustrate daily life here at the end of the 19th century. A few doors along is the **Nahum Gutman Museum**, dedicated to one of Israel's most famous artists. Born in Russia in 1898, Gutman is best known for his painting, but he is also admired for his drawings and children's books.

A short walk away is the Jaffa terminus of the rail line from Jaffa to Jerusalem, which opened in 1892. Nearby buildings have been turned into **HaTachana**, a popular complex with restaurants, boutiques and cultural events.

Suzanne Dellal Center
🏠 6 Yehieli St 🌐 suzanne dellal.org.il

Rokach House Museum
♿ 🏠 36 Shimon Rokach St
🕐 10am–2pm Thu–Sat
🌐 rokach-house.co.il

Nahum Gutman Museum
♿ 🏠 21 Shimon Rokach St
🕐 10am–2pm Mon–Fri, 10am–3pm Sat 🌐 gutman museum.co.il

HaTachana
🚻 😊 🏠 HaMered St, on the corner of Kaufmann St
🕐 10am–9pm Sun–Thu, 10am–3pm Fri, 10am–10pm Sat 🌐 hatachana.co.il

→
Colourful decorations at the Suzanne Dellal Center in Neveh Tzedek

⓮ Sheinkin Street

📍 D3

Once the ultimate symbol of Tel Aviv's counterculture, with cheap flats, independent boutiques and hip cafés, chic-shabby Sheinkin Street has moved decidedly upmarket. Although it now costs a fortune to live here and most of the shops are high-end, young Tel Avivians still flock to the area to stroll and sit in cafés, especially on Friday afternoons.

The street is named after one of the founders of Tel Aviv, Menahem Sheinkin (1871–1924), who was killed in a tram accident in Chicago, United States.

⑮
Bialik Street

📍 D3

Bialik Street is one of Tel Aviv's most historic thoroughfares. At No 14 is the **Rubin Museum**, the former residence of one of Israel's most famous painters, Reuven Rubin (1893–1974), who also became a diplomat in 1948, representing Israel in Romania. The house now contains a permanent collection of his works, including local landscapes, Biblical and historical themes, and people. The third floor has the artist's preserved studio and a documentary film, and there is also a historical archive of his life. Changing exhibits feature the work of other Israeli artists.

A few doors along, **Bialik House** (Beit Bialik) is the former home of Haim Nahman Bialik (1873–1934), Israel's national poet. The house has been kept as it was during Bialik's time, and includes a library and paintings by some of Israel's best-known artists.

A little south of Bialik Street, Bezalel Street is home to a colourful and popular street market renowned for its cut-price fashions. There are also many food stalls that offer local cuisine.

Rubin Museum
🏛 📍 14 Bialik St
🕐 10am–3pm Mon–Fri (to 8pm Tue), 11am–2pm Sat & public hols
🌐 rubinmuseum.org.il

Bialik House
🏛 📍 22 Bialik St 📞 (03) 724 0311 🕐 9am–5pm Mon–Thu, 10am–2pm Fri & Sat (book ahead)

> **A little south of Bialik Street, Bezalel Street is home to a colourful and popular street market renowned for its cut-price fashions. There are also many food stalls that offer local cuisine.**

EAT

Pastel
Modern brasserie in the Tel Aviv Museum of Art.

📍 E2 📍 A27 Sha'ul Hamelech Blvd
🕐 Noon–midnight daily
🌐 pastel-tlv.com

💲💲💲

Alena
Elegant place, with dishes inspired by Greece and the Levant.

📍 D4 📍 Norman Hotel, 23–25 Nachmani St
🕐 7–11am, 12:30–2:30/3pm & 6–10pm daily 🌐 thenorman.com

💲💲💲

Kitchen Market
Contemporary gourmet Mediterranean cuisine overlooking the sea.

📍 F1 📍 1st Floor, Hangar 12, Tel Aviv Port
🕐 Noon–4pm & 6:30–11pm Mon–Sat, 6–11:30pm Sun
🌐 kitchen-market.co.il

💲💲💲

416
One of the city's award-winning vegan restaurants.

📍 E3 📍 16 Ha'arba'a St, 📞 (03) 775 5066
🕐 Noon–11pm daily

💲💲💲

HaBasta
Intimate bistro in grungy Carmel Market.

📍 D3 📍 4 HaShomer St 📞 (03) 516 9234
🕐 Noon–11:30pm Sat–Thu, 8:30–midnight Fri

💲💲💲

Did You Know?

Tel Aviv was originally called Ahuzat Bayit when the city was founded in 1909.

16 Carmel Market

📍 D3 🏠 HaCarmel St
🕐 9am-6pm Sun-Thu, 9am-3pm Fri

Shuk Hacarmel, as it's known locally, is the city's largest and busiest open-air market, a lively place full of the sights and sounds of everyday life and the aromas of fresh food.

In operation since 1920, the market begins near the junction with Allenby Street, with stalls selling cheap clothing, household items and electronics, before switching to fresh fish, meat, fruit and vegetables, spices and herbs, breads and biscuits, and nuts and seeds. Bargains can often be had at the end of the day.

Many of the side-streets off HaCarmel specialize in different food produce.

17 ANU - Museum of the Jewish People

📍 F1 🏠 University Campus, Gate 2, Klausner St, Ramat Aviv 🕐 10am-7pm Sun-Wed, 10am-10pm Thu, 9am-2pm Fri, 10am-5pm Sat
🌐 anumuseum.org.il

Formerly known as Beit Hatfutshot, this museum reopened in 2021 with a new name and three new floors. It is divided into four main sections: The Mosaic, highlighting contemporary Jewish identity and culture; The Journey, encompassing Jewish history; The Foundations, covering the universal messages of Judaism and the Bible; and The Synagogue. Initially opened in 1978, the museum broke new ground by telling a story using creative exhibits and technological means rather than displaying artifacts. The revamped museum has developed this concept with the advantages of 21st-century technology to make Jewish culture and history meaningful for people of all faiths. There is also a children's gallery, a fully digitalized genealogy database, and film and music archives.

↑ Locals and visitors strolling and relaxing in Meir Garden

18 Meir Garden

📍 D3 🏠 King George V St
🚌 14, 18, 24, 25

Tel Aviv's first public park – laid out in the 1930s in honour of Tel Aviv's first mayor, Meir Dizengoff (1861-1936) – is a fine, shady spot to relax or have a picnic lunch. The park is fairly small, but there are plenty of benches, a shaded playground for children and an attractive large koi pond dappled with lily pads. At the park's western corner stands a

dynamic, city-run LGBTQ+ community centre, which runs a wide variety of services and events.

Across King George V St is 16-storey **Metzudat Ze'ev**, named after Ze'ev Jabotinsky (1880–1940), the Russian-born founder of right-wing Revisionist Zionism. It serves as the administrative head-quarters of the Likud party and also houses the small Jabotinsky Museum. The museum's exhibits present the life and world view of the fascinating founder of right-wing Zionism, whose ideology combined free market economics, liberal democracy and nationalism.

Metzudat Ze'ev
📍 38 King George St
🌐 jabotinsky.org

🔟⁹

Eretz Israel Museum

📍 F1 🚌 2 Haim Levanon, Ramat Aviv 🕐 10am-4pm Mon, Wed & Sat, 10am-8pm Tue & Thu, 10am-2pm Fri
🌐 eretzmuseum.org.il

Built around the site of Tel Qasile, where excavations have revealed layers of human habitation that date back to 1200 BC, this excellent museum depicts the history and culture of the land of Israel.

It comprises a number of themed pavilions, all of which contain permanent exhibitions. One has a very fine collection of ancient and Islamic-era glass, and others are devoted to coins, ancient pottery, Judaica, the copper mining industry, postal history and philately, and ancient crafts. In addition, there is an art installation titled

←

Engaging exhibits on Jewish history and culture in ANU - Museum of the Jewish People

→

An art installation of ceramic flowers in the grounds of the Eretz Israel Museum

"Blossoming with Age" consisting of some 10,000 ceramic flowers made by hundreds of Israeli senior citizens from all over the country. They are set out as a colourful garden among trees and bushes in the museum grounds.

Additionally there's a square with a collection of beautiful mosaic floors from early synagogues, churches and mosques; an old olive oil press; a reconstructed flour mill; and a 1925 fire engine given by the city of New York to Tel Aviv's volunteer fire brigade in 1947.

2️⃣0️⃣

Nachalat Binyamin

📍 D4

The second neighbourhood in Tel Aviv (the first was along nearby Herzl Street), Nachalat Binyamin was established in late 1909. It is now a pedestrian mall lined with Eclectic-style buildings from the 1920s featuring Classical, Moorish and Art Nouveau elements. There is a plentiful selection of restaurants, bars and shops, and a colourful,

creative arts and crafts fair is held here every Tuesday and Friday.

Next to Nachalat Binyamin is the Yemenite Quarter (Kerem HaTeymanim), home to Carmel Market. Its maze of small streets – and those of Nachalat Binyamin – predate Tel Aviv's expansive masterplan, which was drawn up by Scottish urban planner Sir Patrick Geddes at the request of Mayor Meir Dizengoff in 1925.

SHOP

Nachalat Binyamin Arts and Crafts Fair
This twice-a-week arts and crafts fair, with tables staffed by the artists themselves, is a great place to pick up creative gifts and Jewish ritual objects.

📍 D3 🏠 Nachalat Binyamin St 🕐 10am-4:30 or 5pm Tue & Fri (to 5 or 6pm in summer) 🌐 nachlat-binyamin.com

A SHORT WALK
OLD JAFFA

Distance 1.5 km (1 mile) **Nearest bus stop**
Flea Market/Yefet **Time** 25 minutes

According to the Bible, Jaffa (then called Joppa) was founded
in the wake of the great flood by Noah's son Japheth.
Archaeologists have unearthed remains dating back to the
20th century BC, establishing Jaffa as one of the world's oldest
ports. However, with the growth of Tel Aviv, Jaffa, which had
flourished under the Ottomans, went into decline. Following
Jewish victory in the 1948 War, it was absorbed into the new
city to the north. The core of the old town has since been
revived as an attractive arts, crafts and dining centre.

Ha-Pisga garden
lies on top of
the ancient "tel"
(mound) of Jaffa.

**Ha-Pisga open-air
amphitheatre** is
used for concerts
during the summer.

START

FINISH

MIFRAZ SHLOMO

The **Mahmoudiya
Mosque** dates
from 1812 and is
still in use today.

**A 19th-century
sabil** (fountain)

HA-ALIYAH HA-SHNIYA

**Napoleonic
cannons**

The **Sea Mosque**
was the mosque
of local fishermen.

← The decorative façade
of the 19th-century
Mahmoudiya Mosque

→ The Artists' Quarter, which houses studios, galleries and residences

Locator Map
For more detail see p170

This compact area of old Arab houses and narrow stone alleys has been transformed into the **Artists' Quarter**.

Ha-Simta Theatre

Ilana Goor Museum of Ethnic and Applied Art

Synagogue

Did You Know?

Roman columns from Caesarea *(p190)* were used to build the Mahmoudiya Mosque.

The **House of Simon the Tanner** *is traditionally held to be where the apostle Peter once stayed (Acts 9: 43).*

Underneath the picturesque **Kedumim Square** *is the Visitors' Centre, with exposed Roman-era exhibits.*

The small, Greek Orthodox **St Michael's Church** *dates from the 19th century.*

The **Monastery of St Peter** *is built in Latin American Baroque style.*

The **Monastery of St Nicholas**, *built around 1667, still serves Jaffa's Armenian community.*

The Wishing Bridge *is said to bring true the wish of anyone crossing it if they touch the statue of their zodiac sign.*

| 0 metres | 50 |
| 0 yards | 50 |

N

→ An arched alley leading to the Greek Orthodox St Michael's Church

Haifa's Baha'i Gardens, cascading down the slopes of Mount Carmel

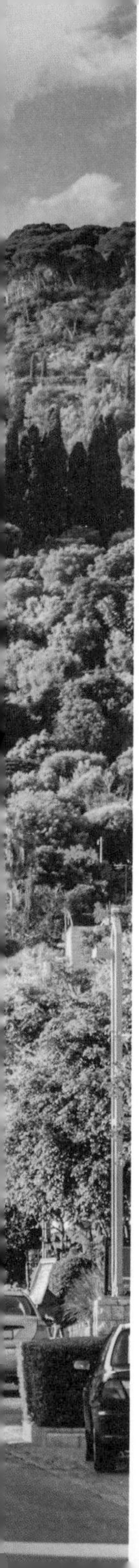

MEDITERRANEAN COAST AND GALILEE

Human life in this region began more than 500,000 years ago, as evidenced by the discovery of numerous prehistoric artifacts on the western slopes of Mount Carmel. By the time of the Pharaohs and the Phoenicians, the area was part of a major trade network: Mediterranean coastal ports connected the Holy Land with empires across the sea, and caravans followed the Via Maris south to Egypt and northeast to Damascus and beyond. In around 720 BC, the Galilee-based Kingdom of Israel was destroyed by the Assyrians, but Jewish life thrived in the region during the Second Temple period (538 BC–AD 70). Jesus of Nazareth grew up here at the start of the 1st century AD, and later preached in Jewish villages around the Sea of Galilee. Following the destruction of the Second Temple by the Romans in AD 70, the Galilee provided refuge to Jews – including sages and scholars – driven out of Judaea. During the Byzantine era, Christians gradually became the majority, and in the Middle Ages the region became part of the Crusader kingdom, with Akko as its capital, before returning to Muslim Arab rule. The fertile coastal plains and rolling hills in Galilee attracted Jewish immigrants in the 19th century, and today the region has a mixed population of Jews, Muslim and Christian Arabs, and Druze.

MEDITERRANEAN COAST AND GALILEE

Must Sees

1. Caesarea
2. Haifa and Mount Carmel
3. Akko
4. Nazareth
5. Sea of Galilee
6. Beit She'an

Experience More

7. Megiddo
8. Safed
9. Golan Heights
10. Tiberias
11. Hula Nature Reserve
12. Belvoir Castle
13. Beit Alpha
14. Zichron Ya'akov
15. Mount Tabor
16. Dan Nature Reserve
17. Hamat Gader
18. Beit She'arim
19. Tzipori
20. Rosh HaNikra
21. Upper Galilee Museum of Prehistory

ROSH HANIKRA 20

Nahariyya

Shavei Tsiyon

Shomrat

AKKO 3

Bay of Haifa

Kfar Masaryk

Kiryat Yam

HAIFA 2

Kiryat Ata

Tirat Carmel

2

Nesher

MOUNT CARMEL

Kiryat Tiv'on

BEIT SHE'ARIM 18

Neve Yam

Daliyat el-Carmel

Yokne'am

Geva Karmel

Nakhsholim

Fureidis

ZICHRON YA'AKOV 14

Bat Shlomo

Binyamina

CAESAREA 1

Pardes Khana-Karkur

Sdot Yam

Mediterranean Sea

Khadera

Mikhmoret

Baqa el-Gharbiya

Yama

Nazlat Isa

Ma'abarot

Netanya

Kfar Yona

Nitsanei Oz

Tul Karem

Udim

Kur.

Kalkilya (Qalqilya)

Imati

Ra'anana

Herzliya

Kfar Saba

Ramat ha-Sharon

Yarkhiv

Mas'ha

Tel Aviv

Jaffa

TEL AVIV
p168

Kholon

Ben Gurion International Airport

Rantis

0 kilometres 15

0 miles 15

N
↑

Did You Know?

Pontius Pilate (who ordered the crucifixion of Jesus) served as prefect in Caesarea in the 1st century AD.

❶ ⚔

CAESAREA

📍 B2 🏠 Off Rd 2, 55 km (34 miles) N of Tel Aviv 🚌 76 and 77 from Khadera
🕐 8am–4pm Sat–Thu (summer: to 6pm); 8am–3pm Fri (summer: to 4pm)
🌐 parks.org.il

Founded by Herod the Great and named for Augustus Caesar, this grand port city is one of Israel's major archaeological sites. The extensive – and fascinating – Roman ruins include a spectacular theatre and the attractive port itself.

At the height of his power, in 29–22 BC, Herod the Great built a splendid city over the site of an ancient Phoenician port. Its prosperity lasted until AD 614, after which its history became more unstable. During the early 12th century and the Crusades, Caesarea again became an important port city, but by the late 13th century it had been destroyed by the Mamelukes and was left to be reclaimed by the sand, with only a small Arab village remaining. The importance of these great hidden ruins was not realized until the 1940s.

Most of the main sights lie in the Caesarea National Park. If entering from the south, you will first see the huge restored Roman theatre, with seats for 4,000 spectators. A short distance to the west, on a small promontory, a group of half-submerged walls indicate the site of Herod's palace. Further inland are the ruins of one of the largest hippodromes in the Roman Empire. On the coast by the inner harbour is the Crusader citadel, surrounded by walls dating back to around AD 1250. Enclosing this whole area are the ruins of the Crusader city walls, within which lies the unique Underwater Archaeological Park. The four complexes at this park enable divers to see the techniques used to build the ancient port, as well as remnants of wrecked ships.

North of the ancient city is a Roman aqueduct dating from the Herodian period. Extending for 17 km (11 miles), it carried water from the foothills of Mount Carmel to Caesarea. A short way to the south of the site, the Caesarea Museum has interesting artifacts from the Roman city.

💬 INSIDER TIP
Concerts

In Roman times, locals and visiting mariners flocked to Caesarea's semi-circular theatre to enjoy dramas and comedies. Today, the ancient performance space (often referred to, incorrectly, as the Caesarea Amphitheatre) is a popular and prestigious venue for pop and rock concerts by major Israeli and international artists. It also hosts the annual Caesarea Jazz Festival.

←

The picturesque ruins of the Roman aqueduct on Caesarea Beach

1 The ancient harbour now houses cafés and restaurants, and makes an excellent spot to watch the sunset.

2 The Underwater Archaeological Park features sunken ships and cargo, ancient anchors and marine life.

3 The eastern gatehouse of the Crusader city is built in the Gothic architectural style, with features including a ribbed vault ceiling.

The terraces of the Baha'i Gardens, with views over the city and Haifa Bay ↑

②

HAIFA AND MOUNT CARMEL

🅰 B2 ⏴ 95 km (59 miles) N of Tel Aviv ✈🚉🚌
ℹ 48 Ben Gurion St; www.visit-haifa.org

Israel's third-largest city, Haifa is built around and on Mount Carmel. A small village for most of its history, things changed in 1868 with the arrival of German Christians known as Templers, who brought with them modern European technology. Today, Haifa is a proud model for Jewish-Arab coexistence and is home to a prestigious science and technology research university.

① ⊘

Baha'i Gardens and Shrine of the Bab

⏰ Ha-Ziyonut St ⏰ Daily (shrine: morning only) 🚫 Shrine: one month in summer; see website for details 🌐 ganbahai.org.il

Haifa has been a holy site for followers of the Baha'i Faith since 1909, when the remains of the religion's founder, the

Báb (executed in Iran in 1850), were interred here. Today, his tomb is marked by the gold-domed Shrine of the Báb (1953), which stands at the bottom of the magnificent Baha'i Gardens, famed for their dazzling views of Haifa Bay. Tours of the, flower-filled terraces of the gardens begin 1 km (half a mile) north of Carmel Center, along gorgeous Yefe Nof Street, and last 45 minutes. Reservations

---

🏔 GREAT VIEW
Haifa Bay

For breathtaking views of Haifa Bay, stroll north along Yefe Nof Street from Gan Ha'Em park in Carmel Center, to the Baha'i Gardens' viewing platform (at No 61).

---

are not necessary but it's a good idea to arrive half an hour before the start time. Dress modestly (shoulders and knees must be covered).

---

②

Carmel Center

The lively area around the upper station of Haifa's six-station Carmelit metro (actually a funicular railway) is known as Carmel Center. The neighbourhood is populated with cafés and restaurants, and offers breathtaking Mediterranean panoramas from Yefe Nof Street. Nearby attractions include Gan Ha'Em (a public garden) and the adjacent zoo, and two excellent museums: the **Tikotin Museum of**

Japanese Art, which houses a fascinating collection of Japanese artifacts; and the **Mané-Katz Museum**, which holds exhibitions of works by Emmanuel Mané-Katz, a Russian-born painter affiliated with the École de Paris.

Tikotin Museum of Japanese Art
🎟 🏠 89 HaNasi Ave
🕐 10am-7pm Sat-Thu, 10am-1pm Fri �📶 tmja.org.il

Mané-Katz Museum
🎟 🏠 89 Yefe Nof St
🕐 10am-4pm Sun-Wed, 4-7pm Thu, 10am-1pm Fri, 10am-3pm Sat �📶 mkm.org.il

---

③
Stella Maris

🏠 Stella Maris St 🕐 8am-12:30pm & 3-6pm daily �📶 carmelholylanddco.org

It was on Mount Carmel, back in Crusader times, that the Catholic religious order known as the Carmelites was founded. The order considers the Prophet Elijah to be their spiritual father, so it is no coincidence that the Stella Maris ("Star of the Sea") Carmelite Monastery, on the northern tip of Mount Carmel, is a short, steep walk up the slope from Elijah's Cave *(p195)*. The monastery is also accessible by cable car from the Bat Galim coast, and houses a beautiful church that dates from 1836.

---

④
Wadi Nisnas

While much of Haifa has changed greatly since the Mandate period, the mostly-Christian Arab neighbourhood of Wadi Nisnas looks very much as it did before 1948, with low-rise stone houses on narrow lanes, small shops and a fruit-and-vegetable market. On HaWadi Street, two rival falafel restaurants – HaZ'kenim (No 18) and Michelle (No 21) – sell some of the city's best all-in-a-pita meals. A little to the west is **Beit HaGefen**, an Arab-Jewish cultural centre that works to foster inter-religious and intercultural dialogue and Arab cultural expression through art exhibits and Arabic-language children's theatre. It also runs engaging experiential tours of the city (book in advance).

Beit HaGefen
🎟 🎟 🏠 2 HaGefen St
🕐 10am-3pm Sun-Thu, 10am-2pm Fri & Sat �📶 beit-hagefen.com

> ### BAUHAUS IN HAIFA
>
> The British Mandate authorities envisioned Haifa's port serving the entire Levant, and the area around it was developed in the 1930s with these big dreams in mind. Although much of the architecture is today run down, it is impressive in its modernism. Lots of Bauhaus buildings can be found on and near Herzl Street in Hadar HaCarmel, and also around Carmel Center.

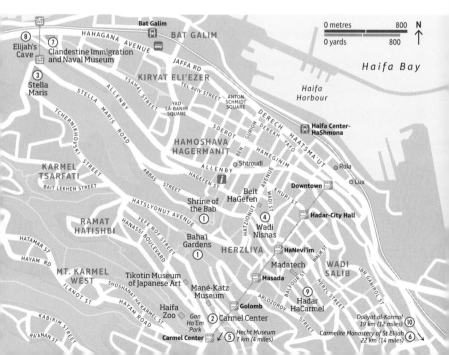

⑤

Hecht Museum

🏛 199 Abba Hushi Blvd, Haifa University ⏰ 10am–4pm Sun–Thu (to 7pm Tue), 10am–1pm Fri, 10am–2pm Sat 🌐 mushecht.haifa.ac.il

At this gem of an archaeology museum, the prize exhibit is the hull of a wooden trading ship, originally 13.5 m (44 ft) long, that sank near Kibbutz Ma'agan Micha'el about 2,400 years ago. Another highlight is a collection of inscribed seals and Jewish coins from the time of the Bible. The permanent exhibition offers an excellent insight into the civilization of the seafaring Phoenicians, while exhibits in the Art Wing include the Ghez Collection, which consists of works by 18 Paris-based Jewish artists who perished in the Holocaust.

⑥

Carmelite Monastery of St Elijah

🏛 22 km (14 miles) SE of Haifa ⏰ 9am–5pm daily 🌐 muhraqa.org

Known as Al-Mukhraka ("the place of the fire") in Arabic,

this hilltop Catholic monastery stands on what some believe to have been the site of the epic confrontation between the Prophet Elijah and the pagan prophets of Ba'al (1 Kings 18). Like Haifa's Stella Maris Monastery (p193), it is run by the Carmelite Order. Visitors to the complex can tour a small chapel, completed in 1883, and enjoy fine views in all directions.

⑦

Clandestine Immigration and Naval Museum

🏛 204 Allenby Rd ⏰ 10am–4pm Sun–Thu

The centerpiece here is the Af Al Pi Chen ("Nevertheless"), a converted Canadian Navy landing craft that was used for clandestine immigration operations during the British Mandate (p52). It was captured by the UK's Royal Navy in 1947 as it tried to smuggle 435 Jewish refugees from Europe into British-ruled Palestine. The museum also presents

the fascinating history of the Israeli Navy – highlights include an exhibit on the capture of the Egyptian destroyer Ibrahim Al-Awal in 1956; the conning tower of the INS Dakar, an Israeli submarine purchased from the UK that disappeared in 1968; and the submarine INS Gal, commissioned in 1976.

MODEL OF COEXISTENCE

Haifa is proud that its diverse communities – which include Jewish refugees and their descendants, Christian and Muslim Palestinians, Jews from the former USSR, Ahmadi Muslims, ultra-Orthodox Jews, Druze and Baha'i volunteers – have long managed to get along with each other. The annual Holiday of Holidays, held each December, is a shared celebration of the season's Jewish, Muslim and Christian festivals.

↑ Views over the Jezreel Valley from the Carmelite Monastery of St Elijah

EAT

Rola

Situated down in the gritty port area, Rola is renowned for serving refined, flavourful versions of traditional dishes from Syria and Lebanon, including some prepared in a *taboon* (traditional clay oven).

🏠 33 HaNamal St
🕐 Noon-midnight Mon-Sat 🌐 rola.rest.co.il

ⓝ ⓝ ⓝ

Shtroudl

Despite its Viennese-sounding name, Shtroudl - in the heart of the German Colony dining strip - serves up light, delectable versions of traditional Arab fare and Italian favourites such as focaccia and pasta, as well as delicious fresh breakfasts.

🏠 39 Ben-Gurion Blvd
🕐 9am-11:30pm daily
🌐 shtroudl.rest.co.il

ⓝ ⓝ ⓝ

Lux

Chef Allaa Moussa uses European techniques that she picked up while working in Michelin-starred restaurants in Sweden to transform top-quality local ingredients (including fresh fish and seafood from Akko) into bold, modern versions of traditional Arab dishes.

🏠 13 HaNamal St
🕐 5pm-midnight Sun-Thu, 12:30pm-midnight Fri & Sat
🌐 lux13.rest.co.il

ⓝ ⓝ ⓝ

---

⑧
Elijah's Cave

🏠 227 Allenby St 📞 (04) 852 7430 🕐 Summer: 8am-6pm Sun-Fri (to 1pm Fri); winter: 8am-5pm Sun-Fri (to 1pm Fri)

Situated at the very northern tip of Mount Carmel, this cave – sacred to Jews, Christians, Muslims and Druze – is where popular tradition holds that the Prophet Elijah hid while fleeing Ahab, King of Israel, in the 9th century BC. The 14-m-(45-ft-) long cave is divided down the middle into sections for women and men, and Jews (especially Sephardim) come here to place petitions in the walls and to pray for the sick (especially the mentally ill), for success in finding a partner and for children.

---

⑨
Hadar HaCarmel

Known as Hadar to locals, this neighbourhood – Haifa's main commercial district from the 1930s to the 1960s – was established by middle class Jews in the 1920s. These days it has inexpensive shopping and a remarkably mixed population that includes immigrants from the former Soviet Union (36 per cent),

↑ Praying inside Elijah's Cave, at the top of Mount Carmel

Arabs (24 per cent), Hasidic Jews and Filipino eldercare workers. A construction boom in the 1930s left the area with a wealth of Bauhaus-style buildings. The old campus of the Technion, built in 1925, is now home to the impressive Madatech, Israel's National Museum of Science, Technology, and Space.

---

⑩
Daliyat al-Karmal

🏠 Route 672, 19 km (12 miles) SE of Haifa

The largest Druze village in Israel, Daliya (as the locals refer to it) sits atop Mount Carmel. Beit Oliphant, built in the late 19th century as the summer home of Sir Lawrence Oliphant (an early Christian Zionist), now serves as Israel's national memorial to Druze soldiers who fell while serving in the Israel Defense Forces. Nearby, the Shrine of Abu Ibrahim honours an 11th-century founder of the Druze faith. Daliya's main street has several Middle Eastern-style restaurants and shops selling Druze textiles.

Akko's picturesque Old City port, bustling with people on a sunny day ↑

3

AKKO

Outside of Jerusalem, Akko (the historic Acre) has the most complete and charming old town in all of the Holy Land. Its origins date back to the Hellenistic period, but its layout was set by the Arabs and their Crusader foes. What can be seen today is largely an 18th-century Ottoman town built on the site of the old.

① ⟨⟩

Knights Halls

🏛️ 1 Weizmann St
🕐 Summer: 8:30am–5pm daily; winter: 8:30am–4pm daily (closes 1 hr earlier Fri) 🌐 akko.org.il

Following the Crusaders' reconquest of Akko in 1191, the Knights Hospitaller (a medieval Catholic military order that also cared for the sick) built this vast complex as its headquarters. It's easy to imagine the clank of knights' armour and the clamour of pilgrims as you walk through its superbly preserved halls. These include the vaulted Refectorium (dining hall), with an arched ceiling held aloft by four massive columns.

② ⟨⟩

Hammam al-Pasha

🏛️ Off El-Jazzar St 📞 (04) 995 1088 🕐 Summer: 8:30am–5pm daily; winter: 8:30am–4pm daily (closes 1 hr earlier Fri)

This is not a museum as such, but a former Turkish bathhouse dating to 1780 and the rule of Ottoman governor Ahmed Pasha El-Jazzar (hence the name of Hammam el-Pasha, meaning "Bathhouse of the Governor"). It was in use until the 1940s and remains in an excellent state of repair. The floors and walls are composed of panels of different coloured marble, and the fountain in the "cold room" (where patrons would relax after

bathing) retains most of its beautiful majolica decoration. A sound-and-light show introduces visitors to the history of Akko and the life of a typical bathhouse attendant.

③

Templars' Tunnel

🏛️ Entrances at Khan al-Umdan and the lighthouse
🕐 Summer: 8:30am–5pm daily; winter: 8:30am–4pm daily (closes 1 hr earlier Fri) 🌐 akko.org.il

The Knights Templar were a Crusader Catholic military order based at Jerusalem's Temple Mount (from which they got their name). After

AKKO'S BAHA'I GARDENS

Bahá'u'lláh (1817–92), founder of the Baha'i Faith, spent the last years of his life in the Mansion of Bahjí, 4 km (2 miles) northeast of Akko's Old City. He was buried nearby, and today his house is a shrine, surrounded by serene formal gardens (www.ganbahai.org.il).

EAT

Uri Buri

Chef Uri Jeramias, aka Uri Buri, is renowned for his minimalistic cooking style, which emphasizes the inherent flavours of his fresh seafood. Don't miss the wasabi sorbet.

🏠 HaHagana St
📞 (04) 955 2212
🕐 Noon–midnight daily

Ⓜ Ⓝ Ⓡ

El Marsa

Based on Galilean-style Arab recipes, chef Allaa Moussa's dishes come with a modern European twist. The dining room affords romantic views of the fishing port.

🏠 13 Nemal HaDayagim
🕐 Noon–midnight daily
🌐 elmarsa.rest.co.il.

Ⓜ Ⓝ Ⓡ

Saladin expelled them from the Temple area in 1187, they reestablished their headquarters in Akko and built this 350-m- (1,150-ft-) long tunnel to link their fortress (on the west side of the city) with the harbour (to the east).

---

④ ✏️

Mosque of El-Jazzar

🏠 El-Jazzar St 📞 (04) 991 3039 🕐 Daily 🕐 Closed during prayers

Akko lay semi-derelict for more than 400 years after its destruction in 1291. Its rebirth came with the rule of the emir Dahr el-Amr and his successor, Ahmed Pasha El-Jazzar ("the Butcher"), both of whom governed the city for the Ottomans in the second half of the 18th century. El-Jazzar,

in particular, was a prolific builder. Among his legacy is the Turkish-style mosque (built 1781) that bears his name and continues to dominate the old town skyline. Its courtyard contains recycled columns from the Roman ruins of Caesarea and, at the centre, a small, elegant fountain used for ritual ablutions. By the mosque are the sarcophagi of El-Jazzar and his son, while underneath are the remains of a Crusader church that El-Jazzar had transformed into a cistern to collect rainwater.

---

⑤ ✏️

Citadel (Underground Prisoners Museum)

🏠 Off Ha-Hagannah St 📞 (04) 991 1375 🕐 8:30am–4:30pm Sun–Thu

Built by the Ottomans as an administrative headquarters, the Citadel later served as a Turkish and then a British prison. During the Mandate era, members of pre-state Zionist militias were held here; nine of them were executed by hanging. Run by the Ministry of Defense (bring your passport to get in), the Underground Prisoners Museum inside the Citadel has exhibits on the prisoners, the cause they fought for, their life in prison and a daring prison break in 1947.

---

⑥ ✏️

Souk and Khans

🏠 Old City 🕐 Souk: 7am–6pm daily

The alleys of Akko's bustling, old-style souk (market) are where locals come to buy fresh fruit, vegetables and locally caught fish, as well as Middle Eastern spices and sweets. A stroll around the neighbouring streets will take you past several Ottoman-era khans (merchants' inns). Khan al-Umdan is easy to spot thanks to its clock tower, while Khan al-Shawarda now houses cafés and restaurants.

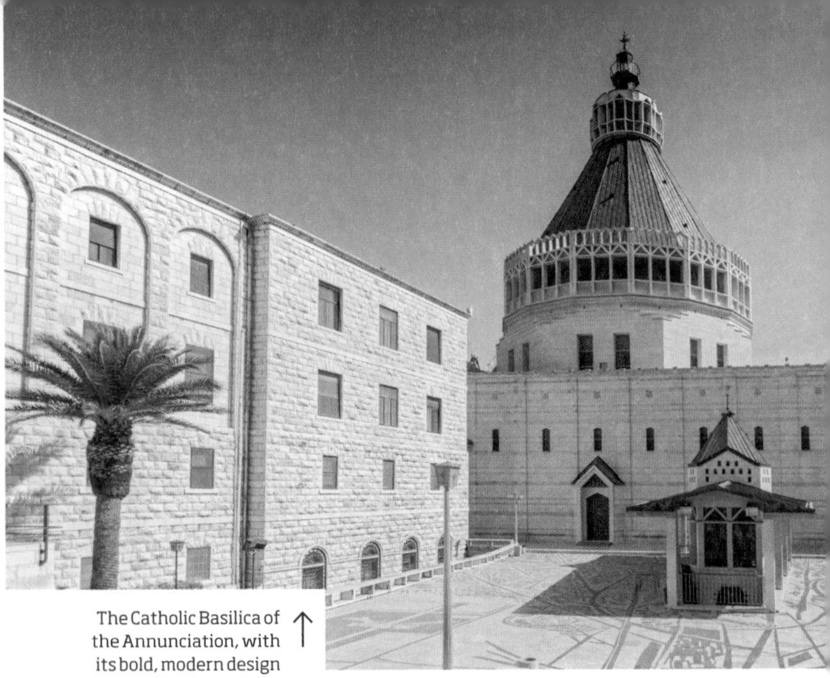

The Catholic Basilica of the Annunciation, with its bold, modern design ↑

4

NAZARETH

🅰B2 🏠102 km (63 miles) NE of Tel Aviv 🚌
ℹ Casa Nova St; www.nazarethinfo.org

Israel's largest Arab city is best known as the site of the Annunciation and Jesus's childhood home, and is today a popular pilgrimage site. Most of the major Christian churches are in the Old City, amid a maze of alleyways that also houses the bustling souk.

① Ancient Bathhouse

🏠Mary's Well Square
🕐9am-7pm Mon-Sat
🌐nazarethbathhouse.org

Discovered by chance in the 1990s, this ancient Roman bathhouse complex includes a *caldarium* (hot water bath), *hypocaust* (heating tunnels) and *praefurnarium* (furnace). It was most likely fed by water from nearby Mary's Well. Tours of the bathhouse end with light refreshments, and above the remains is the Cactus Gallery, a boutique that sells high-quality Palestinian crafts and artworks.

② Greek Orthodox Church of the Annunciation

🏠Church Square
🕐7am-noon & 1-5pm Mon-Sat

According to Greek Orthodox tradition, the spring beneath this church was the site of the Annunciation (the Angel Gabriel's announcement to the Virgin Mary that she would be the mother of Jesus Christ; Luke 1:27-35). The current stone structure dates from the 1760s but there has probably been a church on this site since the Byzantine era.

③ Basilica of the Annunciation

🏠Al-Bishara St
🕐Basilica: 8am-6pm daily; grotto: 5:45am-9pm daily 🌐nazareth-en.custodia.org

Catholic tradition places the Annunciation at the site of this vast, strikingly modern shrine, built atop what is believed to have been the childhood

④
White Mosque

🏠 Souk, Old City ⏰ 9am–about 7pm 🚫 Sun morning

The city's oldest mosque has a long tradition of working for interfaith coexistence. Built between 1785 and 1812, its white colour symbolizes purity, light and interreligious harmony. Visitors are welcome to drop by outside of prayer time; the office, across the courtyard from the street entrance, has head-coverings for women.

---

⑤
Souk

🏠 Market Square ⏰ 8am–about 3pm Mon–Sat

The Old City's souk (market) is the local residents' primary source of fresh vegetables and fruits, spices and cheap housewares. Its winding alleys are lined with tables piled high with produce, and also house craftsmen's shops and a few eateries – one sells inexpensive pita pizzas.

↑ Olives for sale in the souk, Nazareth's lively central market

⑥
Centre International Marie de Nazareth

🏠 15 Al-Bishara St ⏰ 9am–noon & 2:30–5pm Mon–Sat 🌐 cimdn.orgv

Opened in 2012, this complex was founded to foster reconciliation among Christian denominations. Visitors can tour the site's archaeological excavations, watch a multimedia show on Mary and Jesus, and enjoy the views from the rooftop gardens.

home of the Virgin Mary. Consecrated in 1969, the basilica is decorated with images associated with Mary and her life. In the grotto, on the lower level, excavations have revealed the remains of Byzantine- and Crusader-era churches.

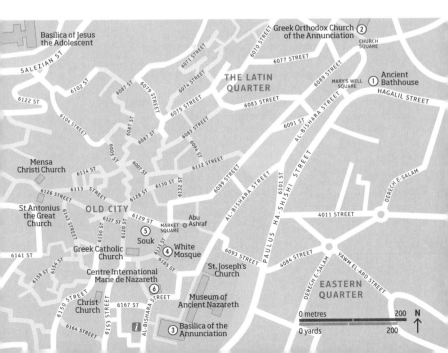

Sunrise over the serene waters of the Sea of Galilee ↑

5

SEA OF GALILEE

⚑ C1-2 ⚐ 135 km (85 miles) NE of Tel Aviv 🚌 From Tel Aviv and Jerusalem 🚢 For groups only from Tiberias to Kibbutz Ein Gev; (04) 665 8008 (phone for times) 🚤 Jesus Boats, Tiberias, www.jesusboats.com; Lido Kinneret Sailing Co, Tiberias, (072) 393 2108 ℹ 19 Habanim St, Tiberias; (04) 672 5666

Famous for its abundance of fish since biblical times, the Sea of Galilee is where Jesus did much of his preaching. Today, this beautiful area is a popular tourist centre, with fascinating historical and religious sites and a varied selection of outdoor activities.

① 🚶

Magdala

⚑ Midgal Junction, Route 90 ⏰ 8am-6pm daily 🌐 magdala.org

This fishing village was the hometown of Mary Magdalene, and was the most important settlement on the Sea of Galilee's western shore until Tiberias (p207) was established in the 1st century AD.

Excavations have uncovered a rare synagogue that was in use here during the time of Jesus, which was dated in part thanks to the discovery of a coin minted in 29 AD. Inside the synagogue, archaeologists unearthed the extraordinary Magdala Stone (a replica is on display here), decorated with depictions of the Second Temple in Jerusalem – among them a seven-branched menorah – that were likely carved by someone who had visited the Temple when it was still standing.

The excavation forms part of the site of a spiritual retreat centre, run by the Mexico-based Legion of Christ. Its centerpiece is Duc In Altum, a striking, modern hall of worship that houses six richly decorated chapels.

②

Tabgha

⚑ Route 87

Situated in the beautiful northwestern corner of the Sea of Galilee, a little way north of Tiberias, Tabgha is traditionally accepted as the place where the New Testament's Miracle of the Multiplication of the Loaves and Fish (Feeding of the 5,000) took place, in which Jesus fed the multitude with just five barley loaves and two small fish. Today, the site is home to two Catholic churches that commemorate this event. The Church of the Multiplication, run by German

12

Types of wood were used to make and repair the Ancient Galilee Boat.

Benedictines, is an austere sanctuary built in 1982 on the ruins (and mosaics) of a Byzantine-era church. A few hundred metres to the southeast is the lakeshore Church of the Primacy of St Peter, built in 1933. Run by Franciscans, it was also constructed on the site of a former Byzantine church.

③ 🖉

Ancient Galilee Boat

🏛 Yigal Allon Center, Kibbutz Ginosar ⏰ 8am–5pm daily (to 4pm Fri) 🌐 yigal-allon-centre.org.il

Discovered in 1986 on the bottom of the Sea of Galilee, encased in protective mud,

↑ The remains of the 1st-century AD Ancient Galilee Boat

this Roman-era boat has been radiocarbon dated to sometime between 50 BC and AD 70 so it may very well have plied the waters of the Sea of Galilee in the time of Jesus. Built – and later repaired – using a variety of different types of wood, the so-called "Jesus Boat" was made with mortice and tenon joints and had a shallow draft to enable inshore fishing.

Displays surrounding the vessel explain how the ancient, waterlogged wood – described by one observer as having the consistency of a coffee-soaked biscuit – was carefully preserved before it was placed on permanent display in 2000.

THE GALILEE IN JEWISH HISTORY

In the Hebrew Bible, the Galilee (Al-Jalīl in Arabic) is first mentioned by name in Joshua 20: 7. In the generations following King Solomon, the region was home to the Kingdom of Israel (Northern Kingdom), which was ultimately wiped off the map by the Assyrians around 720 BC. By the Second Temple period, however, Galilean Jewish life was flourishing. Following the destruction of the Temple and the Bar Kochba Revolt in the 1st and 2nd centuries AD respectively, the Galilee became the centre of Jewish scholarship and renewal. Dozens of synagogues from the Byzantine period, some adorned with lovely mosaics, have been found around the region.

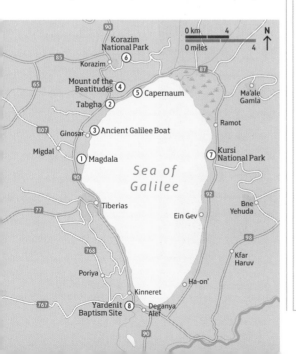

④
Mount of the Beatitudes

🚌 Off Route 90 📞 (04) 671 1223 🕐 8–11:45am & 2–4:45pm

Jesus's Sermon on the Mount (Matthew 5: 7), source of the Lord's Prayer and the eight Beatitudes ("Blessed are…"), is believed to have been delivered at this hillside site, 3.5 km (2 miles) north of Tabgha. A Byzantine church was constructed here in the 4th century, but today's Italian-style Franciscan chapel dates from the late 1930s. Built with financial support from Mussolini, it boasts charming gardens with excellent views.

GREAT VIEW
Sea Views

For an awe-inspiring view of the Sea of Galilee, with flowers and an Italianate chapel in the foreground and intensely blue water in the distance below, head to the Mount of the Beatitudes.

⑤
Capernaum

🚌 Route 87 📞 (04) 672 1059 🕐 8am–4:30pm daily

Capernaum, on the northern shoreline of the Sea of Galilee, was an important Roman town on the trade route between Damascus and Egypt. It was also a focal points of Christ's teachings in Galilee, and was home to a number of his Disciples, including Simon Peter. In Capernaum's fascinating archae-ological precinct, there are surviving houses from the period, as well as a church, built over the ruins of what is said to have been Simon Peter's house. There are also the remains of a synagogue that has been dated to the 4th century AD.

⑥
Korazim National Park

🚌 Route 8277 🕐 8am–5pm Sat–Thu, 8am–4pm Fri (closes 1 hr earlier in winter) 🌐 parks.org.il

According to Matthew 11: 20–24, Jesus was so unhappy with the people of Korazim (and with their counterparts in Bethsaida and Capernaum) for not changing their ways that he cursed them. These days, the excavated ruins of the once-wealthy hillside town include a beautiful synagogue constructed out of local black basalt around AD 400. It is decorated with a mix of Jewish and Hellenistic designs, including plants, geometric shapes, animals and even human forms.

⑦
Kursi National Park

🚌 Route 92 🕐 8am–5pm Sat–Thu, 8am–4pm Fri (closes 1 hr earlier in winter) 🌐 parks.org.il

Situated on the eastern shore of the Sea of Galilee, Kursi is believed to be where the Miracle of the Swine (Matthew 8: 28-32) took place, in which Jesus exorcised demons by casting them into a herd of pigs. Excavations have uncovered a mosaic-adorned church and an extensive Byzantine monastery complex from the mid-5th century AD.

←

Church of the Beatitudes, decorated with colourful floor mosaics *(inset)*

Christians undergoing a baptism ceremony at the Yardenit Baptismal Site ↑

Both were destroyed by the invading Sassanians (Persians) in 614 and again by the great earthquake of 749.

⑧
Yardenit Baptism Site

🏠 Kibbutz Kinneret
🕐 8am–5pm or 6pm Sat–Thu (to 4pm Fri) 🌐 yardenit.com

No one knows exactly where Jesus was baptized, but it could have been at Yardenit, situated about 700 m (2,300 ft) from where the Jordan River flows out of the Sea of Galilee. The hugely popular site has facilities for baptism, including changing rooms (US$2), as well as a restaurant and a shop selling Christian souvenirs. If you don't have the required white baptismal gown (under which you must wear a bathing suit), you can rent or purchase one. Around the site, Mark 1: 9-11 appears on Armenian tile panels in over 100 languages.

THE FIRST KIBBUTZ: DEGANIA ALEF

In 1910, a group of Zionist pioneers arrived in the southwest corner of the Sea of Galilee to farm land that had been purchased five years earlier. They were deeply committed socialists and sought to build a cooperative agricultural community based on socialist principles - although some of the traditional hallmarks of kibbutz life, such as the community dining hall and "children's houses", were a pragmatic response to practical challenges rather than an outgrowth of ideology. The early kibbutzniks believed in equality between men and women, but women nonetheless often ended up in the kitchen.

BEIT SHE'AN

◉ C2 🏛 Beit She'an 🚌 From Tiberiasa 🕐 8am–5pm Sat–Thu, 8am–4pm Fri (closes 1 hour earlier in winter) 🌐 parks.org.il

The best-preserved and most evocative Roman city in Israel, Beit She'an is renowned for its colonnaded thoroughfares and semicircular 7,000-seat theatre. Flattened by an earthquake in 749, some of the stones still lie in a jumble right where they fell.

First inhabited over 6,000 years ago, Beit She'an became an Egyptian administrative centre in the 15th century BC, a Canaanite town around the 12th century BC and then, an Israelite city. But it was as a Hellenistic and then Roman city known as Scythopolis that the city reached its zenith. A member of the Decapolis (a group of 10 Levantine city-states dependent on Rome), it was endowed with impressive public amenities, including temples, bathhouses and public toilets. During the Byzantine era, pagan structures were converted to Christian uses, though the city was also home to Jews and Samaritans. From mid-March to October, a multimedia pageant called She'an Nights is held after nightfall.

→ Visitors examining the remains of the public bathhouse

↓ The remarkably well-preserved ruins of this major Roman city

↑ The impressive Roman amphitheatre, once used for gladiatorial contests

HIDDEN GEM
Ancient Toilets

One of the more unusual structures at Beit She'an is the multiseat public toilet. It features 57 marble seats, under which ran an open sewer that connected to the city's drainage system.

↑ A ruined colonnade lining one of the city's ancient streets, which would once have housed an array of shops

Did You Know?

Beit She'an was home to between 30,000 and 40,000 Roman citizens.

EXPERIENCE MORE

7
Megiddo

🅰B2 🚗Route 66, 35 km (22 miles) SE of Haifa 📞(04) 659 0316 🚌From Haifa & Tiberias 🕐8am–5pm daily (to 4pm winter); closes 1 hour earlier on Fri

This ancient town at the head of the Jezreel Valley was the scene of so many battles that the Book of Revelation in the New Testament says that this is where the final battle between Good and Evil will take place at the end of the world.

The settlement controlled the main communication routes between the East and the Mediterranean, and in the 3rd millennium BC it was already a fortified city. In 1468 BC, its Canaanite fortress was destroyed by the troops of the Egyptian pharaoh Thutmose III and it became an Egyptian stronghold. Megiddo was subsequently conquered and again fortified, possibly by Solomon, and in the 8th century BC it came under Assyrian rule, after which it fell slowly into decline. Extensive excavation of the spectacular mound (or "tel") has revealed 20 successive settlements. Visible remains include defensive walls, a temple, a huge grain silo and the foundations of many buildings. On the eastern side of the "tel" is an old reservoir, with a tunnel that visitors can walk through, leading to a spring outside the city wall.

In 2005, the site joined UNESCO's World Heritage list, reflecting its historical importance and powerful influence on later civilizations.

Did You Know?

The Biblical name "Armageddon" derives from "Har Megedon", or mountain of Megiddo.

8
Safed

🅰C2 🚗120 km (75 miles) NE from Tel Aviv 🚌 ℹ17 Elkabetz St; www.safed.co.il

Safed (Tzfat) has been the foremost centre of Kabbalah (Jewish mysticism) ever since Jews fleeing the Spanish Inquisition found refuge here. One of Judaism's "four holy cities" (with Jerusalem, Tiberias and Hebron), it is home to several historic synagogues. These include the Ashkenazi Ari Synagogue, on the site where the famed Kabbalist Isaac Luria (the Ari; 1534–72) is said to have welcomed the Sabbath; and the Caro Synagogue, named for Joseph Caro (1488–1575), who wrote the Shulchan Aruch (the most important compendium of Jewish law), to whom an angel is said to have revealed the secrets of Kabbalah here. Many renowned Kabbalists and scholars are buried in a Jewish cemetery downhill from the Synagogue Quarter.

Galleries selling ritual objects and Jewish-themed art line Alkabetz Street and its continuation, Beit Yosef Street (Yosef Caro Street). The Artists' Quarter, an Arab neighbourhood before 1948, is home to many artists whose studios can be visited.

Above the centre of town, remnants of the biggest Crusader fortress in the Middle East form part of Citadel Park, which is especially peaceful on Shabbat and Jewish holidays.

→ One of the galleries selling Jewish art in the town of Safed

↑ The ruins of the Nimrod Fortress, in a commanding position on the Golan Heights

⑨ Golan Heights

🗺 C2 🚗 135 km (85 miles) NE of Tel Aviv 🚌 To Katsrin ℹ (04) 685 0208

The strategic Golan plateau was captured by Israel from Syria in the 1967 war. Except during the 1973 Yom Kippur War *(p54)*, the area – which was annexed unilaterally by Israel in 1981 – has since been remarkably quiet.

Streams that drain into the Jordan River offer great hiking trails; some of the best are in the Yehudiya Nature Reserve. Family-friendly Banias Nature Reserve has waterfalls, rich vegetation and a Roman-era palace, while Gamla Nature Reserve houses the ruins of a hilltop Jewish village besieged by the Romans. The area's largest Israeli settlement, Katzrin, offers accommodation, supermarkets, restaurants, a brew-pub and wineries. It is also home to the superb Golan Archaeological Museum and Ancient Katzrin Park, where excavations have uncovered a Byzantine-era Jewish village with an impressive basalt synagogue.

Further north, under the towering slopes of Mount Hermon, is the Druze town of Majdal Shams and the mighty Nimrod Fortress, a ridgetop citadel. It was built by the Muslims in the 13th century to defend the road to Damascus from the Crusaders.

⑩ Tiberias

🗺 C2 🚗 110 km (70 miles) NE of Tel Aviv 🚌 ℹ Archaeological Garden, Rehov ha-Banim; (04) 672 5666

On the Sea of Galilee's western shore, Tiberias was founded around AD 20. A major centre of Jewish scholarship in the 2nd and 3rd centuries AD, elements of written Hebrew were devised here over a millennium ago. It has remained holy to Jews and today, Jewish pilgrims come to visit the tombs of famous scholars such as the Rambam (Maimonides), Yohanan ben Zakai, Rabbi Meir Ba'al HaNess and, up the hill, Rabbi Akiva. South of the centre, Hamat Tveriya National Park has a 4th-century synagogue with a beautiful Zodiac wheel mosaic.

Christian pilgrims are drawn to Tiberias by St Peter's Church and the Monastery of the Apostles (Greek Orthodox). Both are on the lakefront.

EAT

Magdalena
Superior Galilean-style Arab cuisine in one of Israel's most talked-about restaurants.

🗺 C1 🚗 Migdal Junction, Rte 90 🕐 Noon-5pm & 7-11pm daily 🌐 magdalena.co.il

🪙🪙🪙

Baladna
Excellent Galilean Arab cuisine with vegan and pork options, plus a good selection of beer.

🗺 C1 🚗 Jish 📞 (54) 768 7773 🕐 3pm-2am Wed-Sat, 3-11pm Tue & Sun

🪙🪙🪙

Mis'edet HaArazim
Informal place widely known for delicious Lebanese cuisine.

🗺 C1 🚗 Just off Rte 89, Jish 🕐 10am-10pm daily 🌐 2eat.co.il/haarazim

🪙🪙🪙

500 million

Birds migrate through Israel and the Palestine Territories twice a year.

⑪ Hula Nature Reserve

▲C1 🏠Hula Valley, Galilee Panhandle
🚌541, 840 🕒8am-5pm daily (to 4pm Fri); closes 1 hour earlier in winter
🌐parks.org.il

The wetlands of the Hula Valley were drained in the 1950s to fight malaria and create farmland, resulting in unintended ecological consequences. These have been mitigated by the 1964 founding of this nature reserve – Israel's first – and, in more recent decades, by swamp and lake restoration. Today, birds that are migrating between Europe and Africa have a safe spot to rest and feed, attracting bird-watchers from around the world. Trails, a floating bridge and a lookout tower provide observation points to view birds, water buffaloes, fallow deer and otters. Further north, Agamon HaHula is a great place to see flocks of cranes and storks.

⑫ Belvoir Castle

▲C2 🏠Off Route 90, 27 km (17 miles) S of Tiberias
📞(04) 658 1766 🚌To Beth Shean, then taxi
🕒8am-5pm daily (to 4pm Fri); closes 1 hour earlier in winter

This ruined Crusader fortress offers incomparable views of the Jordan Valley. Surrounded by two huge walls, it was built by the Knights Hospitallers in 1168, and besieged many times by Saladin. It capitulated only in 1189 after a year-long siege, with the Muslim leader sparing both the fortress and its defenders in recognition of their great courage. Belvoir was destroyed by troops from Damascus in the 13th century.

⑬ Beit Alpha

▲C2 🏠Off Route 71, 11 km (7 miles) W of Beth Shean
📞(04) 653 2004 🚌 🕒8am-5pm daily (to 4pm Fri); closes 1 hour earlier in winter

The remnants of this 6th-century synagogue were found by chance in 1928 by people from the nearby Hefzi-Bah kibbutz. The ruined walls give an idea of the original building, but the main interest is the magnificent mosaic floor. It depicts the Ark of the Covenant, with cherubs, lions and religious symbols, while the central patterns adopt Roman themes and imagery. The lower part tells the story of Abraham and the sacrifice of his son Isaac.

←
The Hula Nature Reserve, rich in birdlife and a magnet for bird-watchers worldwide

spy ring based here during World War I. HaMeyasdim Street, lined with 19th-century stone buildings, has boutiques, artists' studios and cafés.

14
Zichron Ya'akov

🅰B2 📍30 km (19 miles) S of Haifa 🚌202 (Haifa)

The town of Zichron Ya'akov was established by Jews from Romania in the 1880s, under the patronage of Baron Edmond James de Rothschild. Carmel Winery was founded there in 1882 and is still producing, with tours available. In the town centre, the First Aliya Museum and the NILI Museum recount Zichron's history; the latter focuses on a pro-British

15
Mount Tabor

🅰C2 📍92 km (57 miles) NE of Tel Aviv

Rising above the hills between the Sea of Galilee and Jezreel Valley, perfectly symmetrical Mount Tabor (400 m/1,312 ft) has long been an important Christian pilgrimage site for its association with Jesus's Transfiguration. It also appears in the Old Testament as the place, according to Judges (chapters 4 and 5), where the Prophet Deborah defeated the Canaanite commander Sisera. At the summit, reached along a narrow road with 16 dizzying curves, is a monastery and the majestic Church of the Transfiguration, built in 1924.

16 🚴 Ⓜ 🏛
Dan Nature Reserve

🅰C1 📍Rte 99 🚌36, 58
🕐8am–5pm daily (to 4pm Fri); closes 1 hour earlier in winter 🌐parks.org.il

Fed by a gushing spring that feeds the Dan River, a tributary of the Jordan, this lush area can be explored on foot via three trails.

The excavated ruins of the ancient city of Dan, mentioned repeatedly in the Old Testament, are nearby. In 1979, archaeologists found a mud-brick Canaanite gate (18th century BC) – the oldest of its kind in the world – and a stone gate from the Israelite period (9th century BC). The basalt Tel Dan Stele, found here in fragments in 1993–4, includes the earliest known non-biblical mention of David as the founder of the Israelite dynasty; it can be seen at the Israel Museum in Jerusalem (p156).

STAY

Lishansky Since 1936
Bauhaus-style hotel built by the family of an (in)famous British spy.

🅰C1 📍42 HaRishonim St, Metula 📞(04) 699 7184

Ⓝ Ⓝ Ⓝ

Villa Tehila
Atmospheric boutique hotel in four late 19th-century houses.

🅰C1 📍7 HaHalutzim St, Old Town, Rosh Pina 🌐villa-tehila.co.il

Ⓝ Ⓝ Ⓝ

Safed Inn
Sitting atop Mount Canaan this is a friendly, quirky place.

🅰C1 📍HaGdud HaShlishi St, corner of Merom Kna'an St, Safed 🌐safedinn.com

Ⓝ Ⓝ Ⓝ

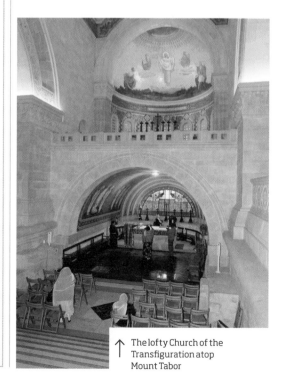

↑ The lofty Church of the Transfiguration atop Mount Tabor

← A group of young people enjoying the hot springs at Hammat Gader

3rd-century Jews, unable to access Jerusalem's Mount of Olives, to choose this as their final resting place. Carved into the limestone hills, many of the Jewish catacombs, and the sarcophagi inside them, are beautifully decorated. They bear inscriptions in Greek, Aramaic, Hebrew and Palmyrene, reflecting the encounter and exchange of influences that took place between the Jewish and Graeco-Roman civilizations.

17

Hamat Gader

🅰C2 🄰105 km (65 miles) NE of Tel Aviv 🚌 🕒8:30am–5pm daily (to 10pm Thu & Fri) 🌐hamat-gader.com

The Romans loved bathing in these hot springs on the northern bank of the Yarmuk River, which today forms the border between Israel and Jordan. All sorts of Israelis – particularly those who have immigrated from the former

USSR – flock here, especially on chilly winter days. In addition to soaking away stress, aches and pains in soothing hot mineral water, both adults and children can swim and play in a water park. At the far end of the resort is a crocodile farm, the only one of its kind in the Middle East, and there are ruins of a Roman bath and amphitheatre that can be explored.

18

Beit She'arim

🅰B2 🄰Off Rte 75, 6 km (4 miles) E of Kiryat Tiv'on 🚌301, 826 🕒Hours vary by season, check website 🌐parks.org.il

A UNESCO World Heritage Site since 2015, Beit She'arim served as a Jewish political and religious centre and as a seat of Torah study in the generations after the catastrophic Bar Kochba Revolt against the Romans (AD 132–135). The Sanhedrin (supreme council of rabbis) was based here for a while, and Rabbi Yehuda HaNasi, the main editor of the Mishnah, lived and was buried here, prompting other 2nd- to

19

Tzipori

🅰B2 🄰Off Route 79, Lower Galilee 🚌 🕒8am–5pm daily (to 4pm Fri); closes 1 hour earlier in winter 🌐parks.org.il

Well-off Tzipori (Zippori), also known as Sepphoris, sat out the Great Jewish Revolt, which ended in the destruction of the Second Temple (AD 70), as well as the Bar Kochba Revolt (AD 132–35), so it was

TOP 5 GALILEE SITES ASSOCIATED WITH JESUS

Nazareth
Much of his youth spent here; also believed site of Annunciation (p198).

Kafr Cana
Near Nazareth, this is where water was changed to wine.

Mount of the Beatitudes
Site of the Sermon on the Mount (p202).

Sea of Galilee
Preached at Capernaum and Kursi (p202).

Mount Tabor
Associated with the Transfiguration (p209).

→ Pale rocks contrasting with the blue Mediterranean Sea at Rosh HaNikra well-placed to become a centre of Jewish learning and spirituality after the devastation of Judea. Today, the site is best known for its Roman and Byzantine-era mosaics, including a breathtaking portrait of a woman nicknamed "the Mona Lisa of the Galilee", and an extraordinary, late-Byzantine-era synagogue floor depicting both a Zodiac wheel and the Ark of the Covenant. Visitors can walk through an ancient water reservoir, 260 m (850 ft) long, carved deep into the rock.

20 ⊘ 🖵

Rosh HaNikra

🅐B1 🚪Northern terminus of Rte 4, Western Galilee 🚌31 ⏱9am–5pm daily (summer: to 6pm Sat–Thu) 🌐rosh-hanikra.com

Just down the cliff (by cable car) from the UN "Blue Line" border between Israel and Lebanon, the wave-battered sea grottoes of Rosh HaNikra radiate every shade of blue, from turquoise to ultramarine, and the scene is given added brilliance by the bright white of the surrounding limestone. A path leads through the cave network, past heaving seas, affording views out to the Mediterranean.

From 1942 to 1948, the rail line from the Suez Canal to Beirut ran by here. A railway tunnel excavated during World War II by British army units from South Africa and New Zealand is now used to screen videos about its history.

21 ⊘ Ⓜ

Upper Galilee Museum of Prehistory

🅐C1 🚪Kibbutz Ma'ayan Baruch 🚌36 ⏱10am–1:30pm daily; longer hours Aug and during Passover 🌐ugmp.co.il

About 12,000 years ago in the Hula Valley, a Natufian-era woman was buried along with her dog. Today, their skeletons – the earliest archaeological evidence ever found of the domestication of canines – can be seen in this superb little museum, which also features an extraordinary collection of hand axes and other tools made by our ancestors of up to 780,000 years ago.

All the artifacts that are on display here were found in the Upper Galilee region. Engaging and informative, the museum provides a captivating insight into prehistoric life.

PAGAN MOTIFS

The Zodiac Wheel, with the sun god Helios in the middle, is instantly recognizable from Roman paganism – so why has it been found depicted on 4th- to 6th-century mosaic floors in synagogues at places such as Beit Alpha and Tzippori? It would seem that even as Jews strove to preserve their faith and civilization by building beautiful houses of worship, their intense encounter with Graeco-Roman beliefs brought about the adoption, and, most likely, the redefinition, of certain pagan symbols, perhaps by groups that tended towards a Hellenized, mystical form of Judaism. It's worth noting that on the synagogue floors, archetypical Jewish symbols, such as Menorahs, are also depicted nearby. They are often accompanied by inscriptions in Aramaic and/or Hebrew (as well as Greek).

Crystallized salt on the surface of the Dead Sea

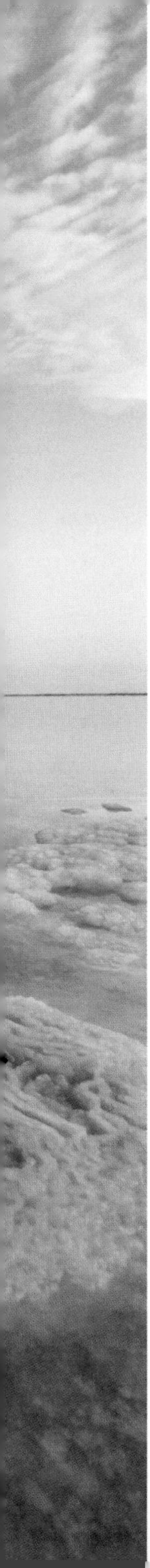

DEAD SEA AND NEGEV DESERT

The chemical properties of the Dead Sea have been utilized since Ancient Egyptian times, when the natural asphalt that rises to its surface was used to embalm mummies. There was little human settlement in this inhospitable area, but in the 1st century BC, Herod the Great built Masada, a mountaintop fortress that in AD 73 was the scene of a desperate last stand by anti-Roman Jewish rebels. Around the same time, a dissenting Jewish sect – possibly the Essenes – found refuge at Qumran, leaving behind a collection of Hebrew manuscripts. Discovered in 1947, they are now known as the Dead Sea Scrolls.

The mountainous, rocky Negev Desert covers about 60 per cent of Israel. The Egyptians began mining copper at Timna around 1400 BC, and according to the Bible both Abraham and Isaac dug wells at Be'er Sheva, which by the 10th century BC was a thriving Israelite city. In the 3rd century BC, the Nabateans established a trans-Negev Incense Route to bring frankincense and myrrh from southern Arabia to the Mediterranean, but their control of the region was ended by the Romans in the 1st century AD. Left largely uninhabited for centuries, the Negev was developed in the 20th century with the establishment of desert *kibbutzim* (collective settlements). Today, the population of the region includes about 250,000 Bedouin Arabs, some of whom still live in desert encampments.

DEAD SEA AND NEGEV DESERT

Must Sees
1 Masada
2 Dead Sea
3 Eilat

Experience More
4 Tel Be'er Sheva
5 Avdat National Park
6 Sde Boker
7 Mitzpe Ramon
8 Makhtesh Ramon
9 Hai Bar Yotvata Wildlife Reserve
10 Kibbutz Lotan
11 Timna Park

*Mediterranean
Sea*

Ashdod

Ashklelon

Sderot

Gaza

GAZA

Netivot

Re'im

Khan Yunis

Ofakim

Rafah

Kerem
Shalom'

Tse'elim

El Kharuba

Bir el 'Abd

El Mazar

Nitzana

Abu 'Aweigila

El Quseima

Bir Gifgafa

Bir Hasana

EGYPT

Bir el Thamada

Nakhl

DEAD SEA AND
NEGEV DESERT

El Thamad

*Gebel
el Tih*

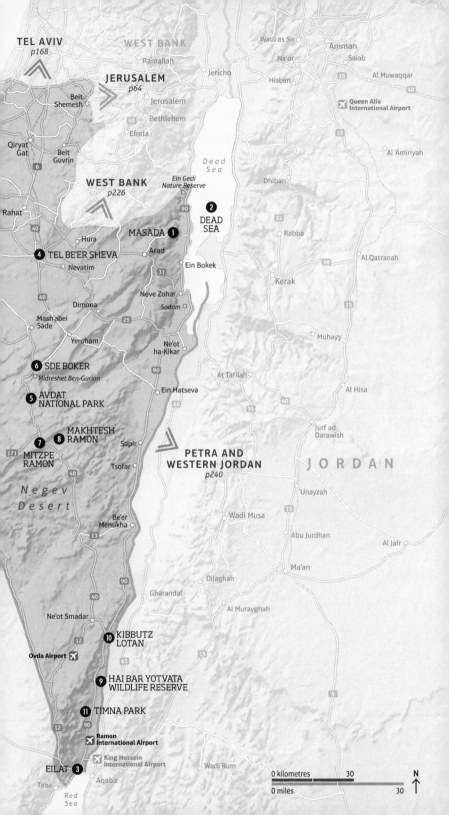

TEL AVIV
p168

WEST BANK

Wadi as Sir
Na'ur   Amman
                    Saiab

JERUSALEM
p64

Ramallah
          Jericho
Jerusalem   Hisban   Al Muwaqqar

Beit
Shemesh   Bethlehem   ✈ Queen Alia
            Efrata   International Airport

Qiryat
Gat   Al 'Amiriyah

Beit   Dead
Guvrin   Sea   Dhiban

WEST BANK   Ein Gedi
p226   Nature Reserve
                                              Rabba
Rahat   ❷
                        MASADA ❶ DEAD
                                 SEA
Hura   Arad   Kerak
                    Ein Bokek
❹ TEL BE'ER SHEVA
    Nevatim   Al Qatranah

                    Neve Zohar
Dimona   Sodom   Muhayy

Mash'abei
Sade
    Yeroham   Ne'ot
                    ha-Kikar
❻ SDE BOKER   At Tafilah   Al Hisa
  Midreshet Ben-Gurion

❺ AVDAT   Ein Hatseva
  NATIONAL PARK

                                              Jurf ad
    MAKHTESH   Darawish
❼ ❽ RAMON   Sapir   PETRA AND   J O R D A N
MITZPE   WESTERN JORDAN
RAMON   Tsofar   *p240*

Negev   'Unayzah
Desert
                                 Wadi Musa
            Be'er
            Menukha   Abu Jurdhan   Al Jafr

                                 Ma'an
                    Dilaghah
❿ KIBBUTZ   Gharandal
  LOTAN
Ne'ot Smadar   Al Murayghah
Ovda Airport ✈

❾ HAI BAR YOTVATA
  WILDLIFE RESERVE

⓫ TIMNA PARK

            ✈ Ramon
              International Airport
            ✈ King Hussein
              International Airport   Wadi Rum   0 kilometres   30
EILAT ❸
Taba   Aqaba   0 miles   30
  *Red
  Sea*   N ↑

1

MASADA

C4 ❑ Off Route 90, 18 km (11 miles) S of Ein Gedi 🚌 From Jerusalem or Eilat
🕐 8am–5pm Sat–Thu, 8am–4pm Fri & hols (closes 1 hr earlier in winter)

Perched atop a plateau that towers over the western edge of the Dead Sea, this isolated fortress is where, in the 1st century AD, 967 Jewish rebels chose mass suicide over submission to Rome. Today a World Heritage Site and a national park, the site contains some fascinating ruins and offers stunning views that stretch all the way to the Jordanian mountains.

Masada was fortified as early as the 1st or 2nd century BC and then enlarged and reinforced by Herod the Great, who added two luxurious palace complexes. On Herod's death the fortress passed into Roman hands, but it was captured in AD 66 during the First Revolt by Jews of the Zealot sect. After the Romans had crushed the rebels in Jerusalem, Masada remained the last Jewish stronghold. It was under Roman siege for over two years before the walls were breached in AD 73.

After the Romans left, the site appears to have been deserted for 200 years, until, in the 5th century, Christian hermits established a monastery here. The remains of a Byzantine church can still be seen.

↑ The Columbarium, which once housed funerary urns

8

Roman military camps were positioned around the base of Masada.

The cable car runs daily; otherwise it is a strenuous 45- to 60-minute climb.

Masada's Calidarium (hot baths) are one of the best-preserved parts of the fortress.

Snake Path

Upper terrace

Middle terrace

Lower terrace

Part of the Northern Palace complex, the Hanging Palace was Herod's private residence.

The Water Gate is at the head of a narrow, winding path to the reservoirs below.

→ The ruins of the ancient mountaintop fortress of Masada

This synagogue is thought to be the oldest in the world.

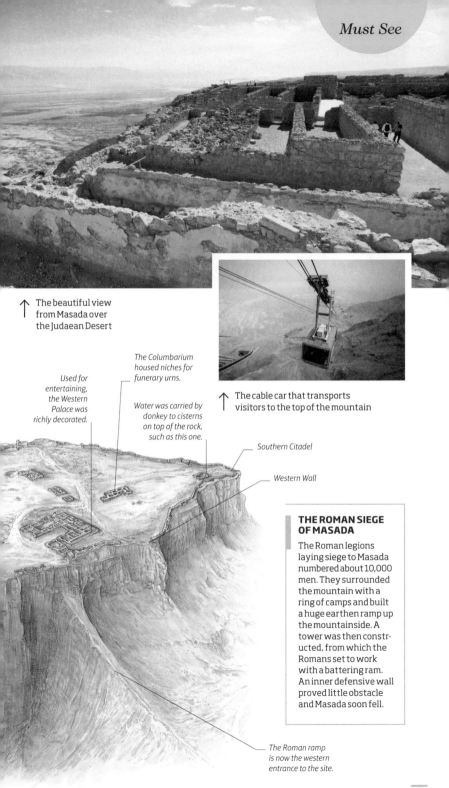

↑ The beautiful view from Masada over the Judaean Desert

The Columbarium housed niches for funerary urns.

Used for entertaining, the Western Palace was richly decorated.

Water was carried by donkey to cisterns on top of the rock, such as this one.

↑ The cable car that transports visitors to the top of the mountain

Southern Citadel

Western Wall

THE ROMAN SIEGE OF MASADA

The Roman legions laying siege to Masada numbered about 10,000 men. They surrounded the mountain with a ring of camps and built a huge earthen ramp up the mountainside. A tower was then constructed, from which the Romans set to work with a battering ram. An inner defensive wall proved little obstacle and Masada soon fell.

The Roman ramp is now the western entrance to the site.

Did You Know?

The salinity of the Dead Sea is around ten times that of ocean water.

②

DEAD SEA

⚑ C3-5 🚌 From Jerusalem

The Dead Sea (which is actually a lake, not a sea) is 76 km (47 miles) from north to south and less than 16 km (10 miles) across. At 411 m (1,348 ft) below sea level, it is also the lowest point on earth. The water is so mineral-laden that it is around 26 per cent solid. The therapeutic qualities of the water, its minerals and its mud have been touted since ancient times, and spas are dotted along its shores.

① ✎

Qumran

⚑ Route 90, 20 km (12 miles) S of Jericho ☎ (02) 994 2235 🕐 8am-5pm Sat-Thu, 8am-4pm Fri (closes 1 hr earlier in winter)

Qumran is known chiefly as the place where the Dead Sea Scrolls were discovered. From 150 BC to AD 68, this remote site was the home of a radically ascetic and reclusive community, often identified with the Essenes. According to their school of thought, the arrival of the Jewish Messiah was imminent, and they prepared for this event with fasting and purification through ritual ablutions. These activities were rudely brought to a halt through conflict with the Romans.

The Essenes largely vanished from history until 1947, when a Bedouin shepherd boy who was looking for a lost goat happened upon a cave full of jars. These jars were found to contain a precious hoard of 190 linen-wrapped scrolls that had been preserved for 2,000 years. Following much study by academics, some of the scrolls are now on view in a purpose-built hall at the Israel Museum (p156).

Visitors to Qumran watch a short film on the Essenes, with audio in eight languages, and view a small exhibition on the community before being directed to the archaeological site at the foot of the cliffs. The trail through the site is wheelchair accessible and has special signage for the visually impaired. From the site you can see the caves above where the scrolls were found.

②

Ein Bokek

⚑ Route 90, 116 km (72 miles) SE of Jerusalem

The largest tourism zone on the Israeli shore of the Dead Sea, Ein Bokek's glittering coastal strip boasts several dozen luxurious hotels, a number of restaurants (most hotel guests take half-board), shops, and a glorious, sandy public beach, completely redeveloped in 2017. Under Israeli law, all waterfront land is public so the beach promenade and its pergolas, showers, changing rooms and bathrooms are all free. Lifeguards are on duty during the day.

←

Salt deposits in the Dead Sea, with the resort of Ein Bokek in the background

③ 🏅

Ein Gedi Nature Reserve

🏛 Highway 90, Dead Sea
📞 (08) 658 4285 ⏰ 8am-5pm Sat-Thu, 8am-4pm Fri (closes 1 hr earlier in winter)

Ein Gedi is famous as a lush oasis in an otherwise barren landscape. Several springs provide plentiful water to a luxuriant mix of tropical and desert vegetation. The site is mentioned in the Bible for its beauty (Song of Songs 1:14) and as a refuge of David who was fleeing from King Saul (I Samuel 24).

Protected as Ein Gedi Nature Reserve, the oasis is a haven for desert wildlife such as ibexes and rock hyraxes, which look like large rodents, while the more remote areas are the abode of the desert leopard. Two gorges are at the core of the reserve; these are crossed by a network of paths. The shortest walking tour takes about an hour and ends at the spectacular Shulamit Falls. Near the reserve's entrance are the ruins of a 5th-century-BC synagogue with mosaics and inscriptions in Hebrew and Aramaic.

↑ Cooling down under a waterfall in Ein Gedi Nature Reserve

④

Sodom

🏛 Route 90, 130 km (81 miles) SE of Jerusalem

Biblical tradition holds that the city of Sodom lay on the southern shore of the Dead Sea (Genesis 19). Its sinful inhabitants, along with those of neighbouring Gomorrah, angered God, and he destroyed the cities with "brimstone and fire". Archaeologists now favour Bab ed-Dhra in Jordan as the likely site, but the name Sodom remains attached to a spot on the Israeli side of the Dead Sea. There is nothing to visit, but nearby are the two spas of Ein Bokek and Neve Zohar, famous for their therapeutic centres, and a public beach with freshwater showers. Inland and 9 km (6 miles) south of Neve Zohar is Mount Sodom, a mountain composed largely of rock salt, boasting incomparable views of the Dead Sea and the Moab mountains in Jordan.

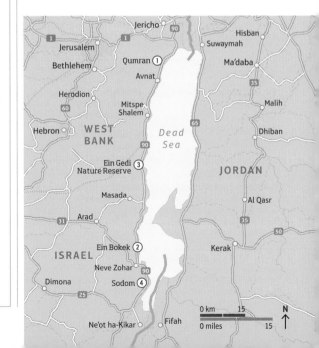

③

EILAT

🅰B7 🚗320 km (200 miles) S of Jerusalem ✈🚌
ℹBeit ha-Gesher St; (08) 630 9111

Lying at the end of the Gulf of Aqaba, on a stretch of Israel's 12-km- (7-mile-) long southern coast, Eilat is the only Israeli town on the Red Sea. This small stretch of coastline was ceded to Israel with the United Nations partition of Palestine in 1947, and Eilat has since developed rapidly, both as a port and as a popular holiday resort. Today, it is filled with hotels and tourist villages, and is a centre for diving and trips into the desert.

①

North Beach

Lined with the city's most luxurious hotels and numerous buzzing cafés and restaurants, North Beach Promenade is the premier place in Eilat to strut your stuff and people-watch. The narrow, coarse-sand beach is well geared to lounging, with free public showers, changing booths and bathrooms, while the more energetic can try an array of water sports such as banana boats, flyboards, jet skis and glass-bottom boat rides. For more places to eat and drink and less-pricey hotels, walk inland along the lagoon.

②

Underwater Observatory Marine Park

🅰Coral Beach 📞(08) 636 4200 🕐9am–4pm daily
🌐coralworld.co.il/en

The large Coral World Underwater Observatory is an oceanographic complex where you can get a close-up view of the marvellous marine life here. It contains 25 tanks with more than 500 species of fish, sponges, corals and invertebrates. The most interesting displays are those with the larger creatures such as sharks and sea turtles. The main spectacle, though, is at the underwater observatory itself, which is 6 m (20 ft) under water and gives a spectacular live view of the local marine life through its large glass windows.

③

Coral Beach Nature Reserve

🅰Coral Beach 🕐9am–6pm Sat–Thu, 9am–5pm Fri (closes 1 hr earlier in winter) 🌐parks.org.il

This small marine nature reserve protects some of Eilat's most robust and vibrant coral reefs. The best way to experience the Red Sea's undersea diversity is

---

💬 INSIDER TIP
Glass-Bottom Boat Trip

If you want to visit the depths of the reef without diving, you can take a trip on Coral 2000. Run by the Underwater Observatory Marine Park, this glass-bottom boat offers a dry tour of the corals from 1.5 m (5 ft) below sea level.

← Eilat's stunning coastline, with its golden sands and brilliant azure sea

observe the marine life from above. Near the shore are shallow wading pools in which children can play.

④ 🤿

Dolphin Reef

🏠 Southern Beach 📞 (08) 630 0111 🕐 9am–5pm daily 🌐 dolphinreef.co.il

This privately run stretch of Red Sea beachfront, 4 km (2 miles) southwest of the city centre, offers a quiet, verdant place to sunbathe, swim and relax, but the main attraction here is a group of semi-wild bottlenose dolphins. Curious creatures, they often approach snorkellers to check them out, offering an opportunity for anyone over age ten to see these highly intelligent sea mammals up close (touching is not allowed).

Did You Know?

Eilat is a popular shopping destination, as the city is exempt from VAT.

to rent snorkelling gear and plunge in with the fish, but if you'd rather stay dry it is also possible to walk out over the reefs on footbridges and

> ▎**DIVING AND SNORKELLING IN EILAT**
>
> The Red Sea is home to some of the world's most astonishing coral reefs that, so far, are unaffected by climate change-caused bleaching. South of Eilat's city centre, a dozen world-class dive centres offer PADI scuba courses and rent out diving equipment. The best spot for snorkeling is the Coral Reef Nature Reserve (masks are available for rent).

⑤ 🦅

International Birding and Research Center Eilat

🏠 Kibbutz Eilot, 2 km (1 mile) N of Eilat 🕐 8am–4pm daily (mid-Feb–mid-May & mid-Aug–Nov: from 6am) 🌐 eilatbirds.com

The salt marshes north of Eilat are the feeding grounds of scores of migratory birds that travel between Africa and Eurasia every spring and autumn. The last feeding stop before crossing the Saharan Desert, this important habitat has been greatly reduced as a result of human development. The International Birdwatching Centre, which seeks to protect what is left of the salt marshes, has an interpretation centre and organizes guided bird-watching tours. In season, the skies are filled with thousands of storks, herons and flamingos. The area is also home to eagles, hawks and buzzards.

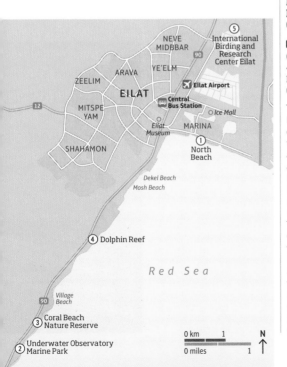

0 km   1

0 miles   1

N ↑

←
The evocative ruins at
Tel Be'er Sheva, site of the
eponymous Biblical city

modern attempts to replicate
their irrigation technology,
can be seen around Avdat.

Sde Boker

🅰B5 🏠Negev Highlands
🚌60, 64 🌐bgh.org.il

David Ben-Gurion (1886–1973),
Israel's first prime minister, was
so inspired by the socialist
pioneers he met in 1952 at
Kibbutz Sde Boker, 50 km
(30 miles) south of Be'er Sheva,
that he chose to live there for
much of the last 20 years of his
life. He was laid to rest 6 km
(4 miles) to the south in the
grounds of Midreshet Ben-
Gurion, a regional academic
and research centre with a field
school (guesthouse), bed-and-
breakfasts, a supermarket and
restaurants. Ben-Gurion is
buried next to his wife Paula
at the edge of a cliff with

EXPERIENCE MORE

Tel Be'er Sheva

🅰B4 🏠6 km (4 miles)
NE of Be'er Sheva 🚌10, 15
🕐8am–5pm daily (to 4pm
Fri); closes 1 hour earlier in
winter 🌐parks.org.il

This UNESCO World Heritage
Site, rising from the desert
5 km (3 miles) east of central
Be'er Sheva, has been identified by archaeologists as
the biblical city of Be'er Sheva.
Excavations have shown that it
was an important walled city
during the Israelite (Iron Age)
period of the 9th and 8th
centuries BC. Water was
supplied year-round by a well
69 m (226 ft) deep and by an
underground reservoir. A First
Temple-period sacrificial altar
with "horns" at each corner, the
first ever found in Israel, was
discovered here in pieces; the
original is now in the Israel
Museum in Jerusalem (p156).

During World War I, in 1917,
Anzac units captured the site
during the British campaign to
take Be'er Sheva from the Turks.

Avdat National Park

🅰B5 🏠Negev Highlands
🚌 🕐8am–5pm daily (4pm
Fri); closes 1 hour earlier in
winter 🌐parks.org.il

Between the 3rd century BC
and the 2nd century AD, the
desert-dwelling Nabateans
controlled the lucrative
"Spice Route" that brought
frankincense and myrrh from
Yemen and Oman to the
Mediterranean world of the
Romans. One of four ancient
Nabatean cities in the Negev,
Avdat's ruins are remarkably
well preserved. The city's
prosperity peaked during the
Byzantine period and so, in
addition to a Roman burial
cave and a bathhouse, the
site is graced by two churches.
Thanks to a sophisticated
system for storing the raging
waters of rare desert down-
pours, the Nabateans were
able to sustain vineyards and
orchards in the wadis around
their cities. Remnants of their
dams and channels, and

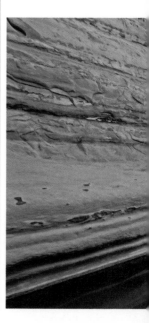

magnificent views of **En Avdat National Park**, beloved by Israelis for its year-round spring, cool pools (swimming prohibited), brookside vegetation (rare in the arid Negev), chalky cliffs and roaming ibexes. The reserve's northern entrance is just outside the gate to Midreshet Sde Boker; trails begin at a parking area 3 km (2 miles) south of there.

En Avdat National Park
🕐 8am–5pm daily (to 4pm Fri); closes 1 hour earlier in winter 🌐 parks.org.il

---

7

Mitzpe Ramon

🅰B5 🚗Rte 40, Negev Highlands 🚌 60, 64, 65, 392 🌐 parks.org.il

Perched on the rim of vast Makhtesh Ramon (*p224*), at an altitude of 900 m (2,952 ft), this high desert

Did You Know?
The ancient Nabatean people harnessed the rare waters of Ein Avdat to maintain agriculture.

town, with a population of more than 5,000, was founded in the 1950s. It is about 82 km (50 miles) south of Be'er Sheva and 150 km (93 miles) north of Eilat. The Makhtesh Ramon Visitors' Center on Ma'ale Ben Tur Street can provide information on walks and hikes; nearby, a Lookout Platform offers breathtaking views of the canyon.

At Bio Ramon, a small wildlife park, you can see small desert animals (owls, lizards, snakes, scorpions) that have been nursed back to health but cannot be returned to the wild.

The workaday warehouses of the old industrial zone have been revitalized as the Spice Route Quarter, where a community of creative and dynamic young Israelis has opened up boutique hotels, restaurants and art studios.

Because of its isolation and freedom from light pollution, Mitzpe is one of the best places in Israel for stargazing, but the high desert gets chilly at night – in winter the town sometimes gets snow – so bring warm clothing.

DRINK

Inspired in part by the ancient irrigation technology of the Nabateans, a number of innovative Israeli vintners have been opening up wineries between Mitzpe Ramon and Sde Boker (along Route 40). Many places offer relaxing, rustic bed-and-breakfast accommodation; here are two of the best.

Boker Valley Vineyards
🅰B5 🌐bokerfarm.com

Desert Estate Carmey Avdat
🅰B5 🌐carmey avdat.com

↓ The spectacular canyon in En Avdat National Park, near Sde Boker

Looking out over the massive crater of Makhtesh Ramon ↑

⑧ Makhtesh Ramon

🅰B5 🚗Route 40, 80 km (50 miles) S of Be'er Sheva 📞(08) 658 8691 🚌From Be'er Sheva

Makhtesh Ramon is Israel's most dramatic natural phenomenon: a crater some 40 km (25 miles) long, 9 km (5 miles) wide, with a depth of 300 m (1,300 ft). It is the largest of three craters in the Negev Desert, which scientists believe were formed more than half a million years ago by a combination of tectonic movement and erosion. Nabataean caravans travelled this way between Petra and Ovdat, and the ruins of an ancient caravanserai stand at the centre of the depression.

On the crater's rim is the town of Mitzpe Ramon, the main base for exploring this part of the desert. The town's visitors' centre has exhibits on the geology of the great

Did You Know?

In spite of the rumours, the Makhtesh Ramon was not the result of an asteroid collision.

> **Makhtesh Ramon is the largest of three craters in the Negev Desert, which scientists believe were formed more than half a million years ago.**

crater and its flora and fauna. It also has hiking maps – but make sure to take plenty of water if you go trekking here. In Mitzpe Ramon you can also arrange to take a tour of the crater by jeep.

⑨ Hai Bar Yotvata Wildlife Reserve

🅰B6 🚗Route 90, 35 km (22 miles) N of Eilat 🚌From Eilat 📞(08) 637 6018 🕑8am–5pm daily (to 4pm Fri); closes 1 hour earlier in winter

Hai Bar was founded with the aim of reintroducing some of the creatures named in the Bible, which have since vanished from the Negev. Most of the animals roam freely, safari-park style, in a 40-sq-km (15-sq-mile) territory in the Arava Valley. Visits can be made by jeep in the company of a ranger guide or you can drive through in your own car. Native species in the reserve (not all of which receive biblical mention) include scimitar-horned

oryxes, wild Somali donkeys, ostriches and the addax antelope with their curved horns. A Predator Centre houses wildcats, caracals (desert lynxes), foxes, leopards and hyenas in spacious enclosures.

⑩ Kibbutz Lotan

🅰B6 🚗Southern Arava 🚌20 from Eilat 🌐kibbutzlotan.com

Situated 55 km (34 miles) north of Eilat, this small kibbutz, surrounded by the glorious scenery of the southern Arava, is known for its Center for Creative Ecology, which specializes in hands-on experimentation with low-impact desert living, including permaculture. Tours take you to the Eco-Park, where innovative technologies are given a trial run, and the EcoCampus, where international participants in the Eco-Experience stay in mud huts while studying desert sustainability, including doing laundry

with a pedal-powered washing machine. The Solar Tea House serves vegetarian and vegan food. Visitors can stay in the guest house or rent a mud hut, and volunteers are welcome.

Timna Park

🅐B6 🅐Off Route 90, Southern Arava 🚌From Eilat 🕐8am-4pm Sat-Thu, 8am-3pm Fri (to 1pm Jul & Aug) 🌐parktimna.co.il

Ancient remains indicate that there were working mines at Timna as far back as 3000 BC, and there is evidence that the Egyptians were mining copper here around 1500 BC. They left behind two temples dedicated to the goddess Hathor, protectress of mines. A hieroglyphic inscription in one of them mentions pharaoh Rameses III offering a sacrifice to Hathor. The mines continued to be worked under the Nabataeans and Romans before eventually being abandoned.

With the added attraction of some curious mushroom-shaped rock formations created by wind erosion, and the distinctive sandstone cliffs known as Solomon's Pillars, the area has been preserved as a nature reserve. An underground passage gives access to the ancient mines, and you can see Egyptian graffiti representing ibexes and hunters armed with bows and arrows.

Timna's bluffs, valleys and rock formations, coloured red, orange and purple by metals and minerals, offer some of the best short desert hikes anywhere in Israel. There are more than 20 trails of varying lengths and difficulty to choose from. Visitors can also cycle on 14 km (9 miles) of single-track bike paths; bicycles can be rented at the visitors' centre, about 30 km (19 miles) north of Eilat.

Inspecting the effects of millennia of wind erosion on the rocks in Timna Park ↑

STAY

Khan Be'erotayim
Far, far from the urban rat race, this isolated desert encampment has eco-friendly mud huts, communal bathrooms and meals from locally sourced ingredients.

🅐A5 🅐Ezuz
🌐beerotayim.co.il

⊚⊚⊚

B'tzel Ha'tmarim Country Lodging
This collection of cosy lodges in the Arava Desert offers basic amenities and views of the Jordanian mountains. It's also a great spot to go cycling.

🅐Kibbutz Yahel, Yahel, Southern Arava 📞(02) 970 6343

⊚⊚⊚

Silent Arrow
Dome-roofed tents with solar lighting are amid the stony expanse of the Negev Highlands. Guided activities include desert archery and stargazing.

🅐B5 🅐1.5 km (1 mile) W of Mitzpe Ramon
🌐silentarrow.com

⊚⊚⊚

Shkedi's Camplodge
Just south of the Dead Sea, this hippy-style, Sinai-inspired compound has a mellow desert vibe and offers basic dorm beds, communal bathrooms, a chill-out bar and nightly campfires.

🅐C5 🅐Ne'ot HaKikar
🌐shkedig.com

⊚⊚⊚

WEST BANK

The 5,628-sq-km (2,173-sq-mile) West Bank consists of the areas of Mandatory Palestine that ended up under Jordanian control at the end of the 1948 Arab-Israeli war. Shortly after Israel captured the area in 1967, right-wing Israelis began establishing settlements on land that they referred to by biblical names: Judea, south of Jerusalem; and Samaria, one-time heartland of the Samaritans, north of Jerusalem. In 1988, Jordan renounced its territorial claims to the West Bank and stripped West Bankers of their right to Jordanian citizenship. Opposition to Israeli military rule sparked the First Intifada (1987–91), a popular rebellion that helped pave the way for the Oslo Accords (1993) and the establishment of the interim Palestinian National Authority, based in Ramallah. Over 130 Palestinian suicide bombings during the Second Intifada (2000–05) led to Israeli raids on West Bank towns and Israel's construction of a "separation barrier" – about 6 per cent of it a concrete wall – and checkpoints to prevent infiltration by Palestinian militants. Today, although the quest for peace seems moribund and the per capita GDP of West Bank Palestinians is just US$3,700 (compared to US$42,000 in Israel), Palestinians continue to build museums, cultural institutions and even wineries – and to welcome both tourists and pilgrims.

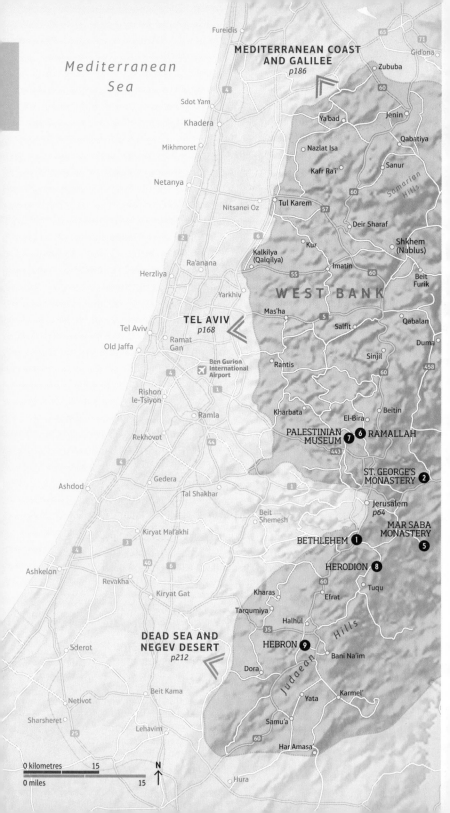

Mediterranean Sea

Fureidis

MEDITERRANEAN COAST
AND GALILEE
p186

Gid'ona

Zububa

Sdot Yam

Ya'bad

Jenin

Qabatiya

Khadera

Nazlat Isa

Sanur

Mikhmoret

Kafr Ra'i

Samarian Hills

Netanya

Nitsanei Oz

Tul Karem

Deir Sharaf

Kur

Shkhem
(Nablus)

Herzliya

Kalkilya
(Qalqilya)

Imatin

Beit
Furik

Ra'anana

WEST BANK

Yarkhiv

Mas'ha

TEL AVIV
p168

Salfit

Qabalan

Tel Aviv

Old Jaffa

Ramat
Gan

Ben Gurion
International
Airport

Rantis

Sinjil

Duma

Rishon
le-Tsiyon

Kharbata

El-Bira

Beitin

Ramla

PALESTINIAN
MUSEUM

7 **6** RAMALLAH

Rekhovot

Ashdod

Gedera

ST. GEORGE'S
MONASTERY **2**

Tal Shakhar

Beit
Shemesh

Jerusalem
p64

MAR SABA
MONASTERY
5

Kiryat Mal'akhi

BETHLEHEM **1**

Ashkelon

HERODION **8**

Revakha

Tuqu

Kharas

Efrat

Kiryat Gat

Tarqumiya

Halhul

Sderot

DEAD SEA AND
NEGEV DESERT
p212

HEBRON **9**

Bani Na'im

Judaean Hills

Beit Kama

Dora

Netivot

Karmel'

Sharsheret

Lehavim

Yata

Samu'a

Hura

Har Amasa

0 kilometres   15
0 miles   15

N

WEST BANK

Must See
1 Bethlehem

Experience More
2 St George's Monastery
3 Jericho
4 Nebi Musa
5 Mar Saba Monastery
6 Ramallah
7 Palestinian Museum
8 Herodion
9 Hebron

Beit ha-Shita

Beth Shean

Sdei Trumot

Dayr Abu Sa'id

Raba

Mekhola

Tubas

Halawah

'Ajlun

Kurayyimah

Jordan River

Damiya

As-Salt

Az-Zarqa

Suwaylih

Russayfah

Al Karamah

Wadi as Sir

Amman

PETRA AND
WESTERN
JORDAN
p240

Na'ur

3 JERICHO

4 NEBI MUSA

Kalya'

Suwaymah

Ma'in

Ma'daba

Queen Alia
International Airport

Netil

Dead
Sea

JORDAN

Malih

Mukawir

Dhiban

Wadi al Hidan

Ariha

WEST
BANK

Wadi al Mujib

Al Qasr

Al
Mazra'ah

Wadi al Karak

Ar Rabbah

①

BETHLEHEM

▲ B3 **●** 7 km (4 miles) S of Jerusalem **▥** Hebron Road
ⓘ Manger Sq; www.vicbethlehem.wordpress.com

Perched on a hill at the edge of the Judaean Desert, Bethlehem is in biblical tradition the childhood home of David, who was named king here as he tended his father's sheep. It is also the birthplace of Jesus Christ and a major site of pilgrimage since the construction of the Church of the Nativity in the 4th century AD.

①

St Catherine's Church

▲ Manger Square **●** (02) 274 2425 **●** Summer: 6:30am-7:30pm daily; winter: 5am-5pm daily **🔇** Sun am for services

Joined to the Church of the Nativity (p232), St Catherine's Church was built by Franciscans in the 1880s on the site of a 12th-century Augustinian monastery, which had replaced a 5th-century monastery associated with St Jerome. The grottoes of the Holy Innocents, St Joseph and St Jerome, were used by Christians as burial places from as early as the 1st century AD and contain within them the tombs of St Jerome and St Paula.

②

Mosque of Omar

▲ Manger Square **●** 4:30am-9:30pm, except during prayers

Built in 1860 on land donated by the Greek Orthodox Church, this mosque is the only Islamic place of worship in the city centre (despite the fact that Muslim residents now outnumber Christians in Bethlehem). It is named after Caliph Omar (Umar) ibn al-Khattab, the 7th-century Muslim conqueror of Jerusalem, who guaranteed Christian religious rights in Bethlehem. Women must be modestly dressed and cover their heads; the women's prayer area is upstairs.

③

Milk Grotto

▲ Milk Grotto St **●** (02) 274 3867 **●** 8am-noon & 2-4:45pm Mon-Sat

This grotto is considered sacred because tradition has it that the Holy Family took refuge here during the Massacre of the Innocents. While Mary was suckling Jesus, so the story goes, a drop of milk fell to the ground, turning it white. Both Christians and Muslims believe that scrapings from the stones in the grotto help to boost the quantity of a mother's milk and also to enhance fertility.

↑ A sculpture of Mary, Joseph and the baby Jesus in the Milk Grotto

↑ A panorama of Bethlehem's sacred historic centre

INSIDER TIP
Banksy in Bethlehem

Many artworks by famed UK street artist Banksy can be seen in Bethlehem. In 2017, he also opened the Walled Off hotel in the city, overlooking the separation barrier *(p227)*.

④ 🗺 🍴 🛍
Bethlehem Museum

🏛 Jerusalem-Hebron St
🕐 8am–6pm daily
🌐 bethlehemmuseum.com/museum-sections

This fascinating modern museum showcases the many contributions of Christians to the heritage of Palestine. Exhibits feature Palestinian embroidery, mother-of-pearl and olive wood carvings, and Roman remains, and look at life in 19th-century Bethlehem and the contributions of Diaspora Palestinians to the countries in which they live. The Al-Karmeh Restaurant inside the museum serves authentic Palestinian cuisine, while the gift shop sells locally made crafts.

⑤
Rachel's Tomb

🏛 Hebron Rd 🕐 1:30am–10:30pm Sun-Thu (to sunset Fri) 🚫 Fri & festivals 🌐 keverrachel.com

On the road to Jerusalem is the tomb of Rachel, wife of Jacob and mother of two of his 12 sons. The tomb is in Jerusalem on the road to Bethlehem just before reaching the crossing into the Palestinian Authority. It is one of the holiest sites in Jerusalem.

The actual "tomb" consists of a rock covered by a velvet drape with 11 stones on it, one for each of Jacob's sons who were alive when Rachel died in childbirth. The structure around the tomb was built in the 1100s by the Crusaders and later altered many times. The site is visited by Jewish women who come to pray for fertility.

TRAVEL IN THE WEST BANK

In order to get to the West Bank, you have to travel through Israel or Israeli-controlled territory. Visitors and locals alike must pass through Israeli military checkpoints such as Checkpoint 300 (between Jerusalem and Bethlehem) and Qalandia (between Jerusalem and Ramallah). Tourists usually have few problems but you may be searched, and if authorities think you're a political activist they may want to ask some questions. Make sure you have your passport and Israeli visa slip.

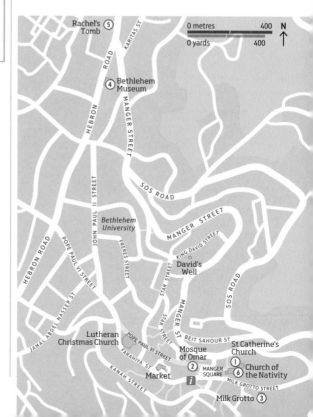

⑥

CHURCH OF THE NATIVITY

🏠 Manger Square 🕐 Summer: 6:30am–7:30pm daily; winter: 5:30am–5pm daily (grottoes closed Sun morning)
🌐 travelpalestine.ps

The traditional site of Jesus' birth has been commemorated by a church since the early 3rd century. Deep inside this important structure, in the Grotto of the Nativity, the precise spot is marked by a 14-pointed silver star.

The first evidence of a cave here being venerated as Christ's birthplace is in the writings of St Justin Martyr around AD 160. In 326, the Roman emperor Constantine ordered a church to be built, and in about 530 it was rebuilt by Justinian. The Crusaders redecorated the interior, but much of the marble was looted in Ottoman times. In 1852, shared custody of the church was granted to the Roman Catholic, Armenian and Greek Orthodox churches, the Greeks caring for the Grotto of the Nativity.

> **The first evidence of a cave here being venerated as Christ's birthplace is in the writings of St Justin Martyr.**

St Catherine's Church (p230)

The Grotto of the Nativity is the church's focal point.

Stairs to main church

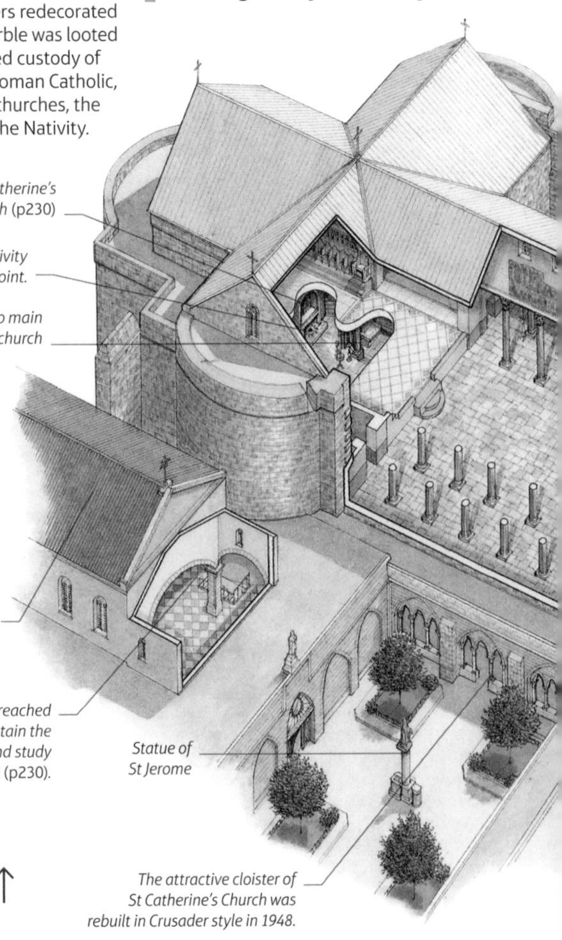

Did You Know?

St Jerome's study is traditionally believed to have been next to the Grotto of the Nativity.

Altar of the Adoration of the Magi (Manger Altar)

Other grottoes, reached by these steps, contain the supposed tomb and study of St Jerome (p230).

Statue of St Jerome

The Church of the Nativity, marking the site of Jesus's birth ↑

The attractive cloister of St Catherine's Church was rebuilt in Crusader style in 1948.

1. A silver star in the floor marks the spot in the Grotto of the Nativity where Jesus is said to have been born.

2. Most of the pink limestone columns in the nave were reused from the original 4th-century basilica.

3. The cloister of St Catherine's Church features a statue of St Jerome.

The wide nave survives intact from Justinian's time, although the roof is 15th-century.

Thirty of the nave's 44 columns carry Crusader paintings of saints and the Virgin and Child.

Wall mosaics once decorated the church.

The narthex was originally a single, long porch, with three large doors leading into the church and three onto the street.

The Door of Humility was reduced in size to prevent carts being driven in by looters.

Trap doors in the present floor reveal sections of mosaic floor surviving from the 4th-century.

THE CRIMEAN WAR AND BETHLEHEM

In the 18th century, France installed a silver star in the Grotto of the Nativity to mark the spot of Jesus's birth – and to stake Catholic claims to the site. In 1847 it was stolen, and the Catholics blamed their long-time rivals, the Greek Orthodox. The battle over the star's replacement ratcheted up tensions between Catholic France and Russia, historic protector of Orthodox Christianity, and directly contributed to the outbreak of the Crimean War in 1853.

EXPERIENCE MORE

❷

St George's Monastery

🅰C3 🚗Route 1, 27 km
(17 miles) E of Jerusalem
📞(054) 730 6557
🚌From Jerusalem
🕐9am–noon daily

The hike from Wadi Qelt to St George's Monastery is one of the finest in the region, and is rewarded by the spectacle of the abbey, hollowed out of the sheer rock wall of a deep and narrow gorge. The monastery was founded in AD 480 around a cluster of caves where St Joachim is said to have learned that Anne, his sterile wife and mother-to-be of the Virgin Mary, had conceived.

In AD 614, invading Persians massacred the monks and destroyed the monastery. It was partially reoccupied by the Crusaders in the Middle Ages, but only fully restored at the end of the 19th century. Some attractive 6th-century mosaics can still be seen, and there is a Crusader-era church with a shrine containing the skulls of the martyred monks.

The monastery can be reached in 20 minutes on foot via a signposted track off the old Jerusalem–Jericho road. From the modern road, hikers can take a more scenic path along the full length of the Wadi Qelt gorge.

---

❸ 🚶 🚴

Jericho

🅰C3 🚗25 km (15 miles)
E of Jerusalem 🚌Bus or
taxi from Jerusalem

Claimed to be the world's oldest city and with rich biblical associations, Jericho is a little way north of the Dead Sea, in the middle of the Judaean Desert. It owes its existence to the Ain es-Sultan Spring (the biblical Elisha's Spring), the same one that, 10,000 years ago in the late Mesolithic period, attracted a semi-nomadic population of hunter-gatherers to first settle here.

According to the Bible, this was the first town captured by the Israelites, led by Joshua. The Book of Joshua tells how,

in order to possess the land promised to them by God, the Israelites brought down the city walls with a tremendous shout and a trumpet blast (Joshua 6).

During Roman times, Mark Antony gave it to Cleopatra of Egypt, who, in turn, leased the town to Herod the Great. At a lower altitude than Jerusalem, Jericho is notably warmer, and Herod wintered in a palace here, as had the Hasmonean rulers before him.

The Bible's New Testament mentions several visits to Jericho by Jesus, who healed two blind men and lodged at the home of the tax collector Zacchaeus (Luke 19: 1–10). Near the centre of town is a

→

The remarkable floor mosaic amid the ruins of Hisham's Palace at Jericho

← St George's Monastery, cut into the rock face, with visiting nuns at prayer *(inset)*

centuries-old sycamore tree up which Zacchaeus was said to have climbed to see Jesus.

Repeated Bedouin raids led to decline around the 12th century, and it wasn't until the 1920s that the town's irrigation network was restored and the area bloomed again. In 1948, the town took in more than 70,000 Palestinian refugees. Most of the camps have since gone, but the Aqbat Jaber camp remains, in the form of a somewhat run-down neighbourhood. Jericho is now run by the Palestinian National Authority.

Other attractions include **Tel Jericho** (also known as Tell es-Sultan), the sun-baked earthen mound that represents something like 10,000 years of continuous settlement. Most striking of all is a large stone tower with great thick walls that dates back as far as 7000 BC.

ISRAELI SETTLEMENTS IN THE WEST BANK

Since Israel captured the 5,628-sq-km (2,173-sq-mile) West Bank (Palestinian Territories) from Jordan in the 1967 War, successive Israeli governments have established 132 Israeli settlements that now have more than 430,000 residents. The ideological hard-core of the mostly Orthodox Jewish settlement movement believes that settling Jews in all parts of the historic Land of Israel, including the West Bank (which they refer to by the biblical names Judea and Samaria), is part of the Messianic process, foretold in the Bible. Radical groups have, without Israeli government authorization, set up dozens more small settlements, many of them on remote hilltops. The international community considers it illegal to establish civilian communities on occupied land and, like many Israelis, sees this as a serious obstacle to a peaceful, two-state solution to the Israeli-Palestinian conflict.

A cable car connects Tell es-Sultan with the 12th-century Greek Orthodox **Monastery of the Temptation** to the north. Like St George's in Wadi Qelt, this holy retreat has a spectacular location, perched high up on a cliff face. The views from its terraces are breathtaking. It is supposedly built around the grotto where the Devil appeared to tempt Jesus away from his 40-day fast (Matthew 4: 1–11).

Hisham's Palace (Qasr Hisham) is an early Islamic hunting lodge built in AD 724 for the Omayyad caliph Hisham. Destroyed centuries ago by an earthquake, the ruins are worth a visit if only to see a gorgeous floor mosaic of a lion hunting.

On the banks of the Jordan River, the **Qasr el-Yehud** baptismal site is popular with those keen to immerse themselves in the historic waters.

Tel Jericho
⊘⊛ 🚪 2 km (1 mile) N of centre ⊙ Daily

Monastery of the Temptation
🚪 2 km (1 mile) N of Jericho ⊙ 8am–4pm Mon–Sat

Hisham's Palace
⊘ 🚪 5 km (3 miles) N of Jericho ⊙ 8am–5pm daily (summer: to 6pm daily)

Qasr el-Yehud
⊛ 🚪 10 km (6 miles) E of Jericho ⓦ parks.org.il

10,000 BC
—
Hunter-gatherers settle in what is now Jericho.

←
Nebi Musa Monastery, surrounded by desert on all sides

④

Nebi Musa

🅰 C4 🚘 Route 1, 10 km (6 miles) S of Jericho 🚌 To Jericho, then taxi

Although the claim is heavily disputed, Muslims revere this desert monastery as the burial place of Moses. There has been a mosque on the site since 1269, built under the patronage of the Mameluke emir Baybars. In 1470–80, a hospice was added for visiting pilgrims. The attractive white-washed structures of the present day date from around 1820. The disputed cenotaph of Moses, with a traditional Islamic green drape, occupies the spartan, domed tomb chamber of the mosque.

⑤

Mar Saba Monastery

🅰 C4 🚘 Off Route 398, 17 km (11 miles) E of Bethlehem 📞 (02) 276 2915 🚌 To Bethlehem, then taxi ⏰ 8am–5pm daily (ring bell)

Out in the wilds of the Judaean Desert, Mar Saba is one of the dozens of retreats

→
Ancient Mar Saba Monastery, blending into the landscape

built in this area from the 5th century on by hermits seeking an austere life of solitude and prayer. This monastery was founded in AD 482 by St Saba, a monk born in Cappadocia, Turkey, whose preachings were said to have impressed the Byzantine emperor Justinian. Despite a massacre of the monks by the Persians in the 7th century (the skulls are preserved in a chapel), the

Did You Know?

Mar Saba is one of the oldest inhabited monasteries in the world.

monastery survived to bloom in the 8th and 9th centuries, when its thick defensive walls housed up to 200 devotees.

Although only around 20 monks now live in Mar Saba, it remains a functioning desert monastery. As seen today, topped by bright blue domes, the complex largely dates to 1834, when it was rebuilt following a major earthquake.

An ornate canopy in the monastery's main church supposedly shelters the remains of St Saba, which were returned to the Holy Land only in 1965, having being carried off by the Crusaders and kept in Venice for seven centuries. The church walls are hung with icons and a lurid fresco depicting Judgment Day.

Women are not allowed to enter the monastery, but the views of Mar Saba from a neighbouring tower (which women are permitted to climb) are alone worth the visit.

Displays at Ramallah's Yasser Arafat Museum, near his former headquarters ↑

Ramallah

A B3 **A** 20 km (13 miles) N of Jerusalem **B** 18, 19, 218, 219 from near Damascus Gate, Jerusalem

The most cosmopolitan city on the West Bank, historically Christian Ramallah (it now has a Muslim majority) enjoys an active cultural life and is renowned for its lively nightlife, with plenty of trendy pubs that serve alcohol. The centre has a selection of international-standard hotels and some of the best restaurants in the Palestinian Territories; for local cuisine, head to the area around Al-Manara Square, a short walk from the bus station. In 2018, the **A M Qattan Foundation**, which focuses on education and culture, inaugurated a US$21 million arts centre in the city. Designed by Seville-based Donaire Arquitectos, the striking modern building houses a gallery space, a 120-seat theatre and a library. The foundation also runs educational outreach programmes that focus on the arts and science.

Ramallah is the de facto capital of the Palestinian Authority, which is why Yasser Arafat's Tomb and the **Yasser Arafat Museum** are here. Charting the history of his life, the museum sits on the grounds of the Muquata'a, Arafat's one-time presidential office and military headquarters (bring ID).

Getting through Israel's Qalandia checkpoint is not usually a problem for Western passport holders but bring your passport and Israeli visa slip.

A M Qattan Foundation
A 22 Al-Jihad Street
W qattanfoundation.org

Yasser Arafat Museum
A Muqata'a
C 10am–5pm Tue–Sun (to 6pm during Daylight Saving Time) **W** yam.ps

7 🖥

Palestinian Museum

🅰B3 🄰Birzeit, 14 km
(9 miles) N of Ramallah
🚌 🕐8:30am–4:30pm Mon–
Fri 🌐palmuseum.org

Along with the A M Qattan
Foundation in Ramallah
(p237), this independent
museum is one of two
modern Palestinian cultural
institutions with a mission to
celebrate Palestinian culture.

Located next to the Birzeit
University (BZU) campus,
not far from Ramallah, the
museum is housed in a world-
class building designed by a
Dublin firm of architects and
is surrounded by lovely
terraced gardens.

Although the Palestinian
Museum has yet to fully grow
into its spectacular, angular
campus, a number of small,
temporary exhibitions, hailed
as being of international
standard, have already been
curated, including one focus-
ing on beautiful embroidered
Jellayeh coats.

> **Dominating the landscape south
> of Bethlehem is the volcano-like
> mound of the Herodian, named for
> Herod the Great.**

8 🎿 🏍

Herodion

🅰B4 🄰Route 60, 32 km
(20 miles) S of Jerusalem
📞(02) 595 3591 🚌 🕐8am–
5pm (to 4pm Fri); closes 1
hour earlier in winter

Dominating the landscape
south of Bethlehem is the
volcano-like mound of the
Herodion, named for Herod
the Great. His circular fortified
palace was built in 24–15 BC
for entertaining, and to mark
the defeat of Antigonus, his
rival. It was long thought
this might also have been
Herod's mausoleum and,
after extensive excavations, a
tomb believed to be his was
discovered in 2007, though
this has been disputed.

During the Second Revolt in
AD 132–5, the site became the
headquarters of the Jewish
leader Bar-Kokhba. In expec-
tation of a Roman attack, the
rebels turned its cisterns into
a network of escape tunnels.
Around the 5th century, the
site became a monastery with

cells and a chapel, where
you can still see carved
Christian symbols. Also
identifiable are a massive
round tower and three semi-
circular ones, ruins of the
palace baths, the triclinium
(dining room) and fragments
of mosaics, all dating from
Herod's time.

At the foot of the mound
are the remains of the Lower
Herodion, with the dry imprint
of a large pool that, in Herod's
day, served as a reservoir
and centrepiece for orna-
mental gardens.

9

Hebron

🅰B4 🄰40 km (25 miles)
S of Jerusalem 🚌

Nestled among hills south of
Jerusalem, Hebron is one of
the most densely populated
towns in the West Bank. It is
famous for its glassmaking
industry, which began in the
Middle Ages and has always
been managed by one single
family. This coloured glass-
ware can be found for sale
in another of Hebron's major
attractions, its medieval
Arab souk, which has some
imposing Crusader-era
vaulted passageways.

→ A Hebron glass blower shaping a fine piece of coloured glass

However, Hebron is a town undermined by troublesome political tensions. It is divided into two zones: the greater area is governed by the Palestinian Authority, but the town centre is occupied by Jewish settlers (p235). Large numbers of Israeli soldiers maintain a constant peace-keeping presence. Friction between the two communities dates back to a 1929 pogrom in which the Arabs massacred Hebron's centuries-old Jewish community. After the Six-Day War of 1967, militant Jews resettled the centre of town. Tension continues to erupt into occasional violence. For your personal safety, ask about the situation before making a trip to Hebron.

Hebron is regarded as a sacred place by the Jewish, Christian and Muslim religions alike; it was here, they believe, that Abraham buried his wife Sarah, in the Cave of Machpelah, purchased from the Hittite Ephron. The cave then became his own tomb and later that of his descendants Isaac and Jacob.

Around 20 BC, Herod the Great sealed the cave and built a great hall over it. Under Byzantine rule the structure was turned into a church and then, after the Arab conquest of 638, a mosque. The Crusaders attempted to reclaim the site for Christianity and built much of the present-day structure, but it was completed by Saladin in the 12th century as a mosque. In the 13th century, the Mameluke ruler Baybars forbade non-Muslims from entering the building.

Following the 1967 War, the mosque remained Muslim, but access was granted to Jews. Today, the complex, known as the **Tomb of the Patriarchs** (Haram al-Khalil in Arabic), is divided into a synagogue and a mosque, each with its own entrance. The site remains a subject of contention between the faiths; in 1994, Jewish colonist Baruch Goldstein entered the mosque and killed 29 Muslim worshippers.

Tomb of the Patriarchs
☎ (02) 996 5333 ◷ 4am-9pm daily (except some religious holidays and during prayer times)

← The ancient remains beneath the mound of Herodion

DRINK

Taybeh Brewing Company
Palestine's oldest and largest brewery gets rave reviews for its crisp, German-style beers and Oktoberfest.

🅰C3 🏠Taybeh Brewery: 8am-4pm Mon-Sat; tours: 9am-2:30pm 🔳taybeh beer.com

Birzeit Brewery
Amber ale, blonde pilsner, stout and seasonal beers under the Shepherds label are the specialities of this family-run brewery.

🅰B3 🏠Birzeit ◷Noon-6pm Mon, Wed & Sat 🔳shepherds.ps

Snowbar
Long the hippest chill-out place in the West Bank's most liberal city, this bar attracts well-off hipsters, creative folk and families.

🅰B3 🏠Ein Sama'an, Ramallah ☎(02) 296 5571 ◷11am-midnight daily

PETRA AND WESTERN JORDAN

Western Jordan was first inhabited in prehistoric times, and by the 1st century BC had become part of a major trading empire established by the Nabateans, who constructed Petra as their central base. Following the decline of the Nabateans, the region came under the rule of the Romans, followed in later centuries by the Byzantines and the Crusaders.

This ancient bedrock that the country sits upon belies the fact that modern Jordan itself is barely a century old. Its land was only partitioned off from Palestine in 1923, and became fully independent in 1946, when the Hashemite kingdom of Jordan was proclaimed. King Abdullah, the grandfather and namesake of the current king, was Jordan's first ruler. It was the vision of the late King Hussein, however, that saw the country truly establish itself on the international scene. His work to establish and maintain peace in the region contributed greatly to Jordan's reputation as an anchor in the often-turbulent sea of Middle Eastern politics. Despite the successive challenges of the crises across the border in Iraq and then Syria, it's a reputation that still holds today.

PETRA AND
WESTERN JORDAN

Gaza

GAZA

Re'im

Mediterranean
Sea

Tse'elim

El Kharuba

El 'Arish

Bir el 'Abd

El Mazar

30

Nitzana

EGYPT

Abu 'Aweigila

El Quseima

31

31

Bir Hasana

Bir Gifgafa

Bir el Thamada

Nakhl

PETRA
AND
WESTERN
JORDAN

El Thamad

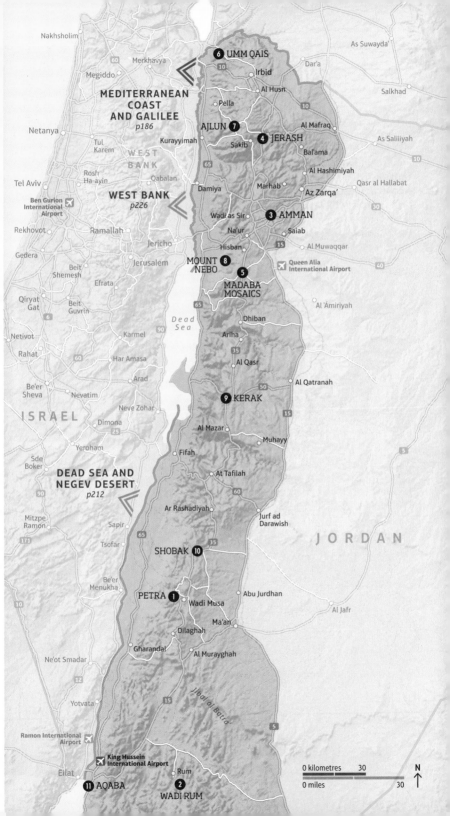

PETRA

🗺️ C5 📍 Wadi Musa, 260 km (160 miles) S of Amman
🚌 To Wadi Musa from Amman & Aqaba 🕐 Site: 6am-6pm
daily (to 4pm winter); museum: 9am-4:30pm daily
(to 5:30pm summer) 🌐 visitpetra.jo

Hewn out of rocky mountains and sandstone gorges, this spectacular
Nabatean city is one of the world's most atmospheric ancient sites.
Known as the "rose-red city", its monumental façades reflect the
swirls of colour that pattern the surrounding hills and valleys.

Petra's marvellously preserved rock-hewn
tombs and temples once encircled a thriving
metropolis. There has been human settlement
here since prehistoric times, but Petra was
just another desert watering hole until the
Nabataeans (p251) arrived. Between the 3rd
century BC and the 1st century AD, they built
a superb city and made it the centre of a vast
trading empire. In AD 106, Petra was annexed
by Rome. Christianity arrived in the 4th century,
the Muslims in the 7th and the Crusaders
passed through briefly in the 12th. Thereafter
Petra lay largely forgotten until 1812, when it
was visited by JL Burckhardt (p249). The hiking
here is excellent, and it is worth spending
more than a day at the site to fully appreciate
all that Petra has to offer.

It is 1.5 km (1 mile) to Petra from the Visitor
Center at the site's entrance, passing across the
Bab el-Siq valley to the Treasury. From there the
path leads into the Outer Siq and widens out
before opening onto the large plain that houses
the City of Petra. You can wander the site on
your own or arrange a guide at the Visitor Center.

↑ The City of Petra's main
street, with the remains
of the Temenos Gate

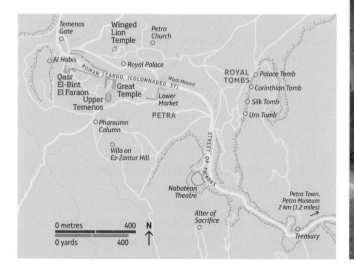

Did You Know?

Petra was the setting
for the final scenes of
*Indiana Jones and the
Last Crusade* (1989).

↑ The breathtaking view
of the Treasury, as glimpsed
from the end of the Siq

↑ The Roman-style theatre, carved into the mountainside around the 1st century AD

FROM THE TREASURY TO THE THEATRE

Set deep in the rock and protected by the valley walls, the magnificent 1st-century-BC Treasury creates a formidable first impression of Petra. As its design had no precedent in the city, it is thought that architects from the Hellenistic Near East were brought in to create it. A colossol doorway dominates the outer court and leads to an inner chamber, at the back of which is a sanctuary with an ablution basin – suggesting that the treasury was in fact a temple.

From the Treasury, the path leads into the Outer Siq, lined on both sides with tombs of all sizes, some half buried by risen ground levels. The tombs display a range of "intermediate" design styles, featuring a huge single-divide crowstep (a set of steps on the top of a gable), Hellenistic doorways and Classical pillars and cornices.

At the end of the Outer Siq, in the midst of this great necropolis, is the Classical Theatre. Started by the Nabataeans and possibly added to by the Romans, it was a project requiring advanced engineering skills.

↑ Walking through the Siq towards the Treasury

TOP 3 TREASURY TO THEATRE FEATURES

Treasury Tholos
The central figure on the façade may be the Petran fertility goddess El-Uzza. Bullet marks in the tholos and urn have been made over the years by Bedouin attempting to release hidden treasure.

Streets of Façades
Carved on four levels, these tightly packed tombs may include some of Petra's oldest façades. Most are crowned with multiple crowsteps.

Theatre Vaults
To access the theatre, there were tunnels either side of the stage. Inside, these were dressed with painted plaster or marble.

THE ROYAL TOMBS

Carved into the base of El-Khubtha mountain, a short detour to the right at the point where the Outer Siq opens out on to Petra's central plain, are the Urn, Corinthian and Palace Tombs. They are collectively known as the Royal Tombs, their monumental size suggesting they were built for wealthy or important people, possibly Petran kings or queens. These tombs and their neighbours are also remarkable for the vivid striations of colour rippling through their sandstone walls, an effect heightened in the warm glow of the late afternoon sun.

First in the sequence is the towering Urn Tomb, reached by a stairway. Its name refers to a relatively tiny urn on top. Further along is the badly eroded Corinthian Tomb, which seems to be modelled largely on the Treasury. Its design has long baffled archaeologists because of

↑ The exteriors of the Palace and Corininthian tombs

its lack of symmetry, which is particularly evident in the different styles of the doorways. Beyond that sits the Palace Tomb, thought to be based on Nero's Golden House in Rome. It had a grandiose façade on five levels, which was taller than the rock into which it was carved.

The atmospheric ↑ interior of the large Palace Tomb

The striking façades
↓ of the monumental Royal Tombs

The Palace Tomb is the largest of all the Royal Tombs.

Each doorway of the Corinthian Tomb is in a different style.

The central aperture contains a statue of a man wearing a toga.

Three burial chambers are carved high in the façade.

Of the four inner chambers, only the middle two connect.

The Silk Tomb is named for its walls, streaked like shot silk.

In AD 447, the Urn Tomb was turned into a church.

Two levels of arches support the Urn Tomb's large terrace.

THE CITY OF PETRA

Just past the Theatre, the Outer Siq opens out into a wide plain. The ruins of the city of Petra are in the middle of this vast basin, and the path alongside the Wadi Musa leads down to the site. Today, fragmented remains of the main street and a few nearby buildings are almost all that is left of the great city that once filled the valley.

The grand Roman-style Cardo would have been Petra's main thoroughfare, fringed with markets and leading to the city's most sacred temple, the Qasr el-Bint. This building, like all the important structures around the Cardo, would have been

↑ The Temenos Gate, with the Royal Tombs in the background

lavishly decorated. Traces of ornate plasterwork and marble veneer can still be seen on its walls and steps.

The colonnaded Cardo, which runs through the centre of the city ↑

JOHANN LUDWIG BURCKHARDT

In 1812, after lying hidden for more than 500 years to all except local Arabs, Petra was rediscovered by an explorer called Johann Ludwig Burckhardt. The son of a Swiss colonel in the French army, he was an outstanding student with a thirst for adventure. In 1809, he was contracted by a London-based association to explore the "interior parts of Africa". Three years later, after intense study of Islam and Arabic, he disguised himself as a Muslim scholar, took the name Ibrahim ibn Abdullah and set out for Egypt. On his way through Jordan, however, he was lured by tales of a lost city in the mountains. To get there, he had to persuade a guide to take him. Using the pretence that he wanted to offer a sacrifice to the Prophet Aaron, he became the first modern Westerner to enter Petra. The site has sparked travellers' imaginations ever since.

City of Petra Highlights

Modern Museum

Among the exhibits are a marble basin with lioness handles found in Petra Church and a small carved plaque of the Nabataean goddess al-Uzza found in the Great Temple.

Qasr el-Bint el-Faroun

▶ The name "Palace of the Pharaoh's Daughter" was a colourful invention of Bedouin mythology. The 1st-century-BC building was probably Petra's main temple, the huge slab of stone at the foot of the steps being an altar to the sun god Dushara, chief deity of the Nabataean pantheon.

Temenos Gate

The imposing entrance to the sacred precinct of Qasr el-Bint had freestanding columns in front of its three massive, possibly metal-clad wooden doors. It probably dates from after the Roman annexation. The carvings of animal deities on its capitals are a Nabataean slant on an otherwise Classical design.

Temple of the Winged Lions

The name refers to the winged lions on the column capitals. It is also known as the Temple of al-Uzza as it may have been dedicated to this deity. The temple's monumental entrance was reached by a bridge across the Wadi Musa. Fragments of plaster painted with dolphins and floral garlands suggest rich interior decoration.

Petra Church

Superbly detailed 6th-century-AD mosaics adorn the aisles of this once large Byzantine basilica. A cache of 152 scrolls found here revealed details of daily life in Byzantine Petra.

The Roman Cardo

The colonnades give the city's main street a Roman feel. They are thought to have been added after the Romans annexed Petra in AD 106. The street has been partly restored by Jordan's Department of Antiquities.

Great Temple

◀ The grand entrance to this 1st-century-BC site led into a colonnaded lower precinct laid with hexagonal paving stones. Under the floor were extensive water ducts and great stairways swept up to a 600-seat auditorium.

OTHER SITES AROUND PETRA

Many of Petra's most famous sights can be visited in half a day. However, having come so far, it would be a pity not to take the time to explore more of this unique capital of a vanished civilization.

Walk to the Monastery

The climb to the Monastery – one of Petra's best preserved and most awe-inspiring monuments – is arduous, but thoroughly worthwhile. The path, which cuts through the wadi, is paved in parts and features more than 800 rock-cut steps. Do the walk in the afternoon, when the sun is not directly in front.

A short detour off the main route, indicated by a signpost, leads to the Lion Triclinium, which has blurred leonine representations of the goddess al-Uzza guarding its entrance. After this, the path rises steeply; there are occasional flights of steps and several interesting carved

> **The path winding down the other side of Jebel Attuf into the Wadi Farasa valley is a spectacular stepped descent, sometimes with sheer drops.**

monuments along the way. Eventually you reach a wide, rock-cut terrace. Immediately to the right is the Monastery, Petra's most colossal temple, dedicated to the deified king, Obodas I, who died in 86 BC. Its powerful architecture is thought to date from the 1st century AD. The interior has one large chamber with an arch-topped niche where the altar stood. It came to be known as the Monastery because of the many Christian crosses carved on its walls.

Did You Know?

The imposing façade of the Monastery is 47 m (154 ft) wide and 40 m (131 ft) high.

Walk to the High Place of Sacrifice

Midway between the Treasury and the Theatre, a rock-cut stairway leads to the top of Jebel Attuf mountain. It is here, at 1,035 m (3,000 ft), that one of the best-preserved of Petra's many places of sacrifice is located. The gradual ascent requires stamina and a good head for heights, and is best attempted in the early morning. The first part of the summit is a large terrace with two 6-m (20-ft) stone obelisks, possibly fertility symbols, and the second is the High Place of Sacrifice. Steps at the far end lead up to the main altar. The adjacent round altar has a basin with a carved channel, which was possibly used for draining the blood of animal and human sacrifices.

The path winding down the other side of Jebel Attuf into the Wadi Farasa valley is a spectacular stepped descent, sometimes with sheer drops. The first thing you see, carved into the rock face, is the Lion Monument, representing the goddess al-Uzza. The path then leads to the delightfully secluded Garden Triclinium, followed by the relatively plain Broken Pediment Tomb, named after its most striking feature. Nearby is the elegant Renaissance Tomb, with the three urns above its entrance. Past this point the Wadi Farasa widens and the descent ends in the main valley, not far from the Qasr el-Bint.

← The façade of the Monastery, framed through a sandstone rock formation

↑ The Tomb of Sextius Florentinus, 2nd century governor of Arabia

Aaron's Tomb

This site is venerated by Muslims, Christians and Jews as the place where Moses's brother Aaron was buried. The white dome of the shrine can be seen from the High Place of Sacrifice, which may be a close enough viewing for most people – the journey there involves a three-hour ride on horseback and a hard three-hour climb. A guide and supplies are essential.

Tomb of Sextius Florentinus

Beyond the Palace Tomb, along a track skirting the cliff, stands the Tomb of Sextius Florentinus. Despite its badly eroded façade, the beautiful and unusual details of its design are clearly visible.

Further north is the Carmine Façade with vivid striations of red, blue and grey. Continuing alongside the Wadi Mataha brings you to a rock-cut complex known as the House of Dorotheos, while on the other side of the wadi is a cluster of homes and tombs known as Mughar el-Nasara.

Little Petra

This northern suburb of Petra, Siq el-Berid, is known as Little Petra because it is like a miniature version of the main city. Situated 8 km (5 miles) north of Wadi Musa town, it is most easily reached by taxi. The journey on foot is hard, but rewarding; a guide is essential.

Little Petra seems to have been a largely residential settlement – it may well have been where Petra's wealthy merchants had their homes. Just outside its Siq-like entrance are a large cistern and a Classical temple. The

THE NABATAEANS

The Nabataeans migrated westward from northeastern Arabia in the 6th century BC, settling eventually in Petra. By the 1st century BC, they had made it the centre of a rich and powerful kingdom, and had built a city large enough to support up to 30,000 people. Key to their success was their ability to control and conserve water. The Romans took over Petra in AD 106 and by the 4th century the Nabateans had left, for reasons unknown.

gorge, shorter than the one leading into Petra, contains a simple temple. As you emerge into the town, the incredible profusion of façades is overwhelming. Flights of steps shoot off in all directions, evoking images of a bustling urban centre. A particular highlight is the beautifully decorated Painted House.

The spectacular desert scenery of Wadi Rum →

2

WADI RUM

🅰 C7 🅾 30 km (19 miles) SE of the Desert Highway (Route 53); turn off 45 km (28 miles) N of Aqaba

The desert landscape of Wadi Rum is one of the most awe-inspiring sights in the entire Middle East. Huge ochre-coloured rock pinnacles, weathered into bulbous, outlandish shapes, rise up 600 m (2,000 ft) from the flat valley floors, like islands in a sea of red sand. Hundreds of hiking and climbing routes wind their way up and around the peaks.

💬 HIDDEN GEM
Rock Map at Jebel Amud

In a cave situated at the base of Jebel Amud, 20 km (12 miles) northeast of Rum village, is a large rock marked with enigmatic indentations and lines. It is thought by some to be a topographical map of the area, dating from around 3000 BC.

This area was once on a major trade route, and evidence of settlement here includes ruins of a temple built by the Nabataeans (p251) and carvings and inscriptions left later by the Thamuds. TE Lawrence, or Lawrence of Arabia, led many guerilla operations in the desert here during World War I; sites with a connection to him include Lawrence's Spring and the spectacular Jebel Makhras, or Seven Pillars of Wisdom (named after his famous book, not, as is often suggested, vice versa). Today, the region, a UNESCO World Heritage Site, is still inhabited by semi-nomadic Bedouin tribes.

There are essentially two main ways to explore the desert of Wadi Rum: through a combination of jeep and hiking, or by camel trekking. Jeeps allow you to travel further and faster, but the more traditional means of transport will bring you much closer to the stillness of the desert. Either way, make sure you carry lots of water and avoid travelling during the midday heat.

Must See

Did You Know?

The 2015 movie *The Martian* was filmed here, with Wadi Rum standing in as the Red Planet.

1 Not far from Rum village, the tranquil Lawrence's Spring was described by its namesake as "a paradise just five feet square". A Nabataean-built water channel can be seen nearby.

2 Rum Village is a rapidly growing Bedouin settlement.

3 The Jebel Umm Fruth Rock Bridge, a dramatic natural phenomenon, is one of several rock bridges in the area. It rises straight from the desert floor and can be climbed and crossed without difficulty.

③

AMMAN

🅰C3 ✈🚌 ℹJordan Tourism Board, El-Mutanabbi St, Jebel Amman (Third Circle); (06) 567 8444

Like Jordan itself, Amman is a modern creation, but one whose roots run deep into history. The hills of Downtown hosted the biblical capital of the Ammonites and the Roman city of Philadelphia, as well as an Omayyad palace. Amman became the capital of Trans-Jordan in the 1920s and today is a bustling, forward-looking Arab city of over four million people.

①

Downtown

The backstreet souks (markets) around Quraysh, El-Malek Faisal and El-Hashemi streets form the commercial hub of Amman. Shops here stock everything from marinated olives to gold jewellery, while pastry stalls, falafel stands and aromatic coffee and spice grinders also compete for the attention of passers-by. There are also several interesting souvenir stalls on El-Hashemi Street. The central King Hussein Mosque, built in

1924 on the site of a mosque erected in AD 640 by the caliph Omar, is the best attended in the city.

Also nearby is the Roman Nymphaeum, a large public fountain built in AD 191 that contained a pool and was dedicated to the nymphs. Jordan's Department of Antiquities is excavating the Nymphaeum as part of an ongoing programme of restoration, with the intention of turning it into an archaeological park with a museum and performance space. There is no timescale for completion.

②

Citadel

🅰Jebel el-Qalaa 📞(06) 463 8795 🕒Summer: 8am-6pm daily; winter: 8am-5pm daily

For thousands of years, Jebel el-Qalaa has served as the fortified heart of Amman. The Ammonite capital of Rabbath Ammon was situated

←

The remains of the Roman temple of Hercules in the Citadel

here, but most of the remains visible today are part of what was an Omayyad Palace, completed around AD 750 and destined to last for only 30 years. The large complex includes a colonnaded street, an impressive audience hall, a Byzantine basilica and the residence of Amman's local governor. The southern Roman Temple of Hercules, with its towering columns and ornately carved stonework, was built at the same time as the city's Roman Theatre and offers fine views over the city.

③

Roman Theatre

🏛 El-Hashemi St 🕐 8am–10pm daily

Amman's most obvious remnant from the past is its impressive Roman Theatre, dating from around AD 170

and with a seating capacity of about 6,000. It's a fine place to sit, meet the locals and take in the city. The back rows of the theatre were added later and carved out of an existing necropolis. At the foot of the theatre are a Corinthian colonnade and the old Odeon (a small theatre or meeting hall). The nearby Hashemite Square is a popular hangout for local families.

④

Jordan Museum

🏛 Omar Matar St 🕐 9am–4pm Sat–Mon, Wed–Thu; 3–6pm Fri 🌐 jordanmuseum.jo

In the Ras Al-Ayn area of Downtown Amman, this modern museum is one of the best in the entire region, giving a detailed insight into Jordanian history and culture, from the first humans to the coming of Islam. Particular highlights among the 2,000 artifacts on display in this stylish building are the surprisingly modern-looking

↑ Examining an ancient statue from Ain Ghazal at the Jordan Museum

8,000-year-old plaster statues found in Ain Ghazal and a separate exhibit dedicated to the Dead Sea Scrolls (p159). One section recounts the development of writing systems in the region, while an extensive display puts the glories of Petra in its regional context. The Living History gallery looks at traditional Bedouin life, while the Modern Jordan exhibition highlights contemporary Jordanian achievements. An upstairs gallery on Islamic Jordan is also planned.

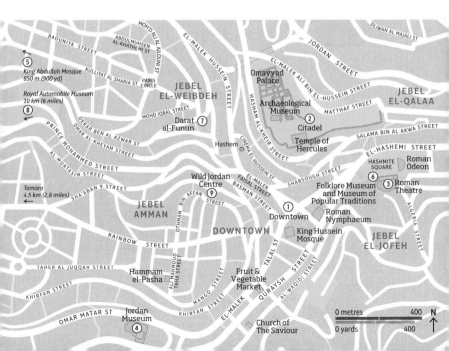

⑤

King Abdullah Mosque

🏠 Suleyman el-Nabulsi St, Jebel el-Webdeh ⏰ 8am-11am & 12:30-2pm Sat-Thu, 9am-10am Fri

Amman's most impressive Islamic monument is the striking King (El-Malek) Abdullah Mosque, completed in 1990 and dedicated by King Hussein to his grandfather. The soaring central blue dome covers the largest religious space in the city – the prayer hall can hold up to 7,000 worshippers. The cavernous, octagonal interior is decorated with elegant Qu'ranic calligraphy and several huge chandeliers. Remove your shoes when you enter the mosque. Women should wear a headscarf (provided). The attached small Islamic museum contains coins and examples of Islamic decorative arts.

⑥

Folklore Museum and Museum of Popular Traditions

🏠 El-Hashemi St 📞 (06) 465 1742 ⏰ Summer: 8am-6pm Sat-Thu, 9am-6pm Fri; winter: 8am-4pm Sat-Thu, 9am-4pm Fri

The vaults below the Roman Theatre are home to these two modest but interesting museums. Exhibits at the Folklore Museum include some traditional costumes, a Bedouin tent, choice examples of the *rababa* (a one-stringed musical instrument) and traditional coffee grinders. The second museum displays Circassian and Armenian silver jewellery, traditionally given to the bride on her wedding day, plus amulets made from Turkish coins and symbols representing the hands of Fatima. There are some fine mosaics from Jerash (*p258*) and the baptism site of Wadi el-Kharrar.

> **INSIDER TIP**
> **Cooking Classes**
>
> Learn to cook Jordanian, Palestinian and other regional cuisines and then sit down to dine on the terrace of the Beit Sitti cookery school (*www.beitsittijo.com*), run by the ebullient Haddad sisters.

↑ The elegant King Abdullah Mosque, with its enormous domed prayer hall (*inset*)

A vintage 1916 Cadillac on display in the Royal Automobile Museum →

⑦ Darat al-Funun

🏠 Nimer bin Adwan St, Jebel el-Webdeh
🕐 10am-7pm Sat-Thu
🌐 daratalfunun.org

This art gallery, pleasant café and small garden dotted with archaeological remains offer a tranquil escape from the nearby Downtown bustle. The rotating exhibits of contemporary art, regular lectures and occasional music concerts make this the best place to tap into Amman's thriving arts scene. The main gallery is housed in a 1920s villa, next to the charming remains of a 6th-century Byzantine church.

⑧ Royal Automobile Museum

🏠 King Hussein Park
🕐 10am-7pm Wed, Thu & Sat-Mon, 11am-7pm Fri
🌐 royalautomuseum.jo

The former King Hussein was passionate about automobiles and this museum, situated 5 km (3 miles) northwest of the city centre, exhibits around 70 classic cars and motorcycles from his personal collection. The vehicles range from a 1916 Cadillac to an array of more modern Lotus, Ferrari and Porsche sporting models. Also on display is the Mercedes-Benz jeep that carried the casket in his funeral procession in 1999.

⑨ Wild Jordan Centre

🏠 Othman bin Affan St, Jebel Amman
🌐 rscn.org.jo

This cutting-edge centre focuses on Jordan's natural heritage. The Wild Jordan Nature shop stocks products made by local development initiatives throughout Jordan, including natural handmade olive oil soaps from Ajlun, worked silver from Dana and Mujib, Bedouin-made candles from Feynan and hand-painted ostrich eggs from the Eastern Desert. The excellent café serves tasty and healthy lunches, and the terrace, in particular, affords fantastic views over Downtown.

This is also the place for information on ecotourism excursions to Jordan's many nature reserves; possibilities include hiking and canyoning in Wadi Mujib, and the chance to see Arabian oryx in the wild at the excellent Shaumari Wildlife Reserve.

EAT

Hashem
An ever-busy Amman icon, Hashem serves up bowls of hummus and *fuul* (stewed beans), mountains of falafel and gallons of mint tea with aplomb.

🏠 Al-Malek St, Downtown 🕐 24 hours

🔵🔵🔵

Tamara
Delicious seafood restaurant; try the house speciality of bass covered with Dead Sea salt. There are also vegan options.

🏠 Al Hayek St, Fifth Circle 📞 (06) 400 0500
🕐 8am-11pm daily

🔵🔵🔵

---

④ ✎ 🖰

JERASH

🔺C3 🚩50 km (31 miles) N of Amman 🚌From Amman ☎(02) 634 2471
🕐Oct-Apr: 8am-4pm Mon-Thu, 9am-4pm Fri-Sun; May-Sep: 8am-7pm
Mon-Thu, 9am-4pm Fri-Sun

Jerash, known as Gerasa in classical times, is one of the most
original and best-preserved Roman cities in the Middle East.
Highlights include the unusual oval-shaped plaza and the Cardo,
a spectacular paved street about 800 m (2,600 ft) long with
chariot tracks still visible in the stones.

Jerash became an urban centre during the 3rd
century BC and from the 1st century BC the
city drew considerable prestige from the semi-
independent status it was given within the
Roman province of Syria. It prospered greatly
from its position on the incense and spice
trade route from Arabia to the Mediterranean.
Trajan's annexation of the Nabataean capital
Petra (p244) in AD 106 brought the city even
more wealth and by AD 130 Jerash was at its
zenith. After a period of decline in the 3rd
century, it enjoyed a renaissance as a Christian
city under the Byzantines. The Muslims took
over Jerash in 635, and it was badly damaged
by earthquakes in the 8th century. The final
blow to the city was dealt by Baldwin II of
Jerusalem in 1112 during the Crusades.

Exploring the City

The city is reached through Hadrian's Arch.
Alongside is the Hippodrome, where
Gerasa's chariot races and other sporting
events were held. Today, re-enactments
of these events take place daily
(except Tue), while the South
Theatre is used as a venue for the Jordan
Festival. The Oval Plaza, with its asymmetrical
shape, is a unique monument from the Roman
world. To its north is the Cardo, which was lined
with the city's major buildings, shops and residences. On the left side is the 2nd-century
Nymphaeum, a lavish public fountain, and
nearby is the impressive Temple of Artemis,
the patron goddess of the city in Greek and
Roman times. Close to the Temple are the
remains of several Byzantine churches. Further
along the Cardo is the Propylaeum Church,
which sits next to the ruins of an Omayyad
Mosque. Beyond lie the unexcavated West
Baths, which preserve a splendid domed ceiling.
   Allow at least half a day to see the ruins,
and finish off at the Museum, which displays
sarcophagi, statuary and coins.

> **Jerash prospered greatly from
> its position on the incense and
> spice trade route from Arabia
> to the Mediterranean.**

1 Hadrian's Arch, which was built in honour of the Roman emperor, stands at the entrance to the city.

2 The Oval Plaza dates back to the 1st century AD. It is 80 m by 90 m (262 ft by 295 ft) and is enclosed by 160 Ionic columns.

3 The main artery through Jerash, the Cardo features regular drainage holes that connect to an advanced underground sewage system.

The impressive remains of the elaborately decorated stage in the South Theatre ↓

MADABA MOSAICS

🅰C4 🏠Madaba 🚌From Amman 🕐St George's Church: 8:30am–6pm daily (from 10:30am Fri & Sun); Archaeological Park: daily

Known as the "City of Mosaics", Madaba is renowned for it spectacular collection of tiled artworks. The most famous of these is the Madaba Mosaic Map of Jerusalem and the Holy Land, comprised of two million pieces of delicately positioned local stone.

According to the Old Testament, the Moabite city of Madaba was one of those conquered by the tribes of Israel. After changing hands several times, it flourished under Roman dominion and by the 4th century AD it had become an important centre of Christianity, with its own bishop. The town weathered invasions by the Persians and Muslims but declined under the Mamelukes, and was abandoned during the 16th century. It was not reoccupied until the late 19th century.

The main attraction is the fabulous mosaic map housed in St George's Church in the town centre. An icon of the Virgin Mary in the church is believed by Christians to incorporate a miraculous blue "helping hand". An Archaeological Park encompasses the remains of several more 6th-century churches, all with impressive mosaics, including one depicting scenes from the legend of Adonis and Aphrodite. The Church of the Apostles on the southern edge of town has a mosaic depicting the sea goddess Thetis surrounded by fish and sea monsters.

↑ The simple exterior of St George's Church, within which lies the Madaba Mosaic Map

← A detail from the Madaba Mosaic Map, showing Jericho and the Jordan River

↑ Admiring one of the works on display at the Archeological Park

THE MADABA MOSAIC MAP

In the late 19th century, a small group of Christians from Kerak moved to the long-uninhabited site of ancient Madaba. In 1884, while clearing the site of an old church to build a new one, the mosaic map was uncovered. It was incorporated into the new St George's Church but was damaged in the process. Ten years later, scholars recognized the historic value of the mosaic, which was probably made during the 6th century.

The colourful interior of ↑
St George's Church with the
mosaic map of the Holy Land

EXPERIENCE MORE

6

Umm Qais

C2 **Q** 100 km (62 miles) NW of Amman **Q** 7am–sunset daily

Umm Qais is the site of the ancient Graeco-Roman city of Gadara. The ruins lie in lush hill country overlooking the Golan Heights and the Sea of Galilee. The city is well known for Jesus's miracle of the Gadarene Swine, when he cast out demons and turned them into pigs (Matthew 8: 28–34). Since 1974, archaeologists have uncovered many impressive Roman remains, including a colonnaded street, a theatre and a mausoleum.

The village is also at the forefront of Jordan's recent community tourism boom, with activities offered under the umbrella of **Baraka Destinations**. Local guides lead visitors on nature trails and hiking and biking tours, or take them foraging for edible plants. There are cooking classes in a family kitchen and even beekeeping with the village apiarist.

Baraka Destinations
W barakadestinations.com

Did You Know?

The ancient theatre of Gadara at Umm Qais was unusual for its time in that the seats had back rests.

7

Ajlun

C3 **Q** 50 km (31 miles) W of Amman **☎** (02) 642 0115

The market town of Ajlun is dominated by the fortress of **Qalat ar-Rabad**, a superb example of Arab military engineering. Built in 1184–5, it was used by the Ottomans up until the 18th century. At a height of more than 1,200 m (4,000 ft), it offers fantastic views over the Jordan Valley.

Qalat ar-Rabad
Q 8am–5pm daily (to 4pm winter)

8

Mount Nebo

C3 **Q** 10 km (6 miles) NW of Madaba **➡** From Madaba, then a 4-km (2.5-mile) walk, or taxi **Q** 7am–7pm daily (to 5pm Oct–Apr)

This mountain is at the end of the long chain skirting the Dead Sea, with panoramic views of the Jordan River and Dead Sea 1,000 m (3,300 ft) below. It was from here that Moses saw the Promised Land just before he died (Deuteronomy 34: 1–5).

In the early 4th century, a sanctuary, mentioned by the pilgrim nun Egeria, was built on Mount Nebo (Fasaliyyeh in Arabic) to honour Moses, probably over the remains of a more ancient construction. During the Byzantine period, the church was transformed into a fine basilica with a sacristy and new baptistry. Monastic buildings were added later.

Since 1933, reconstruction work has been carried out on the church, now known as the Memorial Church of Moses.

Exploring the tunnels of Kerak Castle of the Knights Templar ↑

> **Mosaics decorating the Memorial Church of Moses include a remarkable example in the Old Baptistry depicting farmers, hunters and an assortment of animals.**

Mosaics decorating the inside include a remarkable example in the Old Baptistry depicting farmers, hunters and animals surrounded by geometric decoration. A Greek inscription dates it to AD 531. Next to the New Baptistry, a mosaic cross from the original church stands on a modern altar. Outside, the foundations of the monastery can be seen.

9

Kerak

🅰 C4 🏠 70 km (45 miles) SE of Amman 🚌 🛈 El-Mujamma St; (03) 235 4263

The town of Kerak, on top of a hill with a sheer drop on three sides, is dominated by

←

The imposing 12th-century fortress of Qalat ar-Rabad, which overlooks Ajlun

a magnificent Crusader citadel. Kerak was an important city (and for a time the capital) of the biblical kingdom of Moab. For this reason, Kerak Castle is also sometimes known as Krak des Moabites.

The stronghold was built in 1142 by the Frankish lord of Oultrejourdain, Payen le Bouteiller, to whom the territory had been ceded by King Baldwin II of Jerusalem in 1126. It was the pearl in the chain of fortifications that ran between Jerusalem and Aqaba, and replaced Shobak as the centre of Oultrejourdain. Under Reynald de Châtillon it resisted assaults by Saladin's troops in 1183 and 1184, but finally fell after a siege in 1188.

Arab repairs and additions made in white limestone contrast with the Crusader parts built in dark, volcanic tufa. The upper courtyard, containing a much-damaged Crusader chapel, provides an exceptional viewpoint. From

there, steps lead down to vast, dimly lit, vaulted rooms and corridors below ground. The lower courtyard gives access to a small **Archaeological Museum** displaying various artifacts that were excavated in the local area.

Archaeological Museum
🕙 🅰 Kerak Castle, El-Mujamma St 📞 (03) 235 1862 🕘 9am–5pm daily

---

> **JORDAN TRAIL**
>
> The Jordan Trail *(www. jordantrail.org)* opened in 2015 and is an epic hiking trail that runs for 650 km (400 miles) along the length of the country from Umm Qais to the Red Sea. The trail is divided into eight discrete sections and there is an annual 36-day supported through-hike that runs every March. The four-day route through the spectacular Dana Wildlife Reserve to Petra has been dubbed the Inca Trail of the Middle East.

🔟

Shobak

🅰C5 🚗60 km (37 miles) S of Tafila 📞(03) 213 2138 🚌To Shobak village, then taxi ⏰Daily

Shobak, isolated on a rocky, conical hill in rough, barren surroundings at 1,300 m (4,265 ft) above sea level, is perhaps the most impressively sited castle in Jordan. It was called Krak de Montréal, or Mons Regalis, and was the first outpost (1115) built beyond the Jordan River by King Baldwin I of Jerusalem to guard the road from Egypt to Damascus. It resisted many sieges until 1189, when it fell to Saladin's troops.

The towers and walls are well preserved and decorated with carved inscriptions that date from the 14th-century Mameluke renovations, but the inside is ruinous. Near the gatehouse, a well with more than 350 dangerously slippery, spiral, rock-cut steps descends to a spring.

Large sandy beaches stretch out along the Aqaba coast, bounded by modern hotels, while the steep mountains behind form a spectacular natural backdrop.

1️⃣1️⃣

Aqaba

🅰B7 🚗283 km (176 miles) S of Amman ✈🚌 ℹEl-Koornish St (next to the Fort); (03) 201 3363

The only Jordanian outlet to the sea, Aqaba is a very important commercial port town. This is evidenced by the relentless stream of heavy trucks going to and from Amman on the Desert Highway.

South of the town, however, the crystal clear waters are home to fabulous coral reefs – the main reason for Aqaba's popularity with visitors, with some of the best scuba diving in the world. Closer to shore, many other water sports also help to provide escape from the extreme summer heat. Large sandy beaches stretch out along the coast, bounded by modern hotels, while the steep mountains behind form a spectacular natural backdrop.

Aqaba's long and glorious past also provides it with some notable archaeological sites to visit. It is thought to be near the site of biblical Ezion-Geber, the large port said, but not proven, to have been built by King Solomon.

Aqaba's deep freshwater springs ensured that the town became a popular caravan stop for merchants travelling between Egypt, the Mediterranean coast and Arabia. By the 2nd century BC, the now prosperous town had fallen under the control of the Nabataeans (p251). Such prosperity saw it conquered by the Romans in AD 106, and the Muslims in AD 630.

SCUBA DIVING

Jordan manages to squeeze in some world-class scuba diving on its short Red Sea coastline. Dive centres near Aqaba cater for all levels, and beginners can learn straight off the beach and be swimming among coral almost immediately. There are multiple dive sites within the Aqaba Marine Reserve, which abounds in soft coral, along with the dazzlingly diverse marine life of the Cedar Pride artificial reef.

Under Muslim control, Aqaba became an important stage on the pilgrimage to Mecca, and the Muslims built the fortified town of Ayla nearby to the north. After suffering a major earthquake in 748, the town was rebuilt, and thrived with an increasing sea trade. Following another earthquake in 1068, and the Crusader conquests of the 12th century, the city was abandoned. You can visit the ruins at the Ayla digs, next to the coastal Corniche road. Much of the foundations of walls, towers and a series of buildings still remain, and there's an **Archaeological Museum** next to the tourist office.

Another key archaeological site is the **Mameluke Fort**, which is currently closed for renovation. Built in the 16th century, its portal now bears the coat-of-arms of the Hashemites, placed there after Lawrence of Arabia's troops conquered the port during World War I. The fort also served as a caravanserai, and some restored rooms reflect this more peaceful role.

West past the industrial port and just beyond the ferry terminal is the small

Aqaba Marine Science Station Aquarium, containing some of the most important species of the Gulf of Aqaba. It also displays information on conservation in the Red Sea.

Archaeological Museum
⊘ ⌂El-Koornish St (next to Mameluke Fort) ☎(03) 201 9063 ⌚8am-4pm daily

Mameluke Fort
⊘ ⌂La Côte Verte ☎(03) 201 9063

Aqaba Marine Science Station Aquarium
⊘ ⌂South Coast (near ferry terminal) ☎(03) 201 5145 ⌚7:30am-3:30pm daily

Aqaba's beach and marina and *(inset)* divers out in the Tala bay ↓

NEED TO KNOW

Driving through the Negev Desert

BEFORE YOU GO

Things change, so plan ahead to make the most of your trip. Be prepared for all eventualities by considering the following points before you travel.

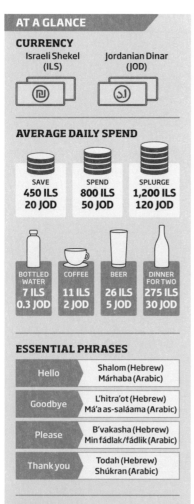

AT A GLANCE

CURRENCY

Israeli Shekel (ILS)

Jordanian Dinar (JOD)

AVERAGE DAILY SPEND

SAVE	SPEND	SPLURGE
450 ILS	800 ILS	1,200 ILS
20 JOD	50 JOD	120 JOD

BOTTLED WATER	COFFEE	BEER	DINNER FOR TWO
7 ILS	11 ILS	26 ILS	275 ILS
0.3 JOD	2 JOD	5 JOD	30 JOD

ESSENTIAL PHRASES

Hello	Shalom (Hebrew) Márhaba (Arabic)
Goodbye	L'hitra'ot (Hebrew) Má'a as-saláama (Arabic)
Please	B'vakasha (Hebrew) Min fádlak/fádlik (Arabic)
Thank you	Todah (Hebrew) Shúkran (Arabic)

ELECTRICITY SUPPLY

Power sockets are type C and H, fitting two- and three-pronged plugs. Standard voltage is 220v.

Passports and Visas

Israel

For entry requirements, including visas, consult your nearest Israeli embassy or check the **Israel Ministry of Foreign Affairs** website, under Consular Services. Israel issues on-arrival tourist visas, usually valid for three months, to most holders of passports from the UK, North America, Europe, Australia, and New Zealand.

Rather than stamping passports, Israeli authorities generally issue an entry card. An Israeli stamp in your passport will bar you from visiting some Arab and Muslim countries, notably Lebanon and Iran.

Israel Ministry of Foreign Affairs
W mfa.org.il

Palestinian Territories

Access to the Palestinian Territories is through Israel. The West Bank's King Hussein/Allenby Bridge crossing with Jordan is controlled by Israel, as are the checkpoints between Israel and the Palestinian Territories. When travelling to and around the Palestinian Territories, always carry your passport and your loose-leaf Israeli entry card as these are likely to be checked.

Jordan

For entry requirements, including visas, consult your nearest Jordanian embassy or check the **Hashemite Kingdom of Jordan** website. To enter Jordan you must have a passport valid for at least six months. Most holders of passports from the UK, North America, Europe, Australia, New Zealand, South Africa, Hong Kong, South Korea and Japan can obtain a single-entry visa, valid for one month, on arrival at Amman's Queen Alia airport or via the Sheikh Hussein/Jordan River crossing from Israel. If entering Jordan via the King Hussein/Allenby Bridge crossing or the Wadi Araba/Yitzhak Rabin crossing, you must obtain your visa in advance from the Jordanian consulate in your home country or in Ramat Gan (near Tel Aviv). Jordan's visa fee is waived if you purchase a Jordan Pass *(p276)* in advance.

Hashemite Kingdom of Jordan
W portal.jordan.gov.jo

Government Advice

It is important to consult both your and the Israeli government's advice before travelling. The **UK Foreign and Commonwealth Office**, the **US State Department**, the **Australian Department of Foreign Affairs and Trade** and the **Israeli Government** offer the latest information on security, health and local regulations.
Australian Department of Foreign Affairs and Trade
W smartraveller.gov.au
Israeli Government
W gov.il
UK Foreign and Commonwealth Office
W gov.uk/foreign-travel-advice
US State Department
W travel.state.gov

Customs Information

You can find information on the laws relating to goods and currency taken in or out of Israel on the **Israel Tax Authority** website. Israel and the Palestinian Authority have a customs union, and there are no customs checks between the two.
Israel Tax Authority
W gov.il/en/departments/israel_tax_authority

Insurance

We recommend you take out a comprehensive insurance policy covering theft, medical care, loss of belongings, cancellations and delays, and read the small print carefully.

Vaccinations

For information regarding COVID-19 vaccination requirements, consult government advice. If you plan on arriving into Jordan from a country where yellow fever is endemic you will need a vaccination certificate.

Money

Israel and the Palestinian Territories use the Israeli Shekel (ILS), while Jordan's currency is the Jordanian Dinar (JOD). Almost all shops and restaurants in Israel take credit cards, as do many in the Palestinian Territories and Jordan. ATMs are easy to find throughout the region.

Travellers with Specific Requirements

Israel offers a good level of accessibility for those with limited mobility. Jerusalem's Old City is not easy to navigate, but there is a wheelchair route starting from Jaffa Gate. City buses have fold-out ramps and Jerusalem's light rail system is wheelchair-friendly. Most Israeli train stations have disabled access, and many national parks and nature reserves have wheelchair routes.
Access Israel has details on sites and services.
In Jordan, only luxury hotels are equipped for the disabled. Cities and most sites are rough terrain, so visits can be difficult.
Access Israel
W aisrael.org

Language

The official language in Israel is Hebrew; in the Palestinian Territories and Jordan it is Arabic. In Israel all signs are bilingual in Hebrew and English, and most people speak some English. In tourist areas in the Palestinian Territories and Jordan, it is usually easy to find English speakers.

Opening Hours

COVID-19 Increased rates of infection may result in temporary opening hours and/or closures. Always check ahead before visiting museums, attractions and hospitality venues.

Because of the many religious holidays in the region, opening hours vary greatly. In Jewish areas of Israel, shops are closed and public transport shuts down on Shabbat (from mid-afternoon on Friday until Saturday after sunset), and on many Jewish holidays. In Christian areas, many shops are closed on Sunday, while Muslim sites and some Muslim-owned businesses are closed on Fridays. In Jordan, smaller historic sites and many museums close on Tuesdays.

Public and Religious Holidays

Dates for public and religious holidays are highly variable, so check ahead before travelling.

GETTING AROUND

Whether you are visiting for a short city break or exploring the desert, discover how best to reach your destination and travel like a local.

AT A GLANCE

PUBLIC TRANSPORT COSTS

ISRAEL

6 ILS

Single journey
Bus and Light Rail

ISRAEL

13 ILS

One-day pass
Bus and Light Rail

ISRAEL

62.50 ILS

Seven-day pass
Bus and Light Rail

TOP TIP
Most public transport stops running on Shabbat, from mid-afternoon on Friday to sundown on Saturday.

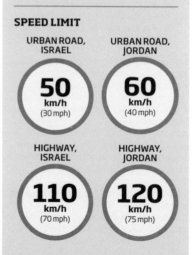

SPEED LIMIT

URBAN ROAD, ISRAEL

50 km/h
(30 mph)

URBAN ROAD, JORDAN

60 km/h
(40 mph)

HIGHWAY, ISRAEL

110 km/h
(70 mph)

HIGHWAY, JORDAN

120 km/h
(75 mph)

Arriving by Air

Israel has two international airports: Ben-Gurion, near Tel Aviv, and Ramon, near Eilat. Thanks to an Open Skies agreement with the European Union, dozens of low-cost airlines link both airports with cities all over Europe. Because of security (reputed to be the strictest in the world), it is advisable to arrive for your flights to and from Israel a full three hours before departure. Israeli airports are open every day of the year except Yom Kippur.

Trains linking Ben-Gurion with Tel Aviv and Haifa operate 24 hours a day, while the new high-speed line between the airport and Jerusalem runs from 6:30am to 7:30pm. All lines are closed on Shabbat and Jewish holidays. Taxis and shared minibuses can also be picked up at the airport.

Jordan's main airport is Queen Alia International near Amman. Royal Jordanian Airlines flies between Amman and Tel Aviv. Express buses into the city depart from outside the arrivals terminal.

Arriving by Land

There are two land border crossings between Israel and Jordan and one between the Israeli-controlled West Bank and Jordan. Closest to Jerusalem is the King Hussein/Allenby Bridge crossing, 16 km (10 miles) east of Jericho. In the south, the Yitzhak Rabin/Wadi Araba crossing is 4 km (2 miles) north of Eilat and 10 km (6 miles) from Aqaba. In the north, the Jordan River/Sheikh Hussein crossing is near Beit She'an, 30 km (20 miles) south of the Sea of Galilee. Check with the **Israel Airports Authority** for opening times. Israel charges a per-person exit fee of 101 ILS (175 ILS at Allenby), while Jordan charges 10 JOD (bring cash).

Land crossings between Israel and Jordan close on Yom Kippur and the Islamic New Year (Eid al-Hijra), while the King Hussein/Allenby Bridge is closed on Yom Kippur, with the Palestinian wing also closed on Eid al-Adha.
Israel Airports Authority
w iaa.gov.il

GETTING TO AND FROM BEN-GURION AIRPORT			
City	Distance	Taxi fare	Train journey time
Jerusalem	52 km (32 miles)	255 ILS	24 mins
Tel Aviv	25 km (15 miles)	132 ILS	16 mins
Haifa	115 km (71 miles)	462 ILS	90 mins

Train Travel

Israel Railways has a growing network that links Akko, Haifa, Karmiel and Beit She'an in the north with Ben-Gurion Airport, Jerusalem and Be'er Sheva in the centre and south, with Tel Aviv's four stations serving as a central hub. For tourists, the most useful (and beautiful) line follows the Mediterranean coast, linking Tel Aviv with Nahariya, near the border with Lebanon. The trains are swift, comfortable and inexpensive but can be crowded on Sunday mornings and Thursday evenings. The express train linking Jerusalem with Tel Aviv, opened in 2018, takes just 28 minutes.
Israel Railways
🗔 rail.co.il

Intercity Bus Travel

Every town and city in the region has a bus station, and interurban services are frequent and affordable. In Israel, intercity bus services are run by over a dozen companies, the largest of which is **Egged**. Details for all services are available on the **Israel Public Transportation Information** website. Advance reservations are not required (or even possible), except to Eilat. Intercity bus services stop for Shabbat, ending in the mid-afternoon on Friday and resuming sometime between mid-afternoon and an hour after sundown on Saturday.

Coach tours, such as those run by **Abraham Tours**, are an efficient way of visiting several sites in one day – something that is not always feasible on public transport.

In East Jerusalem, buses (and shared taxis) to the Palestinian Territories depart from two stations: one on Nablus Road for services to Ramallah and the other on Sultan Suleyman Street for Bethlehem. Change in Ramallah to get to Nablus and Jericho, and in or near Bethlehem for services to Hebron.

Jordan's largest intercity bus company is **JETT**, which runs air-conditioned buses from several stations in Amman to King Hussein/Allenby Bridge, Petra and Aqaba. Booking your seat in advance is advisable.
Abraham Tours
🗔 abrahamtours.com
Egged
🗔 egged.co.il
Israel Public Transportation Information
🗔 bus.co.il
JETT
🗔 jett.com.jo

Local Bus and Light Rail

All of Israel's cities have excellent local public transport, with plenty of information available online in English. Local buses are easy to use, fast, frequent and wheelchair-friendly – for details on services in Jerusalem see the Egged website, and for Tel Aviv check with **Dan**. Tickets are not sold on board and you must buy a **Rav Kav** debit card, which can be purchased at the airport, bus stations or in malls, or downloaded onto your phone. Valid for buses, trains and the light rail, it provides discounts and free follow-on urban rides after an inter-city ride..

In Jerusalem, most of the city's sights are situated along the JLR, an ultramodern tram line that serves downtown West Jerusalem (Jaffa Road), the Old City's Damascus Gate and Mount Herzl, as well as the Central Bus Station; it also uses the Rav Kav system. The 24-km (15-miles) Tel Aviv light rail, which runs underground in the center of the city, is due to open in late 2022.

To get about in Amman, there are city buses, but they can be difficult to navigate because the destination is indicated only in Arabic.
Dan
🗔 dan.co.il
Rav Kav
🗔 ravkavonline.co.il

Taxis

Taxis are generally white with a yellow rooftop sign that is lit up when available. You can hail one on a main street, book by phone or use an app like **Gett**. All taxis have meters and by law drivers must use them. Taxi fares, which are not cheap to begin with, rise by 25 per cent from 9pm to 5:30am and on Shabbat and Jewish holidays.

In Jerusalem, Israeli drivers may sometimes refuse to go to East Jerusalem; Arab drivers are generally willing to go anywhere in the city.

Gett
W gett.com

Shared Taxis

Known in Hebrew as a *sherut* and in Arabic as a *servees*, shared taxis – usually minibuses – operate on fixed routes similar to a bus, but, like a taxi, can be hailed on the street. They can be particularly useful in Israel, as they operate on Shabbat and Jewish holidays. At the start of the route, drivers generally wait until every seat is taken before setting off. There are no set stops; passengers indicate to the driver where they'd like to be let off. Fares are similar to the equivalent bus ride (they cost a bit more on Shabbat and Jewish holidays). Service taxis run by **Nesher** pick up passengers at any address in Jerusalem and take them to Ben-Gurion Airport for 67 ILS per person; reserve a day ahead.

Service taxis are widely used for getting to and around the Palestinian Territories, with the Damascus Gate area of Jerusalem serving as something of a hub. They are also a common form of transport in Jordan.

Nesher
W neshertours.co.il

Driving

Accident rates in Israel have fallen precipitously thanks to education campaigns and aggressive enforcement. Despite this, it is not uncommon to experience aggressive and unpredictable driving from local motorists. While this should not put you off driving in the region, you do need to be cautious.

Car Rental

Most major international car rental companies have offices in Israel, including at Ben-Gurion Airport, though local companies such as **Eldan** sometimes offer better rates.

To rent a car, you must be at least 21 years of age and have a driving licence and an international credit card. Insurance is compulsory as part of any hire package; prices quoted online often do not include insurance, which can double the total cost.

Most Israeli car rental companies do not allow their vehicles to be taken into areas administered by the Palestinian Authority. If you'd like to drive in the West Bank, you can rent from **Dallah** and **Goodluck**, both based in East Jerusalem.

Dallah
W dallahrentacar.com
Eldan
W rent.eldan.co.il
Goodluck
W goodluckcars.com

Driving in the Region

Israel has three toll roads: Route 6, which links the Be'er Sheva area with the Galilee; an express lane from near Ben-Gurion Airport to Tel Aviv; and the Carmel Tunnels, under Mount Carmel in Haifa. Toll charges are automatically taken off the credit card you registered with the hire company, though some may ask you to sign a waiver whereby you agree not to drive on toll roads.

In Jordan, main highways are well surfaced, with proper road markings, but minor roads are often in a poor state. Take care on desert roads, where drifting sand can put the car into a spin.

Parking

In city centres, on-street parking can be very difficult to find, especially if you don't have a local parking sticker, and parking rules, inscribed on yellow signs, are generally only in Hebrew. You are required to pay an hourly fee for parking on blue and white kerbsides (except at night and on Shabbat), which can only be done via a cellphone app, such as **Cellopark** and **Pango**. Driving in Jerusalem and Tel Aviv is therefore best avoided unless essential.

Cellopark
W cellopark.co.il
Pango
W pango.co.il

Rules of the Road

You should drive on the right-hand side of the road throughout the region. Laws requiring that cars stop for pedestrians crossing the street are strenuously enforced. At signals, left turns are permitted only when you have a green arrow; right turns on red are not allowed.

The drink driving limit in Israel is a BAC (blood alcohol content) of 50mg of alcohol per 100ml of blood; in Jordan it is zero.

Children in private cars must ride in backward-facing car seats until age one (recommended until age two), be strapped into car seats until age three and sit on booster seats until age eight (recommended until age ten).

Hire cars come equipped with a fluorescent vest and warning triangle. In the event of a breakdown, put on the vest before leaving the car and position the triangle so it warns oncoming cars.

Cycling

If you don't mind hills, the best regions for cycling are the Galilee and Golan Heights. The varied scenery is lovely to cycle through, and the altitude helps to moderate the extreme heat of summer. In Tiberias, **Aviv Hostel** rents out bicycles to ride all the way around the Sea of Galilee (65 km/ 40 miles), mostly on a dedicated cycling path – a full circuit of the lake can comfortably be made in just one day.

The Negev is also popular for cycling, with off-road biking taking you through spectacular desert scenery. The **Israel National Bike Trail** offers routes between Mitzpe Ramon and Eilat. Bikes can be rented at Timna Park (*p225*).

Tel Aviv-Jaffa has an extensive network of bike paths. There are several hire companies from which you can rent bikes, including **Tel-O-Fun**, and some hotels and hostels offer free bikes to their guests.

Jerusalem is hilly and has narrow streets so the city can be challenging to cycle around – caution is advised. **Bike Jerusalem** offers rental and bike tours.

Aviv Hostel
📞 (04) 671 2273
Bike Jerusalem
🔤 bikejerusalem.com

Israel National Bike Trail
🔤 ibt.org.il
Tel-O-Fun
🔤 tel-o-fun.co.il

E-Scooters

Electric scooters have become one of the most popular forms of intra-city transport in Tel Aviv, Jerusalem and Eilat, with **Lime** and **Bird** dominating the rental market.
Bird
🔤 bird.co
Lime
🔤 li.me/electric-scooter

Walking

Jerusalem's Old and New cities are largely pedestrianized and easy to walk around. The centres of Tel Aviv, Bethlehem, Amman and other cities in the region are also very walkable.

Hiking trails can be found across the region. Some of the best trails in Israel are around Maktesh Ramon and Ein Gedi, and up in the Golan Heights, while the West Bank has a number of walking routes with a focus on Palestinian culture and history. The best hiking in Jordan is in and around Wadi Rum and Petra.

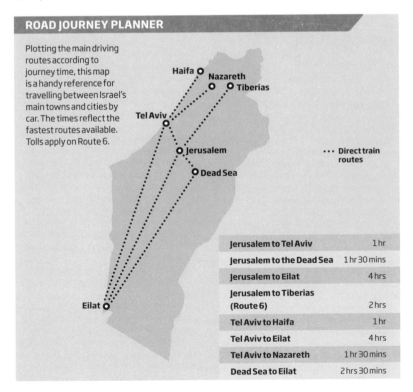

ROAD JOURNEY PLANNER

Plotting the main driving routes according to journey time, this map is a handy reference for travelling between Israel's main towns and cities by car. The times reflect the fastest routes available. Tolls apply on Route 6.

Haifa • Nazareth • Tiberias • Tel Aviv • Jerusalem • Dead Sea • Eilat

••• Direct train routes

Jerusalem to Tel Aviv	1 hr
Jerusalem to the Dead Sea	1 hr 30 mins
Jerusalem to Eilat	4 hrs
Jerusalem to Tiberias (Route 6)	2 hrs
Tel Aviv to Haifa	1 hr
Tel Aviv to Eilat	4 hrs
Tel Aviv to Nazareth	1 hr 30 mins
Dead Sea to Eilat	2 hrs 30 mins

PRACTICAL
INFORMATION

A little local know-how goes a long way in the Holy Land. Here you will find all the essential advice and information you will need during your stay.

AT A GLANCE

EMERGENCY NUMBERS

ISRAEL AND THE PALESTINIAN TERRITORIES		JORDAN GENERAL EMERGENCY
Police	100	**911**
Ambulance	101	
Fire	102	

TIME ZONE

IST/IDT (2 hours ahead of GMT): Israel Daylight Time runs from the Friday before the last Sunday in March to the last Sunday in October.

TAP WATER

Israel's tap water, much of it desalinated seawater, is safe to drink. In the Palestinian Territories and Jordan some tap water is potable but it's advisable to purchase bottled water.

TIPPING

Waiter	10-15 per cent
Housekeeping	10-20 ILS per night
Guide	20 ILS per group member per day
Taxi Driver	Not expected

Personal Security

Violence against tourists and pilgrims is very rare in Israel, the Palestinian Territories and Jordan. However, the political and security situation in the region is volatile, so keep an eye on the local news, stay alert on the streets and steer clear of demonstrations. Among the most sensitive areas are the Temple Mount (Al-Haram ash-Sharif) and Damascus Gate in Jerusalem, Hebron and Israeli checkpoints in the West Bank; the most tense time of the week is Friday after midday Muslim prayers. Should you be unlucky enough to come across a disturbance in the streets, move away from the scene quickly, and make it clear that you are a foreign tourist. Do not drive in ultra-Orthodox areas on Shabbat or you risk having stones thrown at your vehicle.

In Israel, you may have to undergo security checks upon entering hotels, cinemas and malls. At the central bus stations in Jerusalem and Tel Aviv, bags are searched or scanned. Never leave your luggage unattended in public places or the bomb squad may be summoned. Do not accept packages from anyone asking you to carry something for them.

Muggings and other violent opportunistic crimes are rare, but theft of unattended items is common. If you lose something, it is always worth going back to the place where the item was last seen. Avoid leaving valuable objects in full view in your hotel room. Do not leave any items of value inside a car, particularly in the Negev. In the event of theft, contact the police and ask for a copy of the report; you will have to present this to your insurance company when you make your claim.

Both Israel and Jordan have special tourist police who speak English in areas with lots of foreign visitors.

In Israel and the Palestinian Territories, lone women are sometimes subjected to verbal harassment from local males. This problem is most acute in East Jerusalem and in the Old City and surrounding areas, such as the Mount of Olives. In these areas, women are advised not to walk alone in quiet or secluded areas after dark.

In tourist areas of Jordan, lone women may receive unwanted attention from men. If you feel threatened, head straight for the nearest police station.

Homosexuality was legalized in Israel 1988, and LGBTQ+ rights in the country are among the most developed in the Middle East. Tel Aviv is a hugely popular gay destination, with a city-sponsored Pride Parade each June and many gay-friendly events, restaurants and clubs. For local listings, consult **Gay TLVGuide** and **Gay Tel Aviv**. The scene in Jerusalem is much smaller, and conservative religious attitudes in the city mean same-sex couples can face hostility in public. However, the city still has a solid LGBTQ+ community and holds an annual gay pride parade. The **Jerusalem Open House of Pride and Tolerance** provides support for the LGBTQ+ community.

In the Palestinian Territories and Jordan, there are no formal laws against homosexuality, but the law does not provide any explicit protections for LGBTQ+ persons. Circumspect behaviour is strongly advised.

Gay Tel Aviv
ⓦ travelgay.com
Gay TLVGuide
ⓦ gaytelavivguide.com
Jerusalem Open House of Pride and Tolerance
ⓦ joh.org.il

Health

The standard of care in Israeli hospitals – to which seriously ill tourists in the West Bank are referred – is similar to that of other Western countries. Jordan has good private hospitals in Amman. Medical care is costly so do not travel without comprehensive medical insurance.

Excellent pharmacies are easy to find in the region. If you need a specific medicine, it is wise to travel with your own supplies; bring details so that a pharmacist can, if necessary, find a local equivalent. The Jerusalem Post lists pharmacies in Israel that stay open late and on Shabbat and other holidays.

Drinking large quantities of water is essential to avoid heat stroke and dehydration, which can be severe in the region's high summer temperatures. Low humidity causes your body to lose liquids quickly, so drink even if you don't feel thirsty, and wear a hat.

Smoking, Alcohol and Drugs

In Israel smoking is illegal on public transport and in shops, restaurants and bars (except in completely separate, specially designated areas). In the West Bank and Jordan, however, laws and enforcement are weak so cigarettes and *nargilehs* (water pipes) are ubiquitous in restaurants and pubs.

The drinking age in Israel is 18 and alcohol is widely available throughout the country, except in Muslim areas. In the Palestinian Territories, alcohol is generally available in places with a Christian population. In Jordan, alcohol is served in upscale hotels and in a limited number of bars and nightclubs. Drink driving limits (*p273*) are strictly enforced throughout the region.

All illicit drugs, including cannabis, are illegal in Israel, the Palestinian Territories and Jordan, and punishments for trafficking can be harsh. Israel decriminalized the use of cannabis in 2017 but fines can still be imposed.

ID

Israeli law requires that all persons over the age of 16 – both tourists and Israelis – carry ID with them at all times. A passport (including your entry card to Israel) is required to visit the Palestinian Territories.

WEBSITES AND APPS

Go Israel
Israel's Ministry of Tourism has a plethora of helpful information and advice at new.goisrael.com.

Israel Nature and Parks Authority
For details on Israel's national parks and nature reserves, visit www.parks.org.il.

This Week in Palestine
For information on concerts, festivals and exhibitions being held in the Palestinian Territories, check out thisweekinpalestine.com.

Jordan Tourism Board
For useful information on visiting Petra and the rest of Jordan, see www.visitjordan.com.

Local Customs

Political disagreements regarding the Palestinian-Israeli conflict can produce strong emotions, so the wisest course of action is generally to listen and ask questions rather than express strident opinions. Public displays of affection are taboo in Arab areas; Arabic couples are rarely seen even holding hands. Throughout the region, photography at sensitive locations, such as military installations and border crossings, is prohibited.

Visiting Holy Sites

In secular Jewish areas of Israel, visitors can dress pretty much as they would in any warm Western country. However, Orthodox, ultra-Orthodox, Muslim and Druze Israelis – especially women – wear much more conservative clothing, and visitors to holy sites (synagogues, churches, mosques and the Baha'i Gardens) and ultra-Orthodox areas such as Jerusalem's Mea Shearim should wear similarly modest dress. For men, that means long trousers and sleeves, while women should cover their shoulders, arms (past the elbow) and legs (past the knee). At Muslim sites women may be asked to cover their hair with a scarf, while at Jewish sites women may be asked to wear a skirt (rather than trousers). Cloaks may be provided at some sites for visitors who are deemed to be immodestly dressed. Remove your shoes before entering a mosque. In churches, men should take off their hats, while in synagogues men should put on head covering (any hat is fine).

Mobile Phones and Wi-Fi

Foreign mobile phones generally work in Israel but roaming charges can be very high, so it may make sense to buy a local pay-as-you-go SIM card upon arrival. They are available from service providers such as Pelephone, Cellcom and Partner; bring your passport when purchasing one. Israeli networks cover parts of the Palestinian Territories near Israeli settlements. In Jordan, pay-as-you-go SIM cards are also an affordable option.

In Israel, free public Wi-Fi is widely available, including in cafés and restaurants, on many buses and trains, and in public spaces all over Tel Aviv. In the Palestinian Territories and Jordan, Wi-Fi can be found at cafés, restaurants and accommodation in cities.

Post

Using **Israel Post** to send letters or documents is straightforward but parcels require security inspections. The Palestinian Authority's postal service issues its own stamps but can be slow. In Jordan, posting your letters at a five-star hotel or a main post office, rather than at a post box on the street, can help to speed things up.
Israel Post
🅦 israelpost.co.il

Taxes and Refunds

For purchases in Israel of over 400 ILS, shops with a "tax refund" sticker in the window can arrange for you to get a partial VAT (sales tax) reimbursement when you leave the country. Tourists are exempt from paying VAT (17 per cent) on their hotel bills – show your passport (including your entry card).

Discount Cards

The **Israel Nature and Parks Authority** sells two-week passes that cover visits to three, six or an unlimited number of historical and natural sites (78–150 ILS).

If you're planning to visit multiple sites in Jordan, you can save money by purchasing a **Jordan Pass** before you travel. The cost includes not just the price of your visa, but entry to most tourist sites in Jordan, including Jerash, Wadi Rum and, depending on which option you pick, up to three days entry to Petra.
Israel Nature and Parks Authority
🅦 parks.org.il
Jordan Pass
🅦 jordanpass.jo

STAYING INFORMED

Events in the region can move quickly so it's a good idea to stay abreast of the news during your visit. Israeli cable and satellite TV provides access to news broadcasts from around the world, while the Israel Broadcasting Corporation has news programmes in English, French, Spanish and other languages, and broadcasts on FM frequencies and the internet. Israel's left-of-centre newspaper *Haaretz* publishes a daily (Sunday to Friday) print version in English. The right-of-centre *Jerusalem Post* is published daily (except Saturday) and has cultural supplements and entertainment listings on Friday. Online, the *Times of Israel (www.timesofisrael.com)* provides news on Israel and the Middle East in English and French; +972 *(www.972mag.com)* offers a left-wing perspective; and Ynet *(www.ynetnews.com)* has articles translated from Hebrew. In Jordan, keep an eye out for the *Jordan Times*.

INDEX

L

M

PHRASE BOOK

Hebrew has an alphabet of 22 letters. As in Arabic, the vowels do not appear in the written language and there are several systems of transliteration. In this phrase book we have given a simple phonetic transcription only. Bold type indicates the syllable on which the stress falls. An apostrophe between two letters means that there is a break in the pronunciation. The letters "kh" represent the sound "ch" as in Scottish "loch", and "g" is hard as in "gate". Where necessary, the masculine form is given first, followed by the feminine.

IN AN EMERGENCY

Help!	Hatzilu!
Stop!	Atzor!
Call a doctor!	Azminu rofe!
Call an ambulance!	Azminu ambulans!
Call the police!	Tzaltzelu lamishtara!
Call the fire brigade!	Tzaltzelu lemekhabei esh!
Where is the nearest telephone?	Efo hatelefon hatziburi hakhi karov?
Where is the nearest hospital?	Efo bet hakholim hakhi karov?

COMMUNICATION ESSENTIALS

Yes	Ken
No	Lo
Please	Bevakasha
Thank you	Toda
Many thanks	Toda raba
Excuse me	Slikha
Hello	Shalom
Good day	Boker tov
Good evening	Erev tov
Good night	Laila tov
Greetings (on the Sabbath)	Shabat Shalom
Have a good week (after the Sabbath)	Shavu'a tov
morning	boker
afternoon	akhar hatzohoryim
evening	erev
night	laila
today	hayom
tomorrow	makhar
here	po
there	sham
what?	ma?
which?	eizeh?
when?	matai?
who?	mi?
where?	efo?

USEFUL PHRASES

How are you?	Ma shlomkha/shlomekh?
Very well, thank you	Beseder, toda
Pleased to meet you	Na'immeod
Goodbye	Lehitraot
(I'm) fine!	Beseder gamur
Where is/Where are...?	Efo...?
How many kilometres is it to...?	Kama kilometrim mipo le...?
What is the way to...?	Ekh megi'im le...?
Do you speak English?	Ata/at medaber/medaberet anglit?
I don't understand	Ani lo mevin/mevina
Could you speak more slowly, please?	Tukhal/tukhli ledaber yoter le'at, bevakasha?

USEFUL WORDS

large	gadol
small	katan
hot	kham
cold	kar
bad	lo tov
enough	maspik
well	beseder
open	patuakh
closed	sagur
left	smol
right	yamin
straight	yashar
near	karov
far	rakhok
up	lemala
down	lemata
soon	mukdam
late	meukhar
entrance	knisa
exit	yetzia

toilet	sherutim
free, unoccupied	panui
free, no charge	khinam

MAKING A TELEPHONE CALL

I'd like to make a long-distance call	Haiti rotze/rotza lehitkasher lekhutz lair/laaretz
I'd like to make a reversed-charge call	Haiti rotze/rotza lehitkasher govaina
I'll call back later	Etkasher meukhar yoter
Can I leave a message?	Efshar lehashir hoda'a?
Hold on	Hamtin/hamtini (Tamtin/tamtini)
Could you speak up a little, please?	Tukhal/tukhli ledaber bekol ram yoter?
local call	sikha ironit
international call	sikha benleumit

SHOPPING

How much does it cost?	Kama zeh oleh?
I would like...	Haiti rotzeh/rotza...
Do you have...?	Yesh lakhem...?
I'm just looking	Ani rak mistakel/mistakelet
Do you take credit cards?	Atem mekablim kartisei ashrai?
Do you take travellers' cheques?	Atem mekablim travellers' cheques?
What time do you open?	Matai potkhim?
What time do you close?	Matai sogrim?
this one	zeh
that one	hahu
expensive	yakar
inexpensive/cheap	lo yakar/zol
size	mida
shoe size	mida (midat na'alyim)
white	lavan
black	shakhor
red	adom
yellow	tzahov
green	yarok
blue	kakhol

TYPES OF SHOP

antiques shop	khanut atikot
bakery	ma'afia
bank	bank
barber's	maspera
bookshop/newsagent	khanut sfarim/ve'itonim
butcher's	itliz
cake shop	ma'adania
chemist's	bet merkakhat
clothes shop	khanut b'gadim
greengrocer's	yarkan
grocer's	makolet
hairdresser's	maspera
jeweller's	khanut takhshitim
market	shuk
post office	snif hadoar
shoe shop	khanut na'alyim
supermarket	supermarket
travel agency	sokhnut nesiyot

SIGHTSEEING

bus station	takhana merkazit
bus stop	takhanat otobus
church	knesia
closed	sagur
library	sifria
mosque	misgad
park	park
synagogue	bet haknesset
taxi	monit
tourist information office	merkaz hameida letayar
town hall	bet ha'iria
train station	takhanat rakevet

STAYING IN A HOTEL

I have a reservation	Yesh li hazmana
Do you have a free room?	Yesh lakhem kheder panui?
double room	kheder zugi
room with two beds	kheder im shtei mitot
room with a bath or a shower	kheder im sherutim ve ambatia o miklakhat
single room	kheder yakhid
key	mafteakh
lift	ma'alit
Can someone help me with my luggage?	Mishehu yakhol la'azor li im hamisvadot?

EATING OUT

Have you got a table free?	Yesh lakhem shulkhan panui?
I would like to book a table	Haiti rotze/rotza lehazmin shulkhan
The bill please	Kheshbon, bevakasha
I am vegetarian	Ani tzimkhoni/ tzimkhonit
menu	tafrit
fixed-price menu	tafrit iskit
wine list	tafrit hayeinot
glass	kos
bottle	bakbuk
knife	sakin
spoon	kaf
fork	mazleg
breakfast	arukhat boker
lunch	arukhat tzohoryim
dinner	arukhat erev
starter	mana rishona
main course	mana ikarit
portion	mana
rare	mevushal me'at
well done	mevushal hetev

FOOD AND DRINK

almonds	shkedim
apples	tapukhei etz
apricot	mish mish
aubergine/eggplant	khatzilim
beans	shu'it
beef	bakar
beer	bira
bread	lekhem
broad beans	ful
broccoli	brokoli
butter	khem'a
cabbage	kruv
cake	ugha
carrot	gezer
cauliflower	kruvit
cheese	gvina
cherries	duvdvanim
chicken	off
chickpeas	khumus
chips/fries	chips
chocolate	shokolat
coffee	kafe
cold cuts	pastrama
coriander	kuzbera
courgettes/zucchini	kishuim
crabs	sartanim
cucumbers	melafefonim
dessert	kinuakh
draught beer	bira mihakhavit
dry	yavesh
eggs	betza
figs	te'enim
fish	dag
French beans	shu'it yerokha
fried	metugan
fruit	peirot
garlic	shum
grapes	anavim
grey mullet	buri
grilled	al haesh
grouper	lokus
hard-boiled eggs	betza kasha
herbal tea	tei tzmakhim
hot (spicy)	kharif
ice	kerakh
ice cream	glida
kebab	shipud
lamb, mutton	keves
lemon	limon
liver	kaved
meat	basar
milk	khalav
mineral water	myim mineralim
nuts	egozim
olive oil	shemen zyit
omelette	khavita
onion	batzal
orange juice	mitz tapuzim
(freshly squeezed)	(tiv'i sakhut)
oranges	tapuzim
peaches	afarsekim
pepper (condiment)	pilpel
peppers (capsicums)	pilpelim
pickles	khamutzim
plums	shezifim
potatoes	tapukhei adama
prawns/shrimps	shrimps
red snapper	denis
red wine	yain adom
rice	orez
roast	betanur
salad	salat yerakot
salmon	salmon
salt	melakh
sandwich/filled roll	lakhmania
sauce	rotev
seafood	peirot yam
smoked	me'ushan
soup	marak
spinach	tered
spinach beet	alei selek
(Swiss chard)	
squid	kalamari
steak	steik
strawberries	tut sade (tutim)
stuffed vegetables	memulaim
sugar	sukar
tea	tei
tomatoes	agvaniot
trout	forel
turkey	hodu
vegetables	yerakot
vinegar	khometz
water	myim
white wine	yain lavan

NUMBERS

0	efes
1	akhad
2	shtaim
3	shalosh
4	arba
5	khamesh
6	shesh
7	sheva
8	shmone
9	teisha
10	eser
11	ahadesreh
12	shtemesreh
13	shloshesreh
14	arbaesre
15	khameshesreh
16	sheshesreh
17	shvaesreh
18	shmona'esreh
19	tshaesreh
20	esrim
21	esrim veakhad
30	shloshim
40	arba'im
50	khamishim
60	shishim
70	shiv'im
80	shmonim
90	tish'im
100	mea
200	matyim
300	shlosh meot
1,000	elef
2,000	alpyim
3,000	shlosha elef
4,000	arba elef
10,000	asara elef

TIME

one minute	daka
one hour	sha'a
half an hour	khetzi sha'a
Sunday	yom rishon
Monday	yom sheni
Tuesday	yom shlishi
Wednesday	yom revi'i
Thursday	yom khamishi
Friday	yom shishi
Saturday	shabat
week	shavu'a
month	khodesh
year	shana

ACKNOWLEDGMENTS

DK would like to thank the following for their contribution to the previous editions: Daniel Robinson, Paul Clammer, Fabrizio Ardito, Cristina Gambaro, Massimo Acanfora Torrefranca

The publisher would like to thank the following for their kind permission to reproduce their photographs:

Key: a-above; b-below/bottom; c-centre; f-far; l-left; r-right; t-top

123RF.com: Rostislav Ageev 66-7; Alefbet 103br; Rafael Ben-Ari 112clb; Flik47 49cla; Robert Hoetink 205tl; Ievgenii Fesenko 13br; kavram 104-5; Sean Pavone 112bl; Roman Sidelnikov 132cr; silverjohn 102bl, 128-9, 252-3t; Jacek Sopotnicki 133tr; 17bl, 186-7; Lev Tsimbler 159tr.

4Corners: Stefano Amantini 16c, 62-3; Reinhard Schmid 12clb.

akg-images: Erich Lessing 49cr.

Alamy Stock Photo: 95cr; Seersa Abaza 257tr; age fotostock 77tl; Idris Ahmed 82-3b; Albatross / Duby Tal 8cla, 12t; alefbet 185tc; Nir Alon 37cl, 45tr, 47cr, 78b: Ahmad Atwah 259tr; Dotan Beck 196t; Ryan Rodrick Beiler 77br; Vladimir Blinov 204-5b, 225bl; Citizen59 61cr; Classic Image 49tr; Cosmo Condina Middle East 217t; Mark Daffey 233tr; Yaacov Dagan 210-1b; Design Pics Inc 125br, 194b; Didi 260bl; Fesenko 178tl, 184bl; EmmePi Images 261; Everett Collection Historical 52br; Iwona Fijoł 45cl; Florilegius 108clb; Eddie Gerald 22-3t, 40bl, 40-1t, 79br, 83tr, 111c, 127tr, 133cb, 143t, 143kc, 144tl, 147b; 162bl; 185br; 210tl; EDEN-Jerusalem Economic Development company / EDEN-Jerusalem Economic Development company 138-9; Gal Eitan 264-5b, Rostislav Glinsky 100bl, 113tr; Godong 61tr; Gavin Hellier 159bl; Hemis 37tr, 115t; Yagil Henkin - Images of Israel 36tl, 91tr, 224-5t; Historical Art Collection (HAC) 48t; Robert Hoetink 219tr; imageBROKER 119br, 135cr, 209br; Images & Stories 118t; Hanan Isachar 27tr, 58cr, 98bl, 148b, 222tl; Dov Makabaw Israel 84bl; Israel images 99t; Ivoha 135b, 136-7t; Jack Malipan Travel Photography 80t; Jason Langley 20bl; Jon Arnold Images Ltd / Walter Bibikow 191clb; Andreas Keuchel 59br; Konstantin Kopachinskiy 41br; Yadid Levy 36-7b; Felix Lipov 161crb; Melvyn Longhurst 49tl; LOOK Die Bildagentur der Fotografen GmbH 35cla,160b; lucky-photographer 126-7b; Itsik Marom 26tl, 222-3b; Mauritius Images Gmbh 20cr, 182b; Alon Meir 259tl; North Wind Picture Archives 133tl; Sam Oakes 251t; Christian Offenberg 58-9b; Pacific Press 183tr; Painting 173tr; Pal Szilagyi Palko 108cb; Alberto Paredes 175br; Photobyte 142bl; PhotoStock-Israel 29bl, 46br, 97tr, 176b, 177tr, 180t, 206br; Prisma Archivo 127br, 149t; Mieneke Andewegvan Rijn 96-7b; Juergen Ritterbach 262b; Robertharding / Alexandre Rotenberg 70-71b; robertharding 13t, 23cl, 156clb, 162-3t, 203t, 218t; Alexandre Rotenberg 43crb; Boaz Rottem 28b, 73c; Roman Sidelnikov 236-7b; Eitan Simanor 96tl,145bl; Tom Singleton 200t; Kumar Sriskandan 255tr; Craig Stennett 248tr; Steve Davey Photography 265cr; STOCKFOLIO® 79tl; TravelCollection 55cr; Urban Photography TLV 174; Lucas Vallecillos 81tr, 81b, 116-7t; Jelle Vanderwolf 116bl; Vario Images Gmbh & Co.kg 249cra; Ivan Vdovin 146bl, 205tr; Michael Ventura 201tr; Vvvita 30-1b, 31cl; WaterFrame_tfr 191crb; Jan Wlodarczyk 246bl; World History Archive 51cla,51br, 203br; www.BibleLandPictures.com 100tr; Xinhua / Mohammad Abu Ghosh 47cl; Y.Levy 24tr; Zoonar GmbH 192t; ZUMA Press; Inc. 208t, 239tr; ZUMA Press, Inc. / APA Images / © Mahfouz Abu Turk 43cla.

AWL Images: Jason Langley 86-7; Ken Scicluna 4; Jane Sweeney 23tr.

Bridgeman Images: Ancient Art and Architecture Collection Ltd. / Monastery of Saint Catherine, Mount Sinai, Egypt / *Virgin Enthroned with Two Saints*, 6th century (encaustic on panel) 50cr;British Library, London, UK 50crb; Bibliotheque Nationale, Paris, France / Fr

22495 f.43 Battle between Crusaders and Moslems, from Le Roman de Godefroi de Bouillon (vellum), French School, (14th century) 50t, /Fr 22495 f.69v The Crusader assault on Jerusalem in 1099, from Le Roman de Godefroi de Bouillon (vellum), French School, (14th century) 50bc; De Agostini Picture Library / A. Rizzi / Coin depicting Vespasian with Judaea Capta, Roman coins, 1st century 49bc; / Everett Collection /1947 poster showing Theodor Herzl with the flags of Israel and the Zionist Congress 53tl.
Dorling Kindersley: Magnus Rew 85cr.

Depositphotos Inc: fireandstone 12-3b

Dreamstime.com: Alefbet26 35crb, 202bl; Alexirina27000 221tr; Antonella865 234cr; Rafael Ben Ari 46cra, 173tl, 182tr, 204cr; Kushnirov Avraham 27tl; Badahos 22tl; Beata Bar 11br; Buurserstraat386 73br, 108br; Byelikova 206-7t; Dmitry Chulov 60-1b; Checco 8clb; Deanpictures 161t; Dmitriy Feldman 47tl; Evgeniy Fesenko 18cb, 60cr, 71tr, 120-1, 226-7, 230-1t; Fotokon 44bl, 56-7b, 175cl; Borya Galperin 114b; Jaroslav Girovsky 59tr; Giuseppemasci 75; Rostislav Glinsky 46cr; Jasmina 178-9b; Julia161 111tr; K45025 180-1b; Alexandr Makarenko 149br; Masar1920 266-7; Myroslavabozhko 247tr; Irina Opachevsky 153tl; Ryszard Parys 137br; Sean Pavone 20crb, 119cr; William Perry 90-1b; Ramillah 249bc; RnDmS 26-7c; Rndmst 13cr, 47tr, 47br, 199tr; Salajean 31crb, 244-5; Stanislav Samoylik 32-3t; Jozef Sedmak 152clb, 230b; Roman Sidelnikov 173cl; Siempreverde22 258-9b; Ludmila Smite 10-1b; Jacek Sopotnicki 217cr; Spiroview Inc. / Windows at Hadassah Hospital by Chagall ® / © ADAGP, Paris and DACS, London 2018 165tl; Evgeny Subbotsky 24tl; Petr Švec 72tr; Thomaslusth 34t; Ilia Torlin 29cl; Cezary Wojtkowski 198-9t; Lev Tsimbler 158t; Peter Wollinga 10clb; Zatletic 202cl.

Getty Images: 55bc; J. David Ake 55tr; Anadolu Agency 46bl; Yann Arthus-Bertrand 236tl; Esaias Baitel 54-5t; Joel Carillet 57cl; Christophel Fine Art 51tr; Thomas Coex 73tr, 76cl; Kevin Cullimore 25tl; Cultura Exclusive / Laura Arsie 32ca; Luis Davilla 25tr; Design Pics / Reynold Mainse 132-3b; EunikaSopotnicka 39c; Neil Farrin 22cr; Fine Art 158bl; Ahmad Gharabli 61cra; AFP / Ahmad Gharabli 146t, Atta Hussein 46cl; Gim42 57tr; glennimage 11cr; Godong 33crb; Pavel Gospodinov 253cl; Heritage Images 48bc; Hanan Isachar 124t, 195tl; Michael Jacobs / Art in All of Us Tel Aviv Museum of Art Mural in Meshulam Riklis Hall (1989) Oil and Magna on canvas; 7 x 17.4 m (overall); 275 9 / 16 x 669 5 / 16 © Estate of Roy Lichtenstein / DACS 2018 172-3b; Langevin Jacques 54br; Menahem Kahana 42b; Keystone 52t; Keystone-France 53tr; Evan Lang 234t; Jason Langley 134t; Hector Mata 45b; Wally McNamee 54bl; Ido Meirovich 166-7; Lior Mizrahi 10c; Abbas Momani 235bl, 237tr; MyLoupe 260cr; NurPhoto 56cr; Photo 12 52bc; Atlantide Phototravel 26tr; Popperfoto 53bc, / Rolls Press 54tl; Dan Porges 44-3t; Science Photo Library / Photostock-Israel 18tl, 212-3; Frank Scherschel 53cr; Musa Al Shaer 46cla; David Silverman 47bl; Frédéric Soltan 253cr; Alexander Spatari 11t; Stockbyte / Dan Porges 238-9b; ullstein bild Dtl. 53bl; Peter Unger 263t; Universal History Archive 49bl; UniversalImagesGroup 51tl; Tim E White 41cl; WitR 260cb.

iStockphoto.com: alefbet 101t; alexeys 29crb; Leonid Andronov 42-3t; Javier García Blanco 71tl; Matt Burchell 8cl; Joel Carillet 233tl, 246t, 253bl; clu 256-7b; Danor_a 20t; dominiqueandang 24-5c; DZarzycka 110br, 233cr; Fotofantastika 17t, 168-9; geneward2 150bl; gkuna 95t; hugy 256cl; leospek 24-5c; LindaJohnsonbaugh 191br; Lukasz-Nowak1 111crb; Maniscule 220-1t; master2 38-9t; miljko 29cr; nailzchap 254t; Ivan_off 190-1t; peeterv 2-3 Photos by W. Ebiko 8-9b; Mariusz_Prusaczyk 32bl; Bernhard Richter 109; RnDmS 164b; Rostislavv 108cl; sangaku 92-3; seregalsv 6-7; Jacek_Sopotnicki 30-1t; stellalevi 91cl; tirc83 154; tsafreer 34-5b, 39br; WitR 259cr; worldwidephotoweb 38b.

Courtesy Anish Kapoor: Israel Museum, Jerusalem / Elie-Posner 156br.

Robert Harding Picture Library: Cosmo Condina 216cr; Luis Davilla 247cra, 250bl; Yadid Levy 28tl, 151tr; Richard Maschmeyer 19, 240-1; Eleanor Scriven 244cl, 248-9b; Travel Collection 156-7.

Shutterstock.com: Leo Altman 55crb

Front flap:
123RF.com: kavram cb; silverjohn tc; **Alamy Stock Photo:** Eddie Gerald / EDEN-Jerusalem Economic Development company cla; **AWL Images:** Jason Langley cra; **Dreamstime.com:** Salajean bl; **Getty Images:** Kevin Cullimore br.

Sheet map cover:
Shutterstock.com: Ivoha

Cover images:
Front and spine: **Shutterstock.com:** Ivoha.
Back: **123RF.com:** Alexey Stiop cl; **Shutterstock.com:** Ivoha b, ZUMA Press, Inc. c; **Getty Images:** EyeEm /Hamid Khan tr.

All other images © Dorling Kindersley
For further information see: www.dkimages.com

Illustrators:
Isidoro Gonzáles-Adalid Cabezas (Acanto Arquitectura y Urbanismo S.L.), Stephen Conlin, Gary Cross, Chris Forsey, Andrew MacDonald, Maltings Partnership, Jill Munford, Chris Orr & Associates, Pat Thorne, John Woodcock

Penguin Random House

This edition updated by

Contributor Simon Griver

Senior Editor Alison McGill

Senior Designers
Tania Da Silva Gomes, Stuti Tiwari

Project Editors Parnika Bagla, Elspeth Beidas, Dipika Dasgupta

Assistant Editor Mark Silas

Assistant Designer Bandana Paul

Picture Research Coordinator
Sumita Khatwani

Assistant Picture Research Administrator
Vagisha Pushp

Jacket Coordinator Bella Talbot

Jacket Designer Laura O'Brien

Senior Cartographic Editor
Mohammad Hassan

Cartography Manager Suresh Kumar

DTP Designer Tanveer Zaidi

Senior Production Editor Jason Little

Production Controller Kariss Ainsworth

Deputy Managing Editor Beverly Smart

Managing Editors Shikha Kulkarni, Hollie Teague

Managing Art Editor Bess Daly

Senior Managing Art Editor
Priyanka Thakur

Art Director Maxine Pedliham

Publishing Director Georgina Dee

First edition 2000

Published in Great Britain by Dorling Kindersley Limited, DK, One Embassy Gardens, 8 Viaduct Gardens, London SW11 7BW

The authorised representative in the EEA is Dorling Kindersley Verlag GmbH. Arnulfstr. 124, 80636 Munich, Germany

Published in the United States by DK Publishing, 1450 Broadway, Suite 801, New York, NY 10018

The publishers cannot accept responsibility for any consequences arising from the use of this book, nor for any material on third party websites, and cannot guarantee that any website address in this book will be a suitable source of travel information.

A CIP catalog record for this book is available from the British Library.

A catalog record for this book is available from the Library of Congress.

ISSN: 1542 1554
ISBN: 978 0 2414 6252 2

Printed and bound in Malaysia

www.dk.com

MIX
Paper from
responsible sources
FSC **FSC™ C018179**
www.fsc.org

This book was made with Forest Stewardship Council ™ certified paper – one small step in DK's commitment to a sustainable future. For more information go to www.dk.com/our-green-pledge

A NOTE FROM DK EYEWITNESS
The rapid rate at which the world is changing is constantly keeping the DK Eyewitness team on our toes. While we've worked hard to ensure that this edition of Jerusalem, Israel and the Palestinian Territories is accurate and up-to-date, we know that opening hours alter, standards shift, prices fluctuate, places close and new ones pop up in their stead. So, if you notice we've got something wrong or left something out, we want to hear about it. Please get in touch at travelguides@dk.com